# how to get

# the sound

# you want

Printed in the UK by MPG Books, Bodmin

Published by: Sanctuary Publishing Limited, Sanctuary House, 45-53 Sinclair Road, London W14 0NS, United Kingdom

www.sanctuarypublishing.com

ISBN: 1-86074-348-X

# how to get
# the sound
# you want

michael & tim prochak

# contents

# introduction

*"The music is all. People should die for it. People are dying for everything else, so why not the music?"*
  *– Lou Reed*

**M**usic is the world's universal form of communication. It touches every person of every culture on the globe to the tune of £27 billion a year, and the US recording industry accounts for one-third of that world market. It employs thousands of people, including singers, musicians, producers, sound engineers, record promoters and retail salespeople, and its innovations span everything from the first phonograph to digital recordings and beyond. But as musicians, producers and composers, how much do we really know about the music that surrounds us on a daily basis? Do we know where it comes from? Do we know why it sounds the way it does? Do we have any idea whatsoever where all of these silly labels, fads, styles and genres actually come from, or what – if anything – they really mean?

It's been said that trying to understand the subtle nuances and permutations of musical genre can stimulate a level of philosophical angst similar to trying to grasp the significance of why kamikaze pilots wore helmets or agonising over whether or not illiterate people get the full effect of alphabet soup, so it's small wonder that a number of perennial doubts plague genre theory. For example, are genres really "out there" in the world, or are they merely the constructions of twisted, anal-retentive analysts? Is there a finite taxonomy of genres, or are they infinite in principle? Are genres timeless Platonic essences or ephemeral, time-bound entities? Are genres culture bound or transcultural? Should genre analysis be descriptive or proscriptive? Does anyone really care?

The word *genre* comes from the French (and originally Latin) word for "kind" or "class". The term is widely used in rhetoric, literary theory, media theory, music and, more recently, linguistics to refer to a distinctive type of "text" – although, in this context, text doesn't always have to mean text. For most of its 2,000 years, genre study has been primarily nominological and typological in function. That's to say that its principal task has been the division of a subject into types and the naming of those types, much as the botanist divides the realm of flora into varieties of plants. However, the analogy with biological classification into genus and species misleadingly suggests an objective scientific process. But noooo, as John Belushi used to say; when it comes to genre, objective hardly ever enters into the equation, particularly in music.

The classification and hierarchical taxonomy of genres is not a neutral or remotely objective procedure. There are no undisputed maps of the system of genres within any medium. Furthermore, there is often considerable theoretical disagreement about the definition of specific genres. Essentially, a genre is ultimately an abstract conception rather than something that exists empirically in the world, and one theorist's genre may be another's sub-genre or even super-genre. Indeed, what one classes as technique, style, mode, formula or thematic grouping may be treated as a genre by another. Even themes seem inadequate as a basis for defining genres when – particularly as media and content blur – any theme may appear in any genre, and nowadays it usually does.

For a musician who simply plays what he or she plays, the whole issue of genre may appear to be irrelevant. On the whole, this is a fairly healthy approach. It's better to simply create rather than to get too hung up on labels or definitions. Besides, there are plenty of critics and self-styled pundits out there that will be more than happy to bung a label on what you do and enter into no end of twisted and often facile academic or pseudo-artistic arguments to defend their particular interpretation. But sometimes – particularly when you start to think about recording your music, your use of instrumentation or rhythms, lyric structure, etc – some consideration of genre and the sorts of issues and potential production pitfalls that they are capable of generating can make the whole process a little less fraught and considerably more focused on the real task of producing the sound that you really want. That's why the study of the origins and development of styles and genres can be useful, particularly as a generalised approach, since the nature and creative essence of a style or genre is inevitably determined by all possible factors – melody, harmony, texture, rhythm, formal structure, etc – as well as the actual aim and objective of the composition.

In our ever-increasing digital world, the power of the sequencer and the seemingly ubiquitous sampler have put the ability to produce professional-quality recorded music with a modest home set-up well within the grasp of most serious musicians. As this technology becomes increasingly powerful and easy to use, much of the closed-shop mythology that has traditionally surrounded the recording industry begins to look like an elaborate con perpetrated with an expensive array of smoke and mirrors. And all those apparently "difficult" hidden tricks and secrets that were previously the hermetic preserve of "sound professionals" with expensive studios, loads of kit and huge budgets are gradually being revealed to the wider world of studio novices and practising musicians. Beyond the simple process of recording and playing back, sequencers – particularly personal-computer-based systems – now offer musicians a wealth of music-processing options that can open new avenues of musical exploration and experimentation. Currently, home or DIY recording – or the "desktop digital studio" – is one of the fastest growing and most creative industries in the music community. Like the effect that digital video has had on the television industry, cheaper and more powerful audio systems now offer composers and musicians more direct control over the creative process and are therefore making them less dependent on large studios, engineers and producers. These days, four-track or eight-track MiniDisc/hard-disk recorders are almost as cheap as four-track cassette recorders were a few years ago, and home computers can also double as mixdown decks, providing many aspiring bands with the ability to produce professional-quality demos, if not complete, mastered albums. Also, computer-based digital studios providing 16- and 24-track sequencer mixers, hard-disk recording and unlimited audio effects are becoming the mainstay of home-studio musicians and professional producers alike.

If you do decide that you want to record and create your music with a computer rather than with more traditional studio hardware, some understanding and awareness of musical genre would be an advantage. If you're reading this book, it's assumed that you're already using a modern, computer-based sequencer, that you're familiar with the intricacies of recording and mixing MIDI and audio files and that you're reasonably proficient and comfortable with utilising the functionality of your system. Despite the academic overlap and debate over just what constitutes a genre, as a musician you invariably want to know how to get the best results from your equipment for the type of music you produce. This can include everything from the type of microphones you should use, what sort of sequencer is best suited for your style of music, what advantages there might be in using a sampler and what computer system is best suited for you to how much room you need, how to lay out your studio, how to plan a recording session and examples of good working practice. Unfortunately, the whole craft of recording sound, mixing and production is a massive discipline that would obviously be impossible to examine in any great detail in one single book. For that reason, this book focuses instead on helping practising musicians to understand and identify the underlying roots and characteristics of musical genre, its history and its contemporary manifestations and to judge where – if anywhere – their own particular type of music fits in and what – if any – effects this might have on the overall recording process. The primary aim here is to enhance and stimulate your entire creative process and to ensure that, by helping you identify the genre or genres into which your own music fits, recording that music with your very own desktop digital studio will be rendered relatively painless and, hopefully, as pleasurable and satisfying as possible.

As the old saying goes, information is power, and this book is essentially a compendium of information designed to provoke thought as well as provide some simple practical and creative advice. It's not written particularly for traditional hardcore techies or aspiring sound engineers but rather for serious musicians seeking a deeper understanding of what it is that they do and simply wanting to get the best possible generic sound from their own recording environment. So feel free to read from cover to cover or simply browse and dip into it as and when appropriate to your own particular individual musical requirements or circumstances. Although *How To Get The Sound You Want* has been extensively researched and presents a variety of potentially controversial views, opinions and comments on the very nature and substance of genre, nobody expects you to agree with every variation, classification or permutation. As someone else once said, there are trivial truths and there are great truths. The opposite of a trivial truth is plainly false. The opposite of a great truth is also true.

Music, as James Joyce might have said, is an ineluctable modality, and personally it has always been our firm belief that music is about music, not about labels. It must also be realised that there are often no clear dividing lines between various periods and styles. Generally, they merge and mutate, with the culmination of one style or genre overlapping with the beginnings of a new one. As Wagner once wrote, "The begetter of the artwork of the future is none other than the artist of the present, who presages that life of the future and yearns to be contained therein. He who cherishes this longing within the innermost chamber of his powers lives already in a better life, but only one person can do this thing: the artist." At its best, the study of genre can provide a convenient, informed shorthand for classifying a particular type of music that makes it easy for the artist to understand, appreciate and explain his intent to a wider audience. At its worst, it can simply turn into pompous, inauthentic and downright misleading jargon designed to exclude and intimidate all but a small, smug and twisted inner circle of self-satisfied initiates. But again, it's also been our firm belief that it's a mistake to hold firm beliefs.

## chapter 1

# desktop digital recording and the new world order

*"One must still have chaos in one to give birth to a dancing star."*
*– Friedrich Nietzsche*

The poet and artist William Blake noted that the labours of the artist, the poet and the musician have been proverbially attended by poverty and obscurity. However, he believed that this condition was never the fault of the public but was instead the result of "a neglect of means to propagate such works as have wholly absorbed the man of genius". In his time, Blake was a pioneer in developing printing and engraving and was a great advocate of self-publishing as a means of reaching a greater audience. Today, desktop digital studios, cheap CD production and the web are generating the same kind of hope and excitement in music as printing and self-publishing did in Blake's day, and for many very similar reasons.

Throughout this book, it will become blindingly obvious that genre is a cumulative process, and that styles evolve over time and are then subverted. Styles change through processes of lineage. They borrow, stumble and jam their way into the realm that musos label "original". One of the key factors of this clumsy journey into progress is the advent of new technology. While it may be hard to believe, certain notes in early music were thought not to exist, and it wasn't until scales were mathematically applied that the full range of notes was included by composers. It was later still that musicians had the technology to play them on a single instrument. Today, the evolution of genre could well be viewed as having a direct correspondence with the evolution of instruments and, more recently, music technology.

For example, right now, a new band can record in their sitting room with a four-track or Mac or in a local studio with any of a dozen mix-and-match permutations. A final mix can be mastered to MiniDisc, DAT, CD or simply saved as MP3. Instead of slogging to get signed by some record company that's more concerned about how you look than how you sound, musicians can create a "virtual label" via a website, where they can upload MP3 files for fans to listen to or download and then have the option to either receive the whole album online or order a CD directly from the band.

However, technology and online access is no substitute for talent and imagination, unless it's your life's ambition to become one of the legacy-less legions of sterile manufactured pop artists wallowing in the muck of commercial mediocrity where "most successful" certainly doesn't mean most talented, and where money is more important than music. Effectively, the Internet and burgeoning digital technology can offer an alternative for musicians and unknowns to produce and promote their own music and potentially make it available to a global audience. However, once you get onto the net, you'll discover that cyberspace is a wild, noisy and twisted place and that it's all too easy to get lost in the virtual crowd.

# sequencers

Sequencers can be proper hardware devices such as the Alesis MMT8 or software-centric programs such as Cubase, Logic, Cakewalk, etc. These days, software sequencers are all the rage because they run so easily on a fairly basic Mac or PC. Most of these sequencers can provide dozens of MIDI tracks and dozens more audio tracks, depending on the power of your computer, the speed of your hard drive and the particular interface you're using. You'll find that all sequencers these days use some sort of graphic interface that allows you to copy, divide, move and manipulate blocks of sound or MIDI information, while audio and MIDI recordings are often visible within the same window and you can easily integrate them during the recording process.

What makes sequencers so impressive is the way in which they empower individuals to produce professional-quality music on fairly modest home set-ups. Beyond the simple process of recording and replaying, sequencers also offer a wealth of music-processing options that allow musicians to take their original ideas and experiment with them, generating harmony parts and processing effects, etc, in a way that would have once required a commercial studio full of expensive equipment, session musicians and surly engineers. Using computers and sequencers to capture those magic creative moments as and when they happen now allows musicians to work faster and gives them more freedom to experiment.

# which sequencer?

Assuming that you've already got a Mac or PC system and a few extras, the next task is to choose a sequencer. Contrary to what various magazines might tell you, there's no single best solution to this, and choosing a sequencer depends very much on personal preference and how you like to work. At the present time, there are three main programs to choose from.

### Pro Tools

Pro Tools is the most hacked of all of the available music programs, and there seems to be some sort of elitism that exists in the realm of home recording that says that this is the one you must have. Strangely enough, the program was designed with film scorers in mind and offers minute manipulation and seriously crisp recording for Hollywood composers. At first, it was purely an audio program, but recently a high-end MIDI sequencer has also been added. Being fully automated, it's the popular choice of live dance acts that use sequencers onstage, so the "pro" in Pro Tools isn't just clever marketing. However, the pricing reflects its reputation, and at the time of writing it's the most expensive sequencing program available.

### Cubase VST

Cubase is a name that invokes burnt images of unpopular teenagers with misappropriated Ataris churning out happy hardcore for major labels. Certainly the bedrooms were semen-stained effigies of acid house, but the program was a testament to the potential of individual perseverance. Synonymous with MIDI sequencing, Cubase is the most popular music program available. You can get it in a number of forms and versions and it tends to reside in a medium-to-high price range. It's our program of choice, and we personally think that the results achieved in Pro Tools can be easily replicated in Cubase with just a little bit of extra sweat. Depending on the speed and efficiency of your Mac, Cubase VST can give you up to 64 audio tracks, each with four-band parametric EQ, eight real-time auxiliary effects slots, four real-time master insert effects slots and four real-time insert effects slots per channel. It's got an excellent plug-in architecture for a huge variety of third-party effects and processors, great mixdown facilities and clever time stretch and formant pitch shifting. You can patch to a number of external processing devices and features like "Groove Analysis" allows you to analyse the rhythmic structure of your audio recordings, which can then be applied to the structure and "feel" of your MIDI parts.

Cubase incorporates the use of native audio processing, so you don't actually need any additional hardware to record and process audio. However, the more facilities you decide you need from Cubase, the more processing power you'll need, particularly when you start adding third-party plug-ins or if you want to use a lot of audio tracks. The nice thing about Cubase is that it keeps up with your Mac or PC, and as you increase your processing power you actually unlock even more capacity in Cubase.

### Logic

When it comes to sequencers, the lines were drawn early on, and most producers rabidly stand by their choice of program. And if it's Logic, there's not much you can do to shift them. Available in three different precious metals, Logic caters for all strata of the sequencer market, and in practice it offers a very similar platform to Cubase. In its least valuable metal, you can also buy Logic more cheaply than any of the other three. There are always lots of "bundle" offers advertised in the usual mags, so it's worth shopping around. Sharing its birthplace with Cubase (Germany) isn't the only similarity, either; Logic also includes VST compatibility, like the other sequencing programs, and divides audio and MIDI in the same way as its Steinberg competitor. However, its main claim to fame is its resistance to MIDI latency, and Logic users will often cite this as its finest aspect, although a millisecond added to a bar – inaudible to most – seems fairly negligible in real life.

More often than not, your choice of sequencer will be made primarily on price. Remember that all do a very similar job and that the real factor will be your personal preference and working pattern. If money is no object, you can try all three, but Cubase and Logic seem to be the programs of choice.

However, the big three aren't the only options, although they're probably the best, particularly if you use a Mac, which you should, if you're at all serious about music. Vision, Mixman and even EJay offer usable sequencers for musicians on tighter budgets. You can also bypass the whole software route by buying a hardware sequencer or a phrase sampler, which opens up a whole new set of byways and country lanes, roads far too long to explore now. The advantages accorded by software are price and versatility, boons not always catered for by hardware.

# not-so-optional extras

In both music and recording, we've always been advocates of the heuristic approach. Once you understand the basics of how your sequencer works, the best way to master it is to get in there and start experimenting. Trial and error

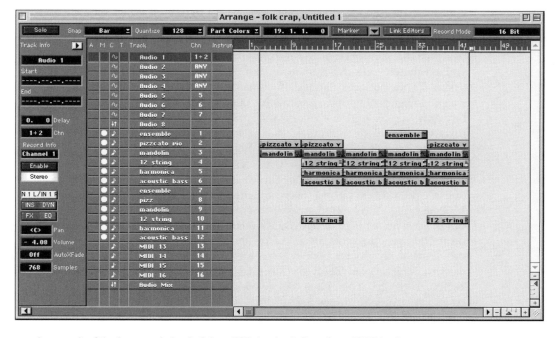

**An example of the Arrange window in Cubase VST showing both audio and MIDI tracks**

is an excellent teacher, and finding things out for yourself is always more valuable then being spoonfed someone else's opinions every step of the way. After all, that's the only way you'll ever develop your own unique approach and creative method. But before we look at some actual studio and recording tips, let's look at some of the other peripheral equipment you'll need to really get the best results out of your sequencer and your own performance.

There's a huge range of samplers, microphones, keyboards, monitors and effects out there that can be used in conjunction with your desktop digital studio, and frankly it would be impossible in a book like this to cover even a fraction of them in any detail. However, there are some items – microphones, for example – which are probably an essential part of any digital studio and which do need some further comment. Also, unless you're happy listening to your playback over headphones, you'll probably want some sort of monitoring system, including an amplifier and speakers. For MIDI-based recordings, you'll also need some sort of input device, such as a MIDI keyboard/synth.

Once your Mac/PC, MIDI and sequencer are sorted out, there are a few additional priorities that you can't really afford to neglect if you're interested in making serious recordings. First, if your budget is tight and you have to cut corners, don't skimp on your microphones, whatever you do. This is one bit of advice that cannot be over-emphasised. Just think about it – the final sound you ultimately produce will never sound better than the original source signal. If your budget is limited, buy one or two high-quality mics rather than several lower-quality ones. As a matter of fact, if money is tight to begin with, buy only one exceptionally good mic. You can do more with one good mic than you can with a number of shoddy models, even though in some instances it might seem like having several cheaper ones would make sessions more convenient. However, if you can afford only one mic, try to find something like an AKG C-414. There's practically no sound that this mic doesn't do at least a good job with, and they usually sell for slightly under £500, although if you shop around you might find them cheaper. If that's still out of your price range, the AKG C-3000 or the Audio Technica 4033 are both pretty decent mics, and these go for under £300. There are also a number other modestly priced condenser mics coming onto the market that are worth taking a look at. My favourite of these at the moment is the Audio Technica AT3035. This mic looks good, it's solid and it will give you a nice balance between accuracy and flattery. It has a convincingly natural sound, which will suit most vocalists, and it's also an excellent option for the recording of acoustic instruments. Best of all, it costs only £200. However, if you're really on a budget, the Shure SM-57 or SM-58 are good performing workhorses that can also be used for reasonable recording. If you can't come up with that, well…how serious are you?

Second, you don't need a 20-space rack full of signal processors (reverbs, delays, etc) to make a pro-quality recording, particularly with the range of VST plug-ins now available. That sort of hardware always looks impressive but, when you come right down to it, it's not essential. If you can afford it, one or two good reverbs and a couple of quality compressors could be useful, and there are currently several decent low-priced reverbs available, including the Alesis Quadraverb, the Lexicon LXP-1 and the Yamaha REV-500. You can also find acceptable low-priced compressors like the DBX 160A and the RNC at reasonable prices, and it's always worth trying to pick up second-hand units as well. While there are advantages to buying some of these hardware processors, you should also check out the range of VST plug-ins that offer digital equivalents of all of these sorts of effects processors. OK, none of the hardware units mentioned here is going to startle the world or give you a Top Ten hit, but if they're used correctly and creatively they can yield surprisingly professional results without sending you to the bank for a second mortgage.

Since you're recording directly to your hard drive, you won't have to worry too much about things like A-DATs or multitrack tape. However, a DAT or MiniDisc recorder can be useful for dubbing down your master mix or for mastering and CD pressing. While the MiniDisc format is a good, cheap digital medium, keep in mind that it does some very funky data compression that can occasionally wreck all of your harmonics and overtones, depending on how you use it.

If you're at all serious about production, at some point you're going to need an external mixing desk. A good one to start with is the 16-channel Mackie, or something like a twelve-channel Spirit Folio. Some people seem to really like Tascam mixers as well, and like everything else it's worth shopping around and checking out second-hand sources. If you can afford it, it's also a good idea to pick up a quality microphone pre-amp. This isn't to say that the pre-amps in all mixers are particularly bad (the ones in the Mackie, for example, are pretty good), but even many mid- to upper-mid-level mixing desks can have mediocre mic pre-amps. The only possible reason for this is that most pro engineers have their own outboard mic pre-amps that they like to work with, and they probably won't use the ones in their consoles anyway, and so the manufacturers figure, "Why jack up the pre-amps and the price when nobody is going to care, anyway?" Some good low-priced pre-amps to look for are the Symetrix and DBX units, although they may not be a great improvement. Really good mic pre-amps cost at least as much as top-notch mics, and if you've got the cash (or the credit) then spring for something in the same league as Avalon or Focusrite models.

Monitor speakers will also have a great impact on the finished sound of your mixes, so don't use those three-way models that came with your JVC stereo system. In the affordable range, you could consider using models like the JBL and the industry-standard Yamaha NS-10, which don't sound all that incredible but seem to mix very well, once you're used to them. The problem with just plugging them into your home stereo is that consumer speakers have things like built-in EQ curves to sweeten their sound, whereas what you want to hear for a mix is the absolute sonic truth. Pro audio monitors don't lie – well, not nearly as much, anyway – and it's also worth keeping a pair of really cheap Sony boombox speakers around or the equivalent to get an unbiased reference once in a while. After a few hours of mixing, your ears tend to go woolly, and you'd be surprised at how a mix can sound like the voice of God over good speakers and like muddy trash over your friend's Audiovox car system, so have at least two sets of monitors – a set of good ones and a set of garbage ones.

If you want a reasonably serious studio system, you can put together an adequate project studio for around £4,000 if you shop around. Anything less and you're probably better off just going out and paying somebody who has some gear to do your recording for you. However, even with all the power and functionality of a sequencer like Cubase, it's worth remembering that you don't have to have 64 tracks to make a damned fine recording. As the old cliché goes, The Beatles' *Sgt Pepper's Lonely Hearts Club Band* was cut to eight tracks (well, actually, two four-track machines synchronised together), and most Mac- or PC-based sequencers already give you a much bigger edge than this, so to create a truly great album you just need to be sure that the peripheral gear you have is top notch and, most importantly, you need a good understanding of how to maximise its potential. Of course, great performances from the musicians never hurts, either.

# planning a recording session

Without going into a lot of detail about how you should plan your recording session, it's worth mentioning a few basic practices with which you might already be familiar. The way in which you actually structure your recording session will, of course, depend on the generic style of your music and the instrumentation and arrangements involved, although in most instances it's best to start by laying down rhythm and bass tracks, either to a click track or to a guide vocal, or perhaps to a main MIDI track. Once you've got the rhythm, bass and chord parts down, you've effectively established the structure and shape of your song and you can build, layer and arrange from there. The nice thing about sequencers like Cubase is that they make it easy for you to adjust the mix as you record new parts so that, by the time you've got everything recorded, you've got a mix that will be pretty close to your desired final sound.

While this may be restating the obvious, it's absolutely imperative that you tune all of your instruments with a tuner before you start any recording session. Despite what a lot of musicians may claim, most of us don't have perfect pitch, or even relative pitch, and getting a properly tuned instrument is one of the first key steps to making a good recording. It also avoids problems later when you start laying down a track with a new instrument only to discover that you've got an out-of-tune instrument somewhere in the previous mix of tracks. Incidentally, most MIDI instruments are tuneable as well, so ensure that all of your instruments are at least in tune with each other, as this will make your life a lot easier.

When you get into recording sessions, you'll discover that there are several different ways of doing the same job and that most people will simply choose the one they like best and use it most of the time. As mentioned earlier, the way in which you organise your session depends entirely on the type of music you're recording, your line-up of instruments and the generic sound you're trying to achieve.

While sequencers running on a suitable Mac or PC fitted with MIDI and audio interfaces will allow you to perform most of the tasks you'd be able to perform in a traditional recording studio, don't forget those important extras such as a reasonable monitoring system, reasonable-quality microphones and perhaps mic pre-amps and external recording facilities such as DAT, MiniDisc or a CD burner. It's also worth mentioning a few simple tips on studio layout which might help to make the whole recording process run a bit smoother.

Unless you only want to use MIDI sound sources that can be generated within your Mac or PC, you'll definitely need an external mixer and some external sound modules. The mixing desk has always been the centre of a traditional recording studio, so you'll want to keep your mixer close to your Mac system so that you can operate both without moving from your ideal monitoring position. MIDI keyboards and samplers can be positioned to one side or even underneath your keyboard position, and you can experiment with racking or tiered arrangements. Just remember that nothing should be placed or racked higher than the bottom of your monitor speakers or anywhere between the monitors and your head. Make sure that your cables are kept out of harm's way and avoid running mains leads alongside signal cables. Don't ever remove any earth leads from any equipment, and if you're use multiplug extension blocks, once you've plugged everything in, leave it plugged in. Plugging in and unplugging mains plugs will weaken contacts and you could end up with dodgy connections or annoying pops and crackles.

Also, make sure that you're using the right cables for your system. Input leads should use screened co-axial cable, while output leads should be good-quality twin-core cable and MIDI leads should be screened twin-core and specifically made for MIDI connections. (Five-pin DIN audio cables are not suitable.) All cables should be kept short, with input leads kept away from mains connectors and monitor screens.

If you usually work alone, try to get hold of a combined mic, pre-amp and compressor for audio work. These work reasonably well for vocal or instrumental recording.

Make sure that you've got a reasonably long mic lead as well, since you'll want to get your mic as far away from your computer and peripherals as possible to avoid picking up hum and fan noise. The layout that we use comprises a computer-style desk housing a G3, monitor, CD burner, Jaz drive and a MIDIman Omni i/o integrated desktop audio station connected to a MIDIman Delta 66 audio card. The top shelf above the monitor holds a Spirit Folio mixer and the bottom shelf is occupied by a Yamaha A5000 sampler. On shelves to the right and immediately behind there's a Roland SoundCanvas keyboard, a mixer, a DAT recorder and additional tape players, while small monitors are positioned on the shelf above the unit just above ear level, and for vocal and other mic recordings the mic can be run out into the kitchen or into a small cupboard with a door that can be closed to block out the majority of extraneous noises. While real voices and miked instruments are affected by the acoustic environment in which they're recorded, you can do quite a lot with sequencers like Cubase to enhance, process and fix that sound, so don't panic if you don't have total isolation facilities or you get a bit of bleedthrough or background noise.

If you're at all serious about your music, trade in those powered computer speakers for a pair of studio monitors and a separate amplifier. You can't make decent music without decent speakers, and most of those designed for computers just aren't up to scratch. Small nearfield studio monitors start at around £100 and will give you a much more accurate picture of the way that your music really sounds.

One of the disadvantages of the digital revolution in music has been a sort of compulsive obsession with perfectly pure audio hygiene. In most cases, a completely clean sound is overrated and rather sterile and generally – unless you're an anal, obsessive audio geek – totally inoffensive to the average ear. The natural world is full of interference and unintended reverberation, and rarely – particularly in live performances – do we hear music played in the acoustic equivalent of an hermetically sealed environment. Let's face it, some genres of music actually benefit from a "lo-fi" approach, and despite what you might hear from the cultural prudes, in many instances a bit of audio dirt can add an important element of warmth and soul to a sound.

Whether you're recording on a digital desktop system in your bedroom or forking out good money for an expensive commercial studio, there are a few things that you should always keep in mind.

# if it sounds good, it is good

Whether you record on your portastudio at home or on a 48-track digital machine in a world-class studio, Duke Ellington's immortal maxim applies. When you get sounds you like, be very reluctant to change things and, if you *do* change things, remember what made your sound good in the first place. Audio is deceptively subtle – the smallest change in EQ, compression, effect or level can make a huge difference. Basically, if it ain't broke, don't fix it.

# if it sounds bad, children, it is bad

If it sounds like crap going onto tape or disk, you can't fix it in the mix. If a track isn't cutting it, change it or kill it. If you aren't EQ'ing, try applying some EQ. If you're not compressing, add some compression. If you're using a mic, try another model. And 'fess up. Admit that either your favourite overdub doesn't work, the musical idea doesn't work or the singer or player is having a bad day or just can't cut it. One way or another, move on.

# screw you guys, i'm going home

When you and your ears get tired, even if more time is booked or your pet overdub hasn't been cut, remember what Cartman says and go home. Slow time in the studio comes in the beginning, getting sounds. Wasted time comes at the end. Remember what's important – vocals, rhythm tracks, solos, sweetening tracks and effects, in that order. Time spent cutting backwards guitar is normally better spent fixing a pitchy vocal or bass, unless of course you're working in a pure dance or ambient genre.

# shiny happy people make good music

Great music is usually made when the engineer and assistant, the musicians, the singers and the producer are all wisecracking and having a good time. If something personal is bugging you, leave it at home. If something in the studio is bugging you, try not to let it ruin a good mood, as this can stop a session dead.

# be prepared

Things always sound different in the studio, and the whole experience can be intimidating, so rehearse and rehearse again (but remember to stop before things get stale). Make sure that you bring everything into the studio with you. Losing an hour of studio time because you don't have a £5 set of strings or a snare head or a nine-volt battery is infuriating, costly and also stops a session dead. And be on time! Be early! The clock starts at the appointed hour, not when you get there, and you *never* have enough time.

# out of time, out of luck

If you have tempo troubles, rehearse at very slow speeds, preferably with a drum machine. Tune up early and often, including drums. If anything sounds like it might be out of tune, check it. Of course, the one exception is the great performance with the minor time or intonation problem, especially vocals. A singer may never get that feeling again, so use an empty track or erase a less important one to try and fix what you have.

# less is more

Mixing is like cooking – one ingredient too many can ruin the dish. Your mix sounds like mush? Try using the Mute buttons. The same goes for effects. Move faders sparingly, one decibel at a time, as pushing up a fader is like turning everything else down. And don't be fooled by volume – monitor at a low level. A mix always sounds great at level ten on the big speakers (which fatigue your ears). The challenge is to make it sound great at level three on the little speakers.

# what to record

Unless you're concentrating solely on dance or MIDI production, the most important elements in the studio are good singers and good songs. No amount of tech will compensate for mediocrity. When you play live, the audience tells you what they like (and will buy). Some songs come alive in the studio, while others die. They're your ears. You decide.

# is there really room for a symphony orchestra?

When it comes to home-based recording, there are some genres that simply aren't practical for creative consideration – at least, not in the traditional sense. Given the space constraints of most home studios, it isn't feasible to try and record classical music performed by a full symphony orchestra. However, this doesn't mean that recording classical music with a full symphony orchestra isn't possible, virtually. Thanks to the advent of samplers and extremely high-quality sample CDs, you can add almost any imaginable instrument to your composition or arrangement and it will be virtually indistinguishable from the real thing. Well, in most cases, it *is* the real thing; it's just not played on the real thing. Friendly and helpful companies such as Time & Space can sort you out with whatever exotic instrumentation you require, and you can have your own orchestra on tap 24 hours a day. Space in a home-based studio can even be a problem for more mundane things like full drum kits and large amps. Again, samplers and sequencers can sort out your drum kit problems, and new devices called *pods* can eliminate the need for a full Marshall stage rig. As studios become more compact, solutions for instrumental recording follow suite. At present, manufacturers offer a competitive range of amp-modelling hardware and software. The premise of which is simple: a unit simulates the genuine sounds of an amp, including effects. This means no miking up and huge savings on space and money.

The current favourites in this field are the aforementioned pod series created by Line 6. A guitar and a bass pod can be picked up for around £200 each, and each unit offers pre- and post-EQ effects, a serious equaliser and a range of classic amp models. It's also possible to create your own user patterns and models, which means that the classic Marshall valve you've always wanted can be created with a few tweaks. Even someone who thinks that the word *mike* is a good wholesome Christian name will get a sound which engineers train for years to achieve. Meanwhile, an alternative to the pod system produced by Johnson J Station provides guitar- and bass-modelling facilities, along with acoustic guitar simulation. Both systems are fully programmable.

# samplers

It's a strange fact that, the people actually make music, the more they become attached to their samplers. There has recently been some debate concerning the continued usefulness of sample technology. Some journalists see samplers as obsolete, arguing that modern sequencers can perform the job of many samplers. This isn't entirely true, however. The idea of writing a book about the home production of (most) generic styles would be inconceivable without sampling technology.

Samplers allow you to use multisamples of real instruments. With them, you can import an entire orchestra to your keyboard with pretty convincing results. Instead of having to buy a lute, you can have a whole collection of medieval instruments. And the uses of samplers don't just stop at multisample instruments.

# which sampler?

OK, this is where things start to get complicated. With most of the major synth manufacturers producing their own models, it's first necessary to select a brand and then try to deal with an ever-amassing series of numbers that follow a seemingly random letter. Brand loyalty is as rampant in buying a sampler as it is in choosing a sequencer. When buying, be sure to try out as many different machines as possible. The only way you'll be truly able to find out which is best for you is to try as many as possible. For personal reference, the sampler world is laid out something like this.

### Akai

Akai is for sampling what Cubase is for sequencing. Their S range of samplers is something of an industry standard and these models are renowned for their easy operating systems and huge sample libraries. Akai became studio favourites purely through popular opinion and hearsay, but the majority aren't always right. In fact, Akai samplers fall down in three major areas:

- Affordability – Although entry-level samplers can be picked up very cheaply, a top-of-the-range Akai will need a serious investment;

- Effects – Akai have never offered a huge variety for effects junkies, and indeed some of their samplers offer no effects boards at all. That said, however, effects boards can be added for a price;

- Manipulation – The other major downfall is Akai samplers' limited beat- and audio-manipulation capabilities. Filters and remix functions are all better catered for by other manufacturers.

## Yamaha

Although still rather new to the sampler market, Yamaha offers three main studio samplers: the A3000, the A4000 and the A5000. With the launch of the A3000 a few years ago, Yamaha managed to create an intuitive sound generator that thrived on creativity. The most recent upgrades improve on the A3000's features, and with the A5000 offering a huge amount of effects, 124-note polyphony and loads of filters, it's the effects junkie's sampler of choice. Its major drawback, however, is its operating system, which sometimes looks like it needs an Enigma machine to decode. For a first-time buyer, this won't be a problem, but producers accustomed to other makes will find themselves trying desperately to rename their sample banks.

## E-mu

Probably Akai's biggest threat in terms of market dominance, EMU samplers combine ease of use with creative capabilities. Makers of the classic SP1200, EMU cater for every range of sample buyer. From high-end to entry-level models, E-mu samplers are known for their sound-manipulation capabilities and built-in beat-mangling processors. The major argument for E-mu models lies in their compatibility with other formats and their huge sound-manipulation potential.

## Roland

Roland offers a number of studio options and has recently been the toast of NAMM (the International Music Products Association) and the music technology world with its release of the VP9000, which allows you to modify pitch and tempo in real time literally at the touch of a knob. On the downside, you can buy a reliable second-hand car for less and it offers only six-part polyphony. In all, it's certainly an indication of the trends that future samplers may follow, although it's not necessarily the best choice for those with bedroom budgets.

## soft samplers

The major drawback of soft samplers is their tendency to hog huge amounts of processor memory, and they rarely offer the same amount of effects or sound-mangling ability. It's also unlikely that you'll want to lug your entire computer to a gig. On the plus side, however, they can be cheaper than outboard samplers, they have quicker loading times and they suit the travelling musician down to the ground if he's running off a Notebook. An iBook with an audio-card sampler and some plug-ins should be all you need to travel the globe, creating music as you go. As with the vast majority of hardware, programmers are constantly developing software alternatives, and these are available from around £200 to upwards of £1,000. Many audio cards incorporate a sampler as part of their set-up.

If you get into using a sampler, you'll soon discover that most sounds can become quite unnatural when transposed too far from their original pitches. Although this can sometimes be a creative advantage, in most instances you'll probably want an instrument to sound as realistic as possible, especially pianos and orchestral instruments. The only way to maintain a natural sound is to take several samples of an instrument at different pitches and then use each sample over a limited part of the keyboard. Ideally, you'd take a fresh sample every semitone, but this gobbles up loads of memory and takes forever. In practice, using the same sample over a range of three or four semitones is generally accurate enough even for the most critical instruments, and often you can get away with far fewer samples. Pianos are very critical, but instruments such as bowed strings and wind instruments are more forgiving. To get the most natural sound possible (even though you're playing from a keyboard), try to play instruments in the same style and with the same intonation with which they're played in real life – for example, don't play chords on instruments like flutes or other instruments that naturally aren't used for chords.

## mixing issues and techniques

It's important to establish the element that will give your mix its identity. This is usually the part that plays or sings the main tune/sound, providing the "story" to a piece of music and therefore is usually the most prominent. This element will also determine the style or genre of your music.

I've mentioned this before, but it's still worth repeating that you should always listen back to mixes on as many different systems as possible. Even if you're using state-of-the-art monitor speakers and a high-quality amp, you should try to listen to your music in a range of different environments before committing to your final mix. Domestic hi-fis, in-car stereo systems and Walkmans, etc, can all be useful in helping you determine whether what you hear will be the same as what other people hear when listening to your music.

Never use headphones to mix. Contrary to popular terminology, there's no such thing as a pair of stereo headphones. When listening through two separate earpieces, music is heard *binaurally*, and the effect is quite different to listening through speakers. It makes accurate mixing all but impossible. On the other hand, headphones are useful for listening closely to your music, as they'll often reveal problems that have been masked by your speakers, such as glitches that crop up during digital editing.

When all of your instruments are up and running, turn off all effects and EQ – unless you're absolutely convinced that you need them – and turn all pan controls to their central positions so that your mix is in mono. Then adjust the level of each instrument until you're happy with the overall balance of sounds.

Leave your bass instrument at the centre of the mix, along with the drum track, if it's a single loop. If the drums track is made up of individual instruments, try panning the bass and snare drums to the centre of the mix and then spreading the other instruments to either side (although not too far). If you're using a single vocal line, leave it at the centre of the mix but try adding a little stereo reverb panned left and right. If you're using more than one vocal, however, pan each left or right in roughly complementary positions.

Position the other instruments across the stereo field. Some sounds – such as percussion and more off-the-wall noises – can be panned fully left or right, with the main instruments spread evenly across the stereo field. Make sure that there are no parts of the song where the sound appears to be too far to the left or right. Listen carefully to your mix, using EQ controls to firm up bass, add sparkle at the high end and clean up the mid range. Tweak your volume levels as required and use reverb to create atmosphere and/or mask problems.

Although there's always potential for creativity, there are established conventions when it comes to panning that you ignore at your peril. Bass instruments, for example, carry the most energy and invariably sound better at the centre of the mix, and if these are panned hard left or right your music will sound off centre. Vocals can be panned a little to the left or right but tend to sound better if there's a balancing vocal or similar instrument panned to the opposite side. Also, remember to pan stereo effects like reverb fully left and right if you want to create width.

When it comes to effects, remember that less is more. If your mix isn't going according to plan, don't swamp it with loads of reverb and chorus, as this will generally make things worse. As you add more and more effects to your parts, they become indistinguishable from each other and the dynamics of the mix are quickly swallowed up in a whirlpool of flanging delays. Try to keep some contrast in your mix by adopting the approach of adding a little reverb here, a little chorus there, etc. Also, try to keep your drums dry (ie with no effects), if you can, as this is the best way of preserving the punchiness of a mix. If you want to make your drums sound live, try adding a touch of reverb on the snare drum alone – it's surprising what a difference this can make. The vocal may also benefit from the tiniest amount of reverb or delay, but nothing too loud or too long, as things can get messy very quickly. Also remember that many chorus effects are in stereo, so the moment you apply one to a part of the mix, the stereo image for the sound that you so carefully set up earlier is lost or at least diffused. In general, use effects where they're needed rather than just sporadically splashing them all over your mix. They *do* sound good, but not on everything simultaneously.

Don't constantly mix at a high volume or at the same volume. Check your mix frequently using a very low volume and at various mid-level volumes and every now and then crank it up to really hear how things hit hard, but be sure to look at your speakers when you do this to make sure you're not overdriving them. When the mix is finished, you should listen to it from start to finish at a high level, but remember to turn it down again if you need to make further alterations. Your ears can get tired and even damaged if you listen to loud music for long periods, resulting in you hearing a muffled version of the sound on which you're working. Don't mess with your ears – you need to keep them in the best condition possible.

Give yourself space and, if possible, try to leave some time between creating a track and mixing it. You'll be amazed at how your perspective changes after you've given yourself a break from a piece of music for a few days or, preferably, a few weeks. If you happen to know someone whose musical opinion you respect, why not ask them to remix your track?

To paraphrase TS Eliot, amateur musicians are influenced; professionals steal. Wherever you're mixing your music, try to listen to some of your favourite tracks to get a feel for the environment in which you're working. If the music sounds too bassy, you'll know to tweak the EQ controls to compensate when mixing your music. Basically, if you're stuck, copy what your favourite band has done – it's the only time you'll get away with it!

Compression has many uses, but it's particularly good at dealing with vocal or instrumental parts which seem to stick out in a mix. By lowering the dynamic range (the difference between a signal's highs and lows), recorded parts can be made to sound more at home with a piece of music. Compression can also be useful to give a mix extra punch, particularly when there's a strong rhythm or bass line, although obviously you'll need a stereo compressor or plug-in to treat a complete mix. These should be used very sparingly, with a low compression ratio setting, but you'll be surprised at how much more energy they can add to a track.

When mixing, try to remember that your sound image doesn't just extend from left to right. Stereo music also has depth, with some instruments "up front" and others "sat back" in a mix. This is mainly achieved through level – the louder an instrument or voice is, the closer it will appear to be – but in real life the further away a sound is, the more high frequencies are lost, so by simply using treble cut and boost it's possible to create a sense of depth.

If you inadvertently end up with distortion on your mix, there ain't much you can do about it. Unfortunately, no one's got around to inventing a distortion filter yet, and using equalisers to cut out some of the more unpleasant frequencies is rarely successful. Short of re-recording the track, your only option is to turn a vice into a virtue and add a nice warm distortion to the offending part, or even the whole track. This should mask the distortion you don't want and could even help give the track a more radical edge. What have you got to lose?

# TrueTape

TrueTape is a newish VST plug-in offering a unique Steinberg technology that emulates the behaviour of a professional analogue tape recorder. While digital audio recording has many of benefits, some musicians have expressed the opinion that digital sound always tends to be somewhat sterile and cold when compared to high-quality analogue recordings. Indeed, a few years ago, Neil Young was particularly outspoken about the evils of digital sound. However, TrueTape claims to remedy this problem by recreating that good old-fashioned open-fire sound of analogue tape saturation at the recording stage. If you're particularly into acoustic music, you might want to play around with this – if your system can handle it, that is.

# considerations

Here are some general tips for getting a better sound, regardless of genre.

- Always listen to the whole track dry, with no effects, no EQ, nothing. This will help you to determine where you want things want to sit in the mix. Of course, if the song you're mixing utilises processed samples, this is impossible. However, a relatively effective way of reducing effects on pre-processed samples is to use a limiter or some form of compression. You can also target the frequency band in which the sample is most effected and reduce the gain, although this can lead to unwanted tonal change.

- Thin out pads, backing vocals and acoustic guitar parts with EQ. Perversely, it adds drama to the dynamics rather than diminishes them.

- Try going into another room and doing something totally unrelated to music and leave your track playing. Now see what needs to be done.

- Smoothe the curve. The radio-friendly "pro" sound of most modern records, although not to everyone's taste, is nevertheless definitely familiar. This polished feel seems to rest in the mid EQ band, with producers tending to cut frequencies between 200Hz and 4kHz and cutting most in the 600Hz-1kHz region. On a graphic equaliser, EQ'ing carried out like this forms a smooth, upside-down curve.

OK, forget the techie crap. On a graphic equaliser, like the one you have in Cubase, equalisation carried out like this forms a smooth, upside-down curve which you can draw in graphically. Professional producers take down the mid range, as middle frequencies have a habit of tiring the ear and blocking out the finer frequencies. This holds especially true on tracks that have a profusion of guitar. The edge that's apparently so desirable is achieved not by boosting the mid range, which seems natural, but by tweaking the top and bottom frequencies so that they interact with contrast.

## chapter 2

# genre theory

*"Musical standardisation gives the music consumer no choice. Products are forced upon him."*
  *– Theodor Adorno*

When it comes to music, tomorrow is a deliberate destination and we can quite literally take steps to get there. Thanks to all of the clever and relatively inexpensive digital technology out there, the spatialised musical future is open for inspection and interaction in real time. The very ability to speculate and conceive of implications and their possible resolutions, to desire a shape for that which is yet to be, means that thinking about any musical future inherently assumes some form of control through classification, whether real or projected. Spatialisation of the temporal is one symptom of that yearning towards control that colours emphatic visions of the future, musical or otherwise. It is also, of course, a plan of action. Participation in a style or genre as an aesthetic criterion can, in a sense, shift the burden of value to a smaller, more manageable unit: the work itself.

In Philip K Dick's novel *Counter-Clock World*, time runs in reverse and commonplace things like shaving or eating breakfast seem like minor miracles when events are viewed in reverse order. Shaving becomes the application of whiskers to the face, meals begin with regurgitation, and so on. This reversal is a possibility when thinking about our own musical future, at least in terms of cultural and generic developments – we may be confused about the direction in which we're actually looking. For example, when listening to a lot of "contemporary" music, or when looking at the implications of sampling and remixing in dance music, that which we see as the future could simply be a regurgitation of the present or even the past. One of the benefits of understanding the nature of the concept of genre is that it allows us to ask ourselves, to what extent is our gaze fixed backward, rather than forward, and how does the meaning of our ideas change, or perhaps not change, because of our failure to perceive the difference?

# historical overview

Music isn't merely an independent art form to be enjoyed for its own sake, particularly in non-Western societies. Instead, it's an integral part of the culture, and music may accompany every conceiveable human activity from the cradle to the grave. Genres or styles of music can include lullabies, games, dancing, work, healing, battle, rites and ceremonies, etc. Ethnomusicologists usually break down music into traditional uses common to nearly all societies. These classifications include:

Lullabies
Games
Work music
Dancing
Storytelling
Ceremonies and festivals
Battle
Communication
Personal symbols
Ethnic or group identity
Salesmanship
Healing
Trance
Personal enjoyment

In our digital age of mass communication, we all have access to an enormous diversity of music. The overall listening potential offered by live music has been greatly expanded by recorded and broadcast music so that our choice of music now spans national, cultural, social and historical divides. Unfortunately, individuals only have time to listen to a fraction of all of this music, and the choices they make in terms of genre and style define what is commonly known as personal taste – and, as we all know, some people have it and some people don't. You'll find that some "musical taste" cultures are associated with more or less distinct subcultures within any given society, and what ethnomusicologists call "aesthetic" musical subcultures usually centre on a particular minority-interest music, such as jazz, classical, ethnic, heavy metal, etc. Minority music usually receives only limited media coverage and exists on the fringes of what these days passes for mainstream culture. Ethnomusicologists also recognise oppositional music subcultures which ostensibly offer loosely organised resistance to conventional social institutions and values and have ideological and/or political components. Jamaican reggae and hip-hop are typical examples of oppositional music. In some cases, music subcultures can be supportive of the power structure of the society in which they exist, or they can be alternative and co-existing. A good example of the former is the more traditional country music in the USA, while an example of the latter could be new age or ambient music. Obviously, when most people subscribe to a musical taste culture, they are generally associating with a particular lifestyle and a wider set of values and fashions. Interpreting these associations, however, can become problematic when you remember that both musical tastes and behavioural problems can always be correlated with a variety of other factors, including personality, social class and education.

It has been argued that no set of necessary and sufficient conditions can mark off genres from other sorts of groupings in ways that all experts or ordinary audiences would find acceptable. Practitioners and the general public make use of their own genre labels – *de facto* genres – quite apart from those put about by smug, dry, academic theorists. We might therefore pretend we're Clive Anderson and ask ourselves, whose genre is it, anyway? And why are all of those people doing silly impressions? But hang on. Still further problems with definitional approaches will become all too apparent in due course.

Although defining genres may not initially seem particularly problematic (particularly if you take a relatively shallow and superficial approach to life), even a semi-scholarly approach can become a theoretical minefield. Over the years, academics have identified four key problems with generic labels:

- Extension – The breadth or narrowness of labels;

- Normativism – Having pre-conceived ideas of criteria for genre membership;

- Monolithic definitions – As if an item belonged to only one genre;

- Biologism – A kind of essentialism in which genres are seen as evolving through a standardised life cycle.

# what it says on the tin

Conventional definitions of genres tend to be based on the notion that they constitute particular conventions of content, such as themes or settings and/or form, including structure and style, which are shared by the "texts" – in this instance music, tune, lyrics, etc, which are regarded as belonging to them. The attempt to define particular genres in terms of their necessary and sufficient "textual" properties is sometimes seen as theoretically attractive, but it still poses numerous difficulties. For instance, in the case of films, some seem to be aligned with one genre in content and another genre in form, and this is also a major issue with music. It has been argued that subject matter is the weakest criterion for generic grouping, because it fails to take into account how the subject is treated.

Besides, it's never all that difficult to find examples that are exceptions to any given definition of a particular genre, and often there are no rigid rules of inclusion and exclusion. Genres aren't discrete systems that consist of a fixed number of listable items. In current popular music, particularly, it's difficult to make clear-cut distinctions between one genre and another. Like it or not, in real life, genres overlap, and there are more than a few mixed genres. Specific genres tend to be easy to recognise intuitively but difficult, if not impossible, to define. For instance, particular features that are characteristic of a genre aren't normally unique to it. Instead, it is their relative prominence, combination and functions that are distinctive, and it's often easy to underplay differences within a genre, since in many ways genres are essentially instances of repetition and difference.

Contemporary theorists tend to describe genres in terms of *family resemblances* among texts (a notion derived from the philosopher Ludwig Wittgenstein) rather than definitionally. An individual text within a genre rarely (if ever) has all of the characteristic features of the genre. The family resemblance approach involves the theorist illustrating similarities between some of the texts within a genre. However, this approach has been criticised on the basis that no choice of a text for illustrative purposes is innocent and that such theories can make any text seem to resemble any other. In addition to the definitional and family resemblance approaches, there is another approach to describing genres which is based on the psycholinguistic concept of *prototypicality*. According to this approach, some examples would be widely regarded as being more typical members of a genre than others. Certain features would identify the extent to which an exemplar is prototypical of a particular genre. After listening to that sort of talk, you can understand why genres have to be seen as fuzzy categories which can't be defined by necessary and sufficient conditions.

The way in which we define a genre depends on our purposes, and the adequacy of our definition – in terms of social science, at least – must surely be related to the light that the exploration sheds on the phenomenon. For instance, if we're studying the way in which genre frames the reader's or listener's interpretation of a text, we would do well to focus on how readers or listeners identify genres rather than on theoretical distinctions. This is particularly appropriate when dealing with music. Defining genres may be problematic, but even if theorists were to abandon the concept, in everyday life people would continue to categorise. Let's face it, people love labels.

In many ways, a genre isn't a system; it's a processes of *systematisation*. Traditionally, genres have tended to be regarded as fixed forms, but contemporary theory emphasises that both form and function are dynamic. It has been argued that genre is not simply "given" by the culture; rather, it's in a constant process of negotiation and change. It's also fairly obvious that – in music, particularly – the boundaries between genres are shifting and becoming more permeable, and that things like "music television" seem to be engaged in a steady dismantling of genre, which can be attributed in part to economic pressure to pursue new audiences. One may acknowledge the dynamic fluidity of genres without positing the final demise of genre as an interpretative framework. At least, you can if you really want to.

As the generic corpus ceaselessly expands, as all bloating corpuses do, genres change over time, as do the relationships between them. The conventions of each genre shift, new genres and sub-genres emerge and others are discontinued (although certain genres do seem particularly long lasting). It has been argued that a new genre is always the transformation of one or several old genres. Each new work within a genre has the potential to influence changes within the genre or perhaps prompt the emergence of new sub-genres that may later blossom into fully-fledged genres. However, such a perspective tends to highlight the role of authorial experimentation in changing genres and their conventions, whereas it's important to recognise not only the social nature of text production but also – especially – the role of economic and technological factors, as well as changing audience preferences. Again, these factors are particularly important in music.

The interaction between genres and media can be seen as one of the forces that contributes to changing genres, and some genres are obviously more powerful than others. They also differ in the status attributed to them by those who produce "texts" or songs within them and by their audiences. As various academics have put it, in the interaction and conflicts among genres, we can see the connections between textuality and power. The key genres in institutions that are *primary definers* – such as news reports in the mass media – help to establish the frameworks within which issues are defined. However, genre hierarchies also shift over time, with individual genres constantly gaining and losing different groups of users and relative status.

Idealistic theoretical approaches to genre which seek to categorise *ideal types* in terms of essential textual characteristics are *ahistorical*. As a result of their dynamic nature as processes, it has been argued that definitions of genre are always historically relative and, therefore, historically specific. Similarly, it has been suggested that no firm logical classification of genres is possible, that their demarcation is always historical or, rather, correct only for a specific moment of history. Some genres are defined only retrospectively, being unrecognised as such by the original producers and audiences. Genres need to be studied as historical phenomena, since ongoing genres and their conventions change over time.

Evolutionary change in genre essentially has three main characteristics. Firstly, it is cumulative, in that innovations are added to an existent corpus rather than replacing redundant elements. Secondly, it is conservative, in that these innovations must be basically consistent with what is already present. Thirdly, it involves differentiation, in that these processes lead to the crystallisation of specialist sub-genres.

# genre genetics

According to social theorist, political scientist, philosopher of aesthetics and hater of jazz Theodor Adorno, there are only two genres in music: serious music, for a musically educated elite; and pop music, for the masses. In his favour, he was most explicit in his condemnation of music as a commodity and the exploitative nature of the whole music and recording industry. In other early studies of musical preferences, a couple of academic types called Fox and Wince distinguished a mere five genres. These included the following:

Pop and rock
Hard rock/rhythm and blues
Jazz
Folk
Classical

In around 1976, while working with the British market, Chapman and Williams came up with ten genres:

Classical
Folk
Reggae
Jazz
Rock
Soul
Progressive
Ballads
Motown
The Osmonds

OK, so the Osmonds were a bit of an aberration, but it *was* 1976 and that end of the '70s has a lot to answer for. By the late '80s, Christenson and Peterson decided that there were 26 classes of music, but only 22 of them were true genres. These included additions such as:

Blues
Heavy metal
Disco
Funk
Punk
Gospel

They also included slightly finer distinctions, such as "art rock", "southern rock", "Christian rock" and "psychedelic rock", as well as "older new wave" and "post-new wave" new music. Several other scholars decided to reduce this list to ten classes but arrived at genres that differed dramatically from those defined earlier. Although they also drew on classical, country and western, jazz, rock, punk, soul and folk music, they also added the following:

Opera
Beautiful music
Big band

Swedish researchers found another ten workable genres, comprising the following:

Classical
Folk
Country
Mainstream pop
Rock
Punk

Reggae
New wave
'60s protest songs
Jazz

By the mid '90s, by analysing the new world order of MTV, musical scholars could distinguish only seven adolescent genres:

Rap
Soul
Country
Heavy metal
Pop
Classic rock
Alternative rock

If you search the Internet for musical genre nowadays, you'll get a variety of listings that usually include all or most of the following:

Acoustic
Alternative
Blues
Classic rock
Classical
Country
Dance
Electronic
Ethnic
Folk
Funk
Fusion
Hardcore
Hip-hop
Instrumental
Jazz
Metal
New age
Pop
Punk
Rap
R&B/soul
Reggae
Rock

Rockabilly
Ska
Soul
Soundtracks
Spiritual
Spoken word

As you can see, any attempt at a genetic analysis of genre will throw up considerable variance and discrepancies. OK, some of the variance undoubtedly derives from what we could kindly refer to as "musical innovation", with newer genres such as rap superseding dated ones such as The Osmonds, for example. Additional confusion and disinformation will be the likely result of what can only be described as careless adoption of those genre labels suggested by music critics and conveniently (and, usually, thoughtlessly) supplied by the music industry. However, as you've probably realised by now, the difficulty in deciding on genres is, for the most part, simply due to the complexity and multidimensionality of the musical products to be classified. Extrapolations of artistic change are usually plotted with reference to a *de facto* belief in a *zeitgeist*, a belief that the diverse facets of a culture can be accounted for in light of a prevailing expression. In this sense, genre can be simply a reflection of the spirit of the times, a summary or a characterisation. However, as long as different investigators continue to focus on different dimensions and use different sets of criteria for their classifications, genre discrepancies are unavoidable and generalisations about genre-to-subculture linkages are seriously tenuous or at best ragged and incomplete.

## chapter 3

# electronica and dance

> *"The poets were willing to discard prosody and even neglect the normal rules of syntax, concerning themselves with the purely sensuous effects of the words – words as sounds and symbols rather than just links in a chain of thought… Impressionist poets and composers both sought to suggest rather than state."*
> – *William Lovelock,* A Concise History Of Music

Sequencers and dance music are happy bedfellows. Throw in all that weird and wonderful digital ju-ju you can generate with various add-ons and effects and you can relax on the waterbed of electronica as well. Unfortunately, a generic boundary is a tiny cot to dance's super-king-sized double bed. It's impossible to cover all approaches to all styles of dance in a single chapter, or even a single book, although we've tried to provide a kind of functional rough outline of some of the more notable categories.

## ambient

It has been reported (although never confirmed) that ambient music found its poetic beginnings in the flat of one Brian Eno. Lying on his bed one afternoon, he was listening to music – what, in particular, isn't recorded – and he suddenly became aware of the sounds outside his flat. Everyday sounds of people, cars and weather were filtered through his flimsy walls to co-exist with the music on his record player. Eno was taken by the subtle interplay of "real" sounds with pre-made music. He was even said to have opened his window.

In a well-rounded, signifying world, you could say that ambient music is the opening of the window. As our world is neither well rounded nor particularly suited for signifying, a dictionary may be of use. In Webster's, music is "the science or art of incorporating pleasing, expressive or intelligible combinations of vocal and instrumental tones into a composition having definite structure and continuity" or, alternatively, "vocal or instrumental sounds having rhythm, melody or harmony".

The definition of *ambient* in Webster's dictionary is "to go around, surround, encompass. An encompassing environment or atmosphere." If one combines the above definitions from Webster's, ambient music would be vocal or instrumental tones that have linear structural qualities and create an encompassing environment. It sounds pretty good, but, as with the majority of our semantic commands of meaning, something is lost in the translation. Ambient music proclaims (and proves) to be outside both tone and linear structure, which means that, in part, ambient music is focused – like the impressionists were – on the effect of sound, the impression made by a signal, rather than the literal translation of melody.

Brian Eno says that a piece of pop music can usually be identified from one-fifth of a second of the music. This means that, in music, the sound itself is more important than other compositional factors. Ambient music takes the focus of pop music further, as other less important factors than the sound are given even less prominence, to the extent of sometimes hardly existing. According to ambient DJ Paul Gaverold, ambient music is "music where the rhythm is less important". According to us, ambient music is sound and texture where the music is less important.

So what do we mean by *sound* and *texture*? A sound may not necessarily be a note – for example, the sound of a waterfall doesn't have the properties that define a note; it doesn't have a defined pitch, length or starting time. Many other sounds also don't have the linear features that might define them as notes, such as the sounds of wind, rain, leaves rustling, an air conditioning unit in operation or a snake hissing.

Working directly with sound rather than symbolising sounds as notes isn't actually a new idea. The French *musique concrète* school used tape reels of recorded sounds and spliced them together with primitive processing techniques, creating clusters or chunks of sounds that changed textures whilst keeping the psychological associations of their original source material. So why work with original sound? Well, signifying the world through melody is a complicated process, because a symbol can never contain as much data as the object itself, as a symbol is, by definition, a generalisation. Therefore, symbolising a sound as a note results in loss of meaning. The proponents of *musique concrète* were interested in the effect of meaning on the listener. To them, the depletion of associated meaning was the depletion of musical significance. Ambient music sets out to play with these aural associations.

# in the beginning

There are many things that can be said to have led up to the beginnings of ambient music, the most important being the progression through disco, techno and rave; the introduction of any sound as being usable in music; the advent of the technology which makes sampling easy; and the experiments in sound made by progressive rock composers. Ambient music also borrows much of its philosophy from the impressionists and minimalist composers.

The progression is as follows. Initially, techno lost most of the melodic content of disco and began to emphasise instead the rhythmic aspects and new sound qualities. The harmonic content tended to play a simpler and less conventional role, going along with the sounds being used for little more than their own sake rather than always as notes in a harmonic and melodic context. Following on from this, rave lost most of the vocal content, lyrics and most of the remaining melodic and harmonic content, while ambient lost the predominance of rhythm, as well as almost all of its melody, lyrics, harmony and the importance of notes as its conceptual basis. This progression went along with the changing possibilities offered with technology and, to some extent, loosely paralleled a similar progression in classical music – from linear, note-based music to composition that may not have linear concepts as a basis. Schoenberg, Berg and Scriabin all used clusters of notes as a melody, while Debussy created washes of sound, rather than progressive melody lines, and Steve Reich saw the evolution of music as a textural wave, rather than a linear structure.

Far back in history, some musical events could be seen now to be leading towards ambient music, or even as actual ambient music themselves. One such example is the instrument called the Aeolian harp, such as the one mentioned in Homer's *Odyssey*. In a way, this produced environmental ambient music. The Aeolian harp is an instrument that is hung outdoors, often from a tree, and is played by the motion of wind across the strings. This is why the ambient genre is so attractive – because, when viewed from a (possibly pretentious) academic level, it can be seen as one of the purest forms of music, as it interacts with and mimics the natural world.

# evolution

The other nice thing about ambient music is that its history can be read as a representation of all experimental music and, to an extent, the evolution of dance. The detail of its philosophy is included here not only because it's particularly interesting but also because some of the concepts brought about by ambient composers seem to be the most promising suggestions for a future theory of music. The ideas covered below also apply to the final chapter, which deals with a possible future for genre.

In a similar process to that which painting and literature underwent, as music progressed it formed the concept of *sound mass*, a cluster-based version of music that minimises the importance of individual notes, as well as regular, discernible rhythms, pitches and melody. Familiar? Sound and texture where music is less important? As sound mass leaves the traditional maps of music, it concentrates instead on the texture or nature of sound, which to an extent confronts the boundary between music and noise. The use of sound mass starts with composers such as Mahler and Stravinsky and progresses to the point at which composers like Ligeti use it as a major focal point in their music.

This musical concept presents sound in a very different way from which it has usually been presented in the past, which is as clearly perceptible notes having easily audible pitch and duration. The music of composers such as Ligeti is often still written as conventional notation and played on conventional instruments or voices, and yet there is often a different note for all 32 violinists in an orchestra, for example. This leads to the individual notes becoming part of the whole sound – the *sound mass* – rather than being audible as discrete entities. This sound mass concept also relates to other composers, including Iannis Xenakis, who worked with the idea of creating musical compositions from the concept of sound grains, each too short to be clearly perceptible on their own (usually five to 40 milliseconds) but which together can be used to define any possible sound. Sound mass works like a wash of sensations, intermingling each upon each. This results in a very different listening sensation to that derived from, say, pop.

Another recent movement in music history that had an influence on the beginnings of ambient music was *futurism*. The futurists were a group of Italian composers who used "noises" as instruments, almost without any success and approval, yet they were influential in opening up the scope of possible sounds that could be used as music. This also led to the thought-based manifesto of *industrial* music, the sampling and manipulation of sounds by *musique concrète* composers made possible by electronic recording media, which is clearly another very important factor leading to the beginnings of ambient music. Meanwhile, *antimusic* was a concept that furthered the expansion of music towards including all possible sounds, and John Cage's piece '4' 33"' introduced the idea that the sounds occurring in the world around us can be heard as music, which at the time was somewhat difficult for an audience to relate to. This piece and the concepts that it presented was a very important step towards the concept of using any sound as music, as in ambient music, and was also a step away from the linear organisation of compositional structure towards the type of structures that occur in natural sounds.

This concept can also be viewed in a literal-centric way. Like deconstructionalism in prose, music based on natural sounds assumes a role in the listener, an actual interaction of associations and "readings" from the brain. Like Lyotard's and, latterly, Barthes' reading of texts, music becomes a *signified object* – a set of natural symbols out of context. In turn, the listener becomes the *signifier* – a personal filter of symbols. The interesting thing about this interaction is that the original context is kept and juxtaposed in a new context. For example, the sound of rain unconsciously has certain emotional and rational responses attached to it, both of which are individual to the listener. Not only are these responses a complex, layered interaction of memory and imagination but, as the stimulus becomes increasingly complex, a new interaction is induced in the act of listening, in which the place in which the listener hears the piece and the other elements of the song all come into play.

Strangely, this re-contextualising of naturally occurring sounds has been happening throughout the history of music. Some birdsong, when slowed down, mirrors passages by Mozart. More consciously, Messiaen created piano music from transcriptions of birdsong, actually slowing down recordings and transcribing them. Messiaen's work was itself an extension of the work of composers such as Haydn, whose "Lark" quartet was a similar attempt to assimilate natural sounds into a musical context. The transcription process used by Messiaen obviously came closer to recreating the "real" sound of a birdsong than that employed by Haydn, who simply imitated the trills in a lark's song; but, at the same time, transcribing a bird's song to the piano obviously limits the pitches to discrete levels and misses the timbre changes that are part of the bird's song. Also, the act of hearing a bird singing isn't just a simple interpretation of melody; it's the process of hearing a mingling of sounds within a surrounding environment. Ambient music samples large chunks of natural sound, either because its proponents are lazy or because they want to create a certain environment faithfully, capturing all of the subtle intricacies of frequency and tone.

Ambient music can also be traced back to minimal music, which used hypnotic, slowly changing progressions that weren't always intended to be consciously heard. The premise behind musical minimalism, like its artistic counterpart, was to have a totally unemotional piece of music – a blank, objective canvas, if you will. The irony (which may well be intentional) is that certain pieces of minimalism are the most emotional compositions ever written. This is because they allow space for the listener to project their own feelings onto them. Ambient music operates on a similar basis, allowing the listener to free-associate with the atmospheres.

## recording ambient music

Well, as the word-heavy introduction may have indicated, there are no straightforward ways of creating the definite article. A lot of chart pop has elements of ambient thrown in but doesn't quite make it with the purists. If you wish to embark on making ambient music, the best technique seems to be to juxtapose sampled sounds with synthesised sounds, a task that can be done quite simply on a sequencer. Cubase VST version 5.0 has quite an agreeable soft synth built into it called Neon, which uses VST plug-ins, and with a modicum of outside control an Aphex Twin-style pad sound can be at your command in minutes. In terms of external synthesis, a good starting point is to use sine waves for melody. If you add a serious amount of attack, the melody becomes a pad. For basses, the traditional dance square wave holds up best under sonic pressure.

In terms of sampling, consult Chapter 1 to find a run-down of options and techniques. In recording ambient music, the traditional technique is to process and trigger natural sounds in a simulation of notes. Of course, you can always simply create a background track of atmospheric sound and run notes over the top. Just remember that you're creating an atmosphere, not a tune. Think big, ethereal background. As one of Eno's oblique strategies says, "Use fewer notes."

## considerations

- You may well want to record natural sounds. For this, a DAT machine and a microphone are the weapons of choice.

- Always think big but reproduce small. If a picture tells a thousand words, a well-placed note can trigger a million melodies.

- Think of drums and rhythms as another melody line and use their interaction like another part in a classical canon.

- Use sample CDs. *Seismic Frequencies* and *Ambient* volumes one and two are our personal recommendations, but you may find the *Cuckooland* series useful. Many house/trance sample CDs also have surprisingly useful sounds.

# dancing in the streets

Dance is something of a leaky umbrella of a genre – it tries to shelter a collection of styles under one ill-fitting banner when all around a rain of other genres and styles pours through the gaps. Hence the sub-genre game. Being a resourceful rain distractor, the dance umbrella ties the new puddles together under tree-like labels, usually borrowing from other established genres for semantic inspiration.

Walk into any record shop and be beguiled by the ever-expanding series of names that producers adopt in order to make their music classifiable. Become even more confused by the amount of genre-jumping music that tries to nestle under the broken umbrella. The aim of the following sections is to break down the genre of dance into some workable sub-genres – simple labels under which still more sub-genres exist. Of course, not every style will fit comfortably within these labels, but most of the major areas are covered here.

As with all of the music in this book, a lot of the best of it (at least, in our humble opinion) is music that could be described as genre defying – not hybrids, as such, but music that is new and inspirational, music that gives rise to new genres and labels, so guide yourself through the signs and treat the labels as being just that – merely labels, words to help our wonderful order-imposing brains classify things.

It's an interesting notion that dance music as it is today wouldn't exist if not for Cubase. Back in the early days, when music was first becoming computer based, it was Cubase and Atari that blazed the frontier, with well over 90% of the classic tunes of the period emerging from smoky bedrooms equipped with Grooveboxes and Atari STs. As a general rule, dance exists in the realms of MIDI, drawing its sounds from a vast array of synths, so sequencers like Cubase are an obvious choice. It's possible to create dance music entirely via MIDI, but as horizons and CPU power expand so audio is also becoming an integral tool. And so, at the risk of sounding old and stupid, here's a very simplistic breakdown of the main dance genres and how they're approached.

House is probably the great grandaddy of dance, the blind idiot godfather of limitless permutations. However, house itself is not a single genre but a broad heading under which dozens of hybrids shelter. To look at dance's family tree is to see the scrawled lineage of white-trash hell always eager to point its inbred roots back to royalty. OK, that's probably an overstatement, but as with any aspect of history, objective records seem pretty thin on the ground. The roots of dance music change species depending on which branch of the tree the writer sits. Ask an ambient producer where dance music came from and you'd probably receive a brief overview of the history of drumming followed by a convincing argument that synthesisers where born in the harmony of Gregorian monks' chanting. The same would apply to a hip-hop producer, although this will vary, depending on which side of the Atlantic they're from. Dance music was clearly invented by the early jazz musicians, who took their cross-rhythms from slave songs.

When sitting in a tree, your view of the world is determined by the branch on which you're sitting, and many writers of dance music find themselves sitting in the tree trying desperately to see through all of the other branches. Objectivity aside, there are certain facts, records and movements that are worthy of note, and to the best of our knowledge they really did happen. Each genre of dance will have a history unique to itself, so we will deal with a sub-genre's specific evolution in its specific section.

# house

House music, the habit-forming four-to-the-floor that helped us build garages and proverbial dwelling of DJs everywhere, started life innocently enough. Its origins stretch back to the '70s, and probably later, if you wish to draw parallels. At that time, disco was firmly established and the club culture that we know and love was being nurtured by its self-conscious funk. The '70s are said to be the drawn-out come-down that inevitably accompanied the '60s, and if this is at all true then house music was a four-in-the-morning thought by one Frankie Knuckles. A New York DJ, Knuckles came to Chicago in 1977 to open an after-hours dance club, the now-infamous Warehouse. (What happens when you take away the ware from house? Indeed.) He drew large crowds because he successfully incorporated popular New York-style mixing and remixing techniques with black urban disco, and his unique style – along with the DJ'ing techniques of popular Chicago jocks like Kenny Jason and Keith "Funkmaster" Farley – paved the way for contemporary or traditional house. These early house grooves were characterised by their raw, steady beat (a slower version of four to the floor), piano riffs and synthesised tremblings. The vocals – like those of disco – weren't of the most piercing variety, but as a reflection of the times, the drug-fuelled sexual innuendoes are pretty accurate. It was the success of the Warehouse and other clubs that led to the birth of Chicago's famous record labels Trax and DJ International.

Over the years, house music grew, splintered off and incorporated other musical styles in much the same way that hip-hop did. To cut a long story short, the genre travelled around the world, evolving as it did so. It visited Belgium, where techno and new beats were invented and added. Britain took it and transformed it into acid house, while in America garage emerged, although not the speed variety that we call UK garage. (Funnily enough, garage music was also named after a club.)

# the main ingredient

Although getting its flavours from electro, hi-NRG, disco and funk, house shares a common ingredient that has pretty much been carried through to today: the beat. At the heart of house is a driving bass-drum beat commonly known as four to the floor. Its very simply a four-square beat, and to produce house you should probably know how to lay it down.

# sequencing a standard house beat

This is probably the simplest piece of drum programming that you'll ever do. First of all, start up your sequencer. (The screen shots on the next page are from Cubase, but the operating systems in most sequencers are pretty similar.) Next, create a four-bar part and loop it up, choosing the MIDI channel on which your drums are playing, which in most cases is channel 10. The default start tempo on Cubase is 120bpm, which is quite reasonable for house, which lies somewhere between 120bpm and 140bpm – ie about the speed of a dancer's heartbeat. Next, select the part and open the drum map/editor and lay down a bass-drum kick on the first beat of each bar. This is your standard house rhythm. Now lay down the classic offbeat hi-hats and the snare.

This somnambulant pulse is the basis for house, the spawning of different

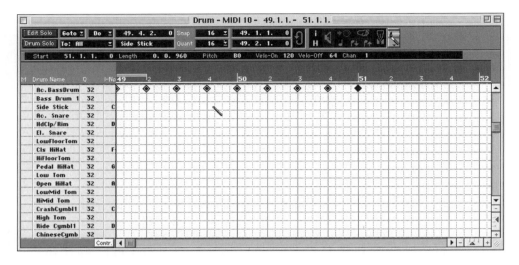

**A conventional four-to-the-floor drum map**

genres. Trance, tech house, dream house, hard house, deep house and funky house all take their single concurrence from the drumbeat. This is the way in which a lot of dance music operates. The defining factor of a genre tends to be the type of drum loop employed, and the music on top can happily jump between styles, and so, if you hear a four-to-the-floor beat pitched at around 130bpm, it's pretty safe to say that you're listening to house.

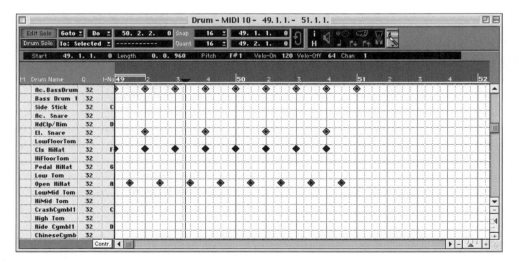

**A typical house drum map**

# house elements

Aside from the four-to-the-floor beat, most house music relies on synthesisers to produce the music. A syncopated arpeggio bass line and pad sounds under a synth lead are the *modus operandi* of this genre. The real difference, however, is in the detail. Like mistaking one girl band for another, in order to spot the ever-expanding series of sub-genres, an ear bordering on the anally retentive must be employed.

# trance

Just like frowning parents, we blame the drugs. A soundtrack to the fine line between ethereal bliss and projectile vomiting, trance is music that is designed for drugs – or, more specifically, MDMA, or ecstasy. This is the sharpened product of rave that emerged as the potential of synths grew. In many respects, it's simply a four-to-the-floor rhythm layered with electronica and soaring pads. It's usually focused around a breakdown, with either side of the song working on the plus/minus build ethic, in which a simple riff is repeated and built upon (with the exception of bass breaks and key changes). From the experimentation of acid house and techno, rave-goers discovered certain traits inherent in trance that made good drugs better. These elements were distilled by groups like Future Sound Of London, Moby, BT and Rabbit In The Moon. The integral factor to trance is the depth of the melodies. Trance always attempts the epic and is designed to extract maximum serotonin levels at desired intervals.

To achieve the trance sound, you need to start with the drums. Most house music uses either the Roland 808 or 909 drum machines. These maps are still available on other Roland drum machines, and nowadays most manufacturers offer similar kits, although with the LM9 VST plug-in it's now possible to load in multisamples and create your own drum kits. 808 samples are readily available over the Internet.

So now you have your drum sound. Like its father, house, trance uses a four-to-the-floor rhythm with syncopated claps or hits, while an arpeggiated bass line dances over the drums, and you can create your own with one of VB's synth basses and Cubase's Arpeggiator. The bass line itself needn't be too bottom-end heavy, as the floor tom carries the really low frequencies. On top of the bass line you need to apply lushly orchestrated pads, and with a bit of time and effort Neon can actually create satisfactory results. For a quick pad, choose a triangle wave, assign a heavy attack and pump the release. Now play with VST's bounteous effects for depth. A common mistake with pads is to saturate them with reverb. They already occupy a huge frequency band, and reverberation expands their range further.

For the main melody either a synth lead or piano are the trusty guns of trance. The Universal Sound Module actually has a very convincing cheese piano that's perfect for floating arpeggios. For a synth lead, applying overdrive to Neon, employing a square wave and jacking your LFO to maximum can give pleasing results.

# hard house

Here's another style that can happily thrive in the oxygen-starved world of MIDI. Hard house follows a similar structural path to house music but is sped up and, as the name implies, is generally harder. To achieve this sound, add mild distortion to your synth lines and phase the hi-hats. Hard house tends to be bass-line driven, meaning that you'll be looking to have a grooving bass melody rather than the floating lead of trance. Experiment with VST instruments and you'll be surprised at the results.

The dance of choice at the time of writing, hard house is…well, harder. When working in this genre, follow a similar direction to the one you'd pursue with trance but think more along the lines of industrial and experiment with analogue bass lines and horn noises. The speed should be about 20bpm faster and it should be far more bass oriented, with symphonic pads replaced by quick stabs of sound. Also, in hard house, the melody tends to rest in the bottom end. Think of higher states of consciousness but also quicker – techno with a four-to-the-floor pulse. In terms of EQ, a gentle curve that knocks out the middle is the standard rule, since this helps to achieve a sense of depth.

Of course, house doesn't end there. Tech trance, deep house and disco all enter in at some point, and for these similar production rules apply. House is a good genre with which to enter into dance-music production, offering accessible drum programming and simple melodies. It's also possible to create house music with a stand-alone version of Cubase 5.0.

# deep house

I don't mean to sound patronising, but deep house is deeper, with hypnotic, funky bass lines and a watery sheen applied to the production achieved by glass-like synths and heavy compression. Meanwhile, the percussion is usually more complex and hints at breakbeats.

# psychedelic trance/goa

Epitomised by Flying Rhino records, psychedelic trance is a darker, longer shade of blue, using slightly darker in tones and relying on atmospheric as well as melodic builds and drops. Combine deep house with Pink Floyd and trance and this is the result.

# nu-skool breaks

Nu-skool is a modern incarnation of old-skool hardcore that's only too happy to display its lineage. Indeed, Hybrid have reworked 2 Bad Mice and Future Sound Of London's 'Papua New Guinea'. The style is marked by spankingly tight breakbeats and advanced production. Nu-skool breaks kind of fit into the intelligent trance mould.

# drum and bass

The clever naming continues. Drum and bass relies on…wait for it…drums and bass to convey its essence. Born out of jungle, which itself was born out of rare groove and Motown, drum and bass relies on a solid and rapid two-step rhythm rolling in at between 160bpm and 180bpm. The two-step beat is driven by a snare that falls on the beat, with a bass drum falling behind every second stroke. The standard drums sounds found on the LM9 are inadequate for drum and bass production, and instead practitioners favour real drums that are time stretched and pitched up to add the desired speed and make room for the spleen-shattering bass frequencies.

If dance music is the robotic creation of contemporary composers, drum and bass is the ghost in the machine, the acceleration of breaks into a concise scientific frenzy, which – like chaos theory – form a bizarre spiritual whole when viewed from afar.

As we've seen from the evolution of other dance styles, the UK underground dance scene has been both an important point of introduction and a source of almost limitless expansion of American dance music forms such as disco, house, acid, techno, electro and rare groove. It's often been noted that England has never really had a dance music of its own – at least, not until jungle. Although jungle's most direct roots lie in the hardcore breakbeat style of techno that was popular in clubs in the late '80s and early '90s, the music's mutation of elements from not only hardcore but also reggae, ragga, hip-hop, jazz and dub, as well as its origins in social and economic factors such as racist and class-based oppression, is a distinctly British mix. Born largely in the working-class suburbs of London's East End and on the east coast, and now popular throughout England as well as Europe and North America, jungle has coalesced into one of the most exciting and distinctive British musical movements since the rock explosion of the 1960s.

# history

Drum and bass has a long and convoluted history, and its roots can be traced through hip-hop, house and hardcore, starting with breakbeat, an underground music that originally came from the USA in the late 1970s. Then, in the late '80s, the house scene erupted in UK, especially in London. As rave culture and acid house moved into the mainstream, house and breakbeat converged into what would later become drum and bass.

Jungle started to emerge from the general dance scene in the 1990s. Record labels such as Kickin' and Shut Up And Dance began to fuse breakbeat, house, hip-hop, reggae, techno and, most importantly, dub to produce what the new genre called jungle. In fact, the name originates from one of the experimental clubs in London, itself called Jungle, where the first fusion experiments were played. (Does anyone have a sense of *déjà vu*? Yet another beat-specific genre being named after its birthing club?)

Jungle was often confused with hardcore at the time, which was quite similar but was directed more towards a 4/4 bass beat rather than a looped asynchronous rhythm. Also, jungle had just made its way to a larger audience, while hardcore was a total novice to the dance scene. Both jungle and hardcore were played at the same raves, and sometimes the artists themselves didn't know whether the track they'd written was jungle or hardcore. Both of the styles co-existed under one roof, and so there was no separate jungle scene.

The defining records of the time were probably 'Johnny' by the semi-comical Johnny Jungle (who, seeing the jocular potential of his name, is now known as Pascal) and 'Hurt You So' by Johnny L on XL Recordings, both of which highlighted the breaking out of the hardcore formula. This provoked other producers – most notably 4Hero, LTJ Bukem, Grooverider and DJ Hype – to start heading in the new direction of breaks. 1993 was the end of the confusion, when hardcore and its twin brother, happy hardcore, moved towards a more progressive rhythm, while jungle remained on the breakbeat side of things. Although still reminiscent of 1992, artists such as Wax Doctor headed the darker bass-line sounds. At that point, jungle had finally gained its own identity, with dedicated clubs starting to have regular jungle nights.

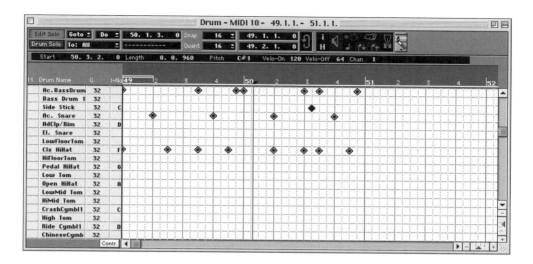

**Above: A drum and bass breakbeat drum map**
**Below: A two-step drum map**

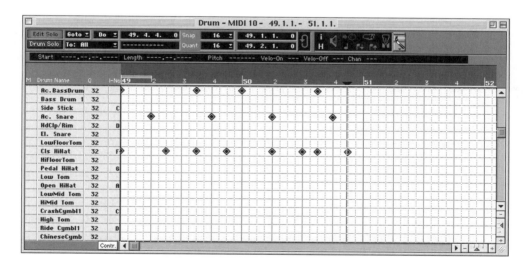

It was at around this time that artists who now occupy places in the annals of dance history began to emerge: Andy C releases the timeless jungle hit 'Valley Of The Shadows', Ed Rush throws the darkcore 'Bloodclot Attack', while LTJ Bukem rolls out the ambient 'Music'. It was – not to understate a point – Moving Shadow's year. Artists such as Omni Trio stormed the jungle scene with 'Renegade Snares' and Foul Play remixed it even better, leaving it in our minds forever. As the producers moved away from hardcore towards breakbeat, their technical skills – which had relieved jungle of the ordinary mockery of the speeded-up vocals – grew in turn. Throughout the '90s, jungle continued to grow and flourish, nourished by the sprinting up of pirate radio stations. However, it was very much a London scene, with the major clubs, labels and artists all converging in Britain's capital.

Like house, which suffered significant monkey syndrome or sub-genreitis, drum and bass is prone to succumbing to the swirling vortex of self-penned styles. Many of these are confusing to the untrained ear (or, possibly, the less anally retentive listener). What follows is a brief summary of the mainstays of its lineage.

# (happy) hardcore

This is an urban, working-class offshoot of techno that was popular in the late '80s and early '90s and is characterised by looping, speeded-up breakbeats and dense, angular bass lines. A more mainstream, rave-oriented brand of happy hardcore remained even truer to the music's acid house roots, drawing wailing divas and upbeat piano and synth lines in close proximity to hardcore's brash rhythms. Notable proponents include Acen, 2 Bad Mice and SL2.

# ragga

Ragga jungle was one of the earliest and most widely embraced forms of drum and bass that didn't rely overtly on the clichés of hardcore techno and was a direct reflection of the rising embrace of drum and bass among the street-level urban population, of which a sizeable portion are commonly of African and Caribbean descent. Ragga jungle is characterised primarily by fast, complex beat patterns, deep, tight bass and the use of soundsystem-type MC chanting sampled from old reggae, ragga and dance-hall records. Ragga also makes jungle's connection to African and Caribbean traditional and popular musics most evident, with rhythms recognisably descendent from Nyabinghi and calypso-style drumming. Artists of this sub-genre include 2 Bad Mice, Rude Bwoy Monty, Shy FX and Amazon II.

# hardstep/jump-up

This is a spare, limber refinement of hardcore and ragga that retains the hardness and rhythmic complexity of both while subtracting much of the bonus fat (rude bwoy chatter, excessive samples, etc). Hardstep also carries more of a sense of progression, varying drum patterns more

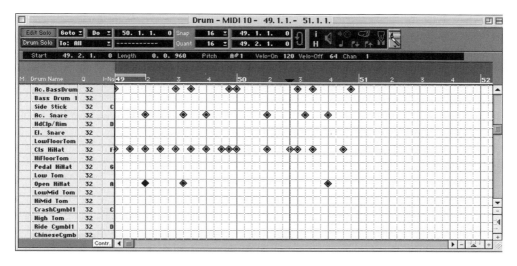

**A hardstep drum map**

musically and focusing on bass as a melodic element. Although slight variations exist between hardstep and the more recently applied jump-up, with the latter generally referring to a sprightlier, more dynamic brand of hardstep, the two are for the most part used interchangeably. Proponents include Ray Keith, DJ SS, Dillinja and DJ Zinc.

# darkside

A somewhat historically rooted term, darkside refers to a more spare and pessimistic style of hardcore that sought to differentiate itself from the more above-ground, mainstream appeal of rave that by the early '90s was producing only the most repetitive and uncreative of music. Darkside artists stripped the bright melodies and speeded-up samples from hardcore and replaced them with gloomy bass lines and less obvious melodic passages more reminiscent of Detroit techno than happy hardcore. Darkside is also something of a bridge between early hardcore and the increasing sophistication of the hardstep and experimental drum and bass of DJ SS, Solo, Source Direct and the Metalheadz artists.

# techstep

Techstep is similar to hardstep in its beat structures and attitude but differs in its use of techno-type elements such as bleeps and synth squelches as well as its dense, heavily treated bass lines. After the softening of drum and bass in the wake of jungle's first wave of widespread popularity (major-label signings, international tours, etc), darker techstep-type jungle has risen to the fore of the underground, proving to be one of the most active and interesting splinter styles in its use of experimentalism. Labels on the bleeding edge of this style include Emotif, No U-Turn, Penny Black and SOUR, and a good introduction exists in Emotif's label compilation *Techsteppin'*, as well as in SOUR's *Nu-Skool Update*. Other artists of the sub-genre include Ed Rush, Nico, Solo and Shapeshifter.

# ambient/intelligent

First used to designate drum and bass styles that drew heavily on atmosphere and environment, the term *ambient* has come to have something of a negative connotation among the hardcore fraternity, referring to loopy, relatively unchallenging rhythmic programming and a predominance of sugary, pop-oriented melodic textures. Most likely, the backlash has as much to do with the fact that it was the softer, jazzier, ambient-style drum and bass that was the first to sever its roots with the underground and gain popularity among a wide audience. Proponents include TPower, Omni Trio, Source Direct, Photek, 4Hero and Dave Wallace.

# recording drum and bass

Like most dance music, similar principles interplay throughout the overall genre of drum and bass. The stylistic differences of the above sub-genres don't actually affect production to any major degree. The basic drum and bass set-up is a computer-based sequencer and a sampler. Laying down a drum and bass track is similar to creating other dance music – structurally, a long drum intro leads to a bass breakdown, while the interplay of pads and atmospheres generally seems to be more akin to ambient music, lifting the listener at concentric points.

# considerations

Like its name suggests, drum and bass relies on the bass for its foremost voice. When you first attempt to create some of your own drum and bass, expect to be first disappointed with the preset bass sounds available to you and then confused that, next to other genre mixes, all of your drum and bass attempts sound muddy and confused. This is due to the vast frequency range that low-band bass takes up. What sounds almost chunky and distinct on quality monitors steals frequencies when played on normal speakers. To help compensate for this, producers usually pitch up the drums (a practice that, to begin with, was an unintentional by-product of speeding up breaks) and use syncopated bass lines – for example, making sure that notes don't fall at the same time as the bass drum. Compressing mixes also helps to add a sense of punchiness by restricting certain frequencies.

Another key element in producing drum and bass is the ability to cut up drums and trigger separate parts of a loop. In the past, this was a long and laborious task. Now, though, Steinberg's ReCycle allows you to open a sample and automatically splice it at the zero points or converging volumes of the waveform, thus preventing that mysterious clicking that often bedevils sample editing. ReCycle also enables you to send cut-up loops to a sampler as sample banks, automatically assigning them a MIDI configuration. You can then export the MIDI map and trigger each part or slice from your sampler, allowing your loops to be played at any tempo without suffering timbre mutation.

# industrial

*"At first, the art of music sought and achieved purity, limpidity and sweetness of sound. Then different sounds were amalgamated, care being taken, however, to caress the ear with gentle harmonies. Today, music, as it becomes continually more complicated, strives to amalgamate the most dissonant, strange and harsh sounds. In this way, we come ever closer to noise-sound."*
– *Luigi Russolo,* The Art of Noises, *1913*

Remember the '80s, that wonderfully overt pimple of a decade that, instead of hiding its pus-filled centre, gleefully pasted red mascara around its edges? A lot of people who were buying the red mascara (and many other colours besides) were new romantics, a breed of teenagers separated from goths by an idealistic coincidence. As the decade dawned, the finely painted line that separated goths from their jolly counterparts dissolved. This coming together of self-conscious youth was partly due to the mainstream successes of bands like The Sisters Of Mercy, Depeche Mode and Joy Division.

The common ground appears to be a nurturing of electronica combined with a comically bleak outlook. As technology progressed through the '90s, this comically bleak outlook became better produced, and for people that found grunge that tad bit blasé industrial became the only genre in which that a well-dressed goth could skulk in solitude.

Industrial is characterised literally by industrial sounds, the noise of metal grating against stone. The din made by factories whose sole output is babies' heads is the sound that best suits the genre. Aside from the '80s pioneers and a possible nod to *musique concrète*, the bands that rule the roost, so to speak, are Nine Inch Nails (Trent Reznor's DIY utility), Skinny Puppy, Einstürzende Neubauten and "come-to-daddy"-period Aphex Twin.

But that, dear reader, is a very occluded view of a much greater whole. Like ambient and minimalism, industrial is a genre founded upon ideas. In fact, ambient music closely parallels the ideas within industrial, but if you thought that the philosophies behind ambient were pushing reason then industrial is happy to pile on more complexities in the pursuit of its aim. The original term *industrial* comes from Genesis P Orridge's seminal group Throbbing Gristle, best known for their literally deafening noise jams and their allegiances with William Burroughs and Brian Gyson. In the late '70s, Throbbing Gristle found time from their endless pursuit of the alchemists' scale to set up a record label called Industrial Records. The term *industrial music,* however is usually accredited to Monte Cazazza, who coined it as a negative label for '70s music's (unsuccessful) quest for "authenticity". The negative connotations of the word *industrial* were soon lost when many '80s bands began describing their styles as such.

However, these bands run into a quandary with industrial purists. The groups who were released on Throbbing Gristle's imprint – including Cabaret Voltaire, ClockDVA and SPK – all combined an interest with transgressive culture with an almost religious pursuit of noise. Throbbing Gristle stood by the idea that noise and frequency had the ability to change states of consciousness, that in their cosmogony the correct combinations of frequency vibrations would "tear a whole in the perceived world". Their claims did have some effect – fans who saw them live have given reports of hallucinations, nausea and general trippiness, as well as experiencing sexual arousal and loss of hearing. Something worth noting is that the word *noise* is used here in its literal meaning, not in the sense of Nirvana's use of feedback or a Mogwai-style loss of control. Throbbing Gristle literally produced noise by whatever means they had, including drills, and this is noise that's pretty devoid of any semblance of melody, in the best possible sense. The original industrial music came in a variety of colours – pink noise, white noise and black noise. The bands that coined the term in the '80s usually stuck to a shade of pale magenta.

Industrial originally evolved with Warp-inspired drill and bass and certain obscure techno producers sampling volcano shudders, but a layman's definition fits groups on Nothing Records (Trent Reznor's label) and some of the heavier, funkier heavy metal labels (think thrash, think factories). Popular industrial musicians such as Front 242 and Ministry *do* draw on the elements of early industrial music, but usually only in reference to the rock and techno arenas, although sometimes this just means aggression, paranoia and dolls with no eyes ("pretty scary, huh?"), a far cry from mugwump-juicing, homo-erotic beatings). Other bands have explored industrial music's relationships with ritual music, *musique concrète*, academic electronic music, improvisation and pure noise. In recent times, through the popularity of ambient music, several artists involved in this more experimental tradition have achieved more popular recognition than before.

Like ambient music, industrial's primary sources of inspiration are the futurist and minimalist movements and guys like Frank Zappa. Mix this up with a healthy splash of drug-induced paranoia, a feeling of unreality and a semblance of hope in the promise of change through pain and you pretty much have industrial.

## how to make industrial music

Arguably the best method for producing this sort of music is to lick the back of a particularly ugly toad and stand under a pylon. (Size is an issue here; the pylon needs to be at least big enough to worry villagers 40 miles away about the risks of leukaemia.) When you've found your toad and your pylon, stand underneath until the subtle carcinogenic pulses are in time with your own heartbeat. This could take anything from an hour to twelve months. When you leave, your body will be attuned to the false rhythm of industrial living. Now find a noise-making device and hit, bow or strum it while screaming/sobbing your fears about cancer and/or madness. Cynical, yes, but it's guaranteed to be genuinely effective. If that sounds too dangerous or stupid (and, after all, not everyone has a pylon within walking distance), you can always make industrial music at home on a standard sequencer.

For mainstream industrial, you'll play most of your songs in the key of *disturbed*. The desired effect is the mixing of musical textures, and a detuned classical guitar over reversed death-rattles is a good place to start. In fact, this is one formulaic device that you *can* bring into home production, the contrast between sweet and ugly. Like the innocent strains of a music box over a spleen-shattering bass drone, industrial thrives off the accentuation of light and dark.

## considerations

- Unlike many genres who nod towards electronic music, there are no set drum loops or genre-defining patterns in industrial. Groups use live drummers just as readily as they use sampled drills and hammers. On the techno front, think crazier and more distorted. For inspiration, listen to releases from Rephlex Records' and Warp Records' techno forays.

- Live instruments are a consideration, and you'll want to mic them up in the traditional sense. However, you might also want to lay extra microphones around amps and speakers to pick up noise and atmospherics.

- A lot of industrial music uses unconventional objects as instruments. Unfortunately there are no hard and fast rules for recording power tools, so you'll have to use your discretion. Industrial is also probably the only genre in which digital distortion and feedback are plus points. In terms of synths and noises, analogue and twisted are the hallmarks of industrial. Manipulate sounds as much as possible and remember that repetition of almost anything produces some inkling of a composition.

- Make use of sample CDs. In terms of dark and clangy, the CDs worth looking at are *Twisted Beats*, *Malice In Wonderland* and the *Cuckooland* series.

# hip-hop

Hip-hop is one of those genres that loves to spin a history for itself. You can trace it back to the earliest and naffest rap music on throughout the breakdance days through a dense rainforest of sub-genres and styles until you end up with Eminem and the recent hip-hop convention where the elder spokesmen of the gangsta culture are suddenly worrying about the sexist, violent themes and obscene language, because radio stations in the George Dubya version of the good ole US of A have stopped playing the more offensive hip-hop in a really big way.

There's normally a lot of confusion about the interchangeability of the terms *hip-hop* and *rap*, and rightly so. Essentially, they're the same thing. Hip-hop likes to think that it keeps its messages political and social, while rap generally just tells your mates how good you are and that you're going to shag their girlfriends. Both styles – until recently, at least – used the standard set-up of two turntables and a microphone. With groups like Roots Manuva, the set-up in hip-hop is now becoming more similar to the set-up used in dance music, with turntables being hooked up to samplers and computers with live instruments. Now far removed from the black ghetto kids in the early '70s flexing their lyrical muscles to the sounds of Motown/disco breaks for fun, in rap and hip-hop today the improvisation is less improvised, and now more than ever hip-hop is a lifestyle lived by the average middle-class white kid. It's a big business now, and its roots are being exploited by the likes of Eminem, although, if the truth is told, the black rappers out there aren't really doing their bit to get rid of the under-educated, oppressed-minorities tag. If one year Dre is singing about shooting the whites and the next year he's helping Eminem to become the biggest-selling artist of all time, even in a genre ostensibly run by white-hating black rappers money is always more important than colour. Anyway, moving swiftly on…

It all started way back in the early '70s with a bloke called Kool Herc. Hailing from Jamaica, he was into chatting lyrics or poetry over dub, toast-reggae records, essentially discounting the early classics, such as Bach and his canons, and forming the first variation on remixing a tune. With this idea in tow, he and a few close friends (known as the Herculoids, not to be mistaken with the rectal disorder) waved down a yellow cab and made their way to New York – more specifically, the Bronx. Unfortunately, the followers felt that Mr Herc's tunes weren't quite wicked enough, feeling that they required newer "of-the-moment" breaks, and so, taking some funk and disco records, they started off afresh. People dug the new style and hip-hop was born and began to rise with almost two-step velocity. Mr Herc was also the first to use two turntables and a microphone – apart from (would you believe it?) Jimmy Saville. With this style and set-up, Herc found that he could play two records that were the same and use an audio mixer to blend the records together, keeping the song going forever.

That's the mixing side dealt with. The mic controllers, or *emcees*, set themselves up as the elite of street boys who found that ounce of inspiration to shout such things as "the roof is on fire" and "one two three, who's the best emcee?". The emcee's job was to have the best rhymes and the quickest licks in order to outdo his fellow emcee and to make himself look dope and his opponent look tired.

One of the main reasons why hip-hop grew at such an extreme rate was the fact that you didn't need any really expensive equipment; all you needed was two record players, a mixer, a mic and some kids who liked dissin'. Also, as radio was the main receptive and positive source of information in the black areas, it was a way of giving the community a kind of glue to hold the populace together. At about the same time, in the West, house was popping its little four-to-the-floor head out of some Illinois sewer and an influx of Europop shite was killing off everything but the little middle-class white kids' shopping lists.

In the mid '70s, the radios started to play to a whiter audience in order to keep the artists afloat. With the white kids starting to get into the hip-hop scene, and with the godlike names of James Brown and George Clinton practically unheard of on the airways, hip-hop was just growing faster and faster. Some of the other dominant styles aired at that time were those of bands like The Rolling Stones and The Grateful Dead.

By the time of Afrika Bambaataa and Grandmaster Flash, hip-hop had faced a large number of stylistic changes. Bambaataa, Flash and Clinton, who all essentially found funk to be a dying style, used a collection of funk records and disco breaks to create the infamous B-boy era of '79. Sylvia Robinson's Sugarhill Gang broke out with 'Rapper's Delight', Flash with 'The Message' and The Universal Zulu Nation with 'Planet Rock'. All well known in the hip-hop world, these geniuses of scratching and mixing started to create the monoliths of the early '80s.

Through the mid to late '80s, crews like NWA and Public Enemy started to talk about issues of police oppression and brutality to the blacks and ghettos. Thereafter, hip-hop started to take on the second definition of the word *genre*: a portrayal of scenes from ordinary life. The outward message of hatred from either side, both blacks and whites, created a racial divide that unfortunately still exists today. A side-effect of this was *gangsta rap*, performed by groups, cliques, crews, gangs, posses, hoods and bloods who were bound to the ghettos, had had enough and wanted out, and they decided to let people know. Hip-hop had assumed an attitude, and through this it jumped from being an esoteric art form to being the third-biggest industry in the world, after country music and porn.

On the flip-side of the '80s, with groups like De La Soul, Naughty By Nature, Tone Loc and LL Cool J, there was a lighter, more novel tone, and this took the heat off the hardcore side of hip-hop. With pink lapels, bad hair, trousers big enough to fill the San Andreas fault and, of course, jewellery, it truly was…umm…nice. The early '90s saw the hip-hop market spread through many different styles – R&B, soul, rap, gangsta, Christian, satanic, rock and novelty (ie an all-girl line-up).

Hip-hop is a lifestyle that has its own language, dress and mindset and is continuously evolving. Fortunately, due to corporate greed, most of these earlier styles died away quite quickly and quietly. Unfortunately, with

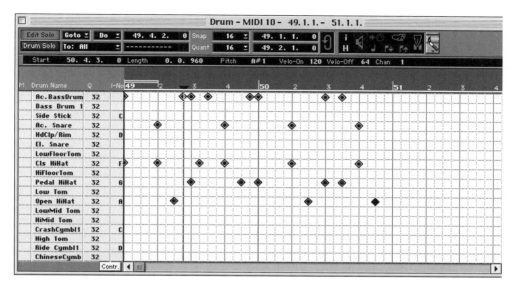

**A hip-hop drum map**

people like Sean "Puffy" Combs creating more and more slipstream pop shit, the market just gets bigger and more confusing and less worth listening to.

# how to make hip-hop

Beats per minute usually range from 96 to 140, and these beats tend to be very sparse, usually relying on the interplay between the kick and snare for their impact, while the hi-hats tend to be a minor fill-in. Traditionally, this has been done essentially to give the rapper enough headroom to display his "vocal prowess".

# trip-hop

Trip-hop is a complex melding of lush soundscapes infused with a rich layering of soulful guitar riffs, jazzy horns and atmospheric strings interwoven with innovative sampling and grounded in a hip-hop beat, slowed to a brooding, moody tempo. It's a genre so startlingly refreshing and innovative that the term trip-hop itself only came into existence in the mid '90s in an attempt to describe a musical style that defies all known musical categories. Trip-hop is an obscure offshoot of the umbrella term of electronic music and draws from a kaleidoscope of influences including jazz, hip-hop, dub and drum and bass. The essence of trip-hop is the sampling and remixing of snippets of music from the recordings of other artistes. As such, trip-hop has often been accused of being merely a hybrid sample which stitches together imitations of other genres and is undeserving of being termed a musical genre in its own right.

The question with trip-hop, as with most dance forms, is – as Plato may have asked – should an art form which employs mimicry be discredited? In *The Republic*, where he deals with the function of art in the republic, Plato discusses the imitative quality of art, the appeal of art and poetry and the effects of poetry and drama. Written in the form of a dialogue between Socrates and Glaucon, the main thrust of the argument asserts that God is the one and only true creator and that all other forms of creativity are but mere imitations of the original idea conceived by Him. Socrates charges the creative arts for being deceptive and far removed from reality and asserts the argument that creativity opposes logic and reasoning, appealing only to the emotions. The dialogue culminates in a call for the banishment of the creative arts from the republic. Plato accuses the creative arts – such as painting and poetry – of being "the imitator of the thing which others produce" and "the producer of the product" of being "three removes from nature".

Extrapolating Plato's theory, we could say that trip-hop music is of far less value, as the genre is in a way rather self-referential. To be brutally frank, or equally earnest, trip-hop is music that draws material from previous recordings by other musicians. However, interposed with Plato's theory on mimetic art is the fact that the production of trip-hop music does require a certain level of skill that is non-imitative in nature, although production techniques do share similarities with other dance genres. To produce good trip-hop music requires a mastery of technical procedure and musical talent. Technical competence is required to operate the spinning deck, mixers and synths, for instance. Furthermore, there is a particular vocabulary of techniques involved with sampling. A sample mix is usually grounded by a drum and bass line that holds a repeating rhythm. The rhythm forms a foundation that is open to any and every sound that can be woven into the mix to form a harmonious symphony, from instrumentation that enters in harmony with the beats to ambient sounds, vocals and rapping that may fall in and fade out. Care has to be taken to ensure that all of this audio input is manipulated in such a way that it blends in with the underlying rhythm set-up within the composition.

There are also what's known as *rhythm drop-outs* that occur in trip-hop when repeating beats stop and something else – such as an echo, for example – falls in. Another criterion for producing good trip-hop is the musical talent required to pick out samples and sounds that gel, and compositional competence is required to interweave layers of instrumentation and orchestration, while an acute sensitivity to rhythm is required to adjust the rotation of a sample to the precise speed of the music. Then there is *scratching*, the act of briefly turning the vinyl disc in the opposite direction to produce, literally, a scratching sound, which could be considered a whole new art form in itself. (Of course, it's arguable whether or not scratching counts as music, and whether decks qualify as real instruments or merely production tools.) Co-ordination is critical to scratching, from entering at the precise moment to knowing the exact sequence of movements necessary to produce the right tone and rhythm.

To illustrate the particular level of skill needed to produce trip-hop, check out some of the works by Portishead, a band recognised by critics as one of the pioneers of the genre and who won the prestigious Mercury music prize in 1994 for their genre-defining debut album, *Dummy*. Portishead's videotaped live recording at the Roseland Ballroom, *PNYC*, is an excellent visual document of the skill involved in the production of trip-hop. Their set features a live orchestra consisting of string and brass sections, which illustrates Portishead's ability to co-ordinate layers of instrumentation to produce a polyphonic composition. Geoff Barrow's adeptness at scratching and sampling is crystallised in the performance of 'Only You' (*PNYC*, disc one, track six), in which he scratches to a sample of 'She Said' by The Pharcyde. As his hand deftly skims the disc, Barrow picks out the word "flip" in the line "flip like that", scratching in time with the beat and distorting and emphasising the word.

In spite of all of the justification in terms of the skill required to produce it, critics of trip-hop would undoubtedly still discredit it for its reliance on sampling and mimicry. This sentiment is echoed by Plato, who states, "If he had genuine knowledge of the things he imitates, he would rather devote himself to real things than to the imitation of them." Proponents of trip-hop generally do have a "genuine knowledge" of musical technique, and indeed a thorough understanding of music is needed before an artist can sample from it. The reason why trip-hop artists such as Portishead, Massive Attack and Tricky propose to imitate rather than, as Plato says, "devote [themselves] to real things" is perhaps justified by the need to draw on precedence to provide a reference point from which innovation and revolution may take place. After all, as we've been trying to stress throughout this book, it's often difficult to achieve a breakthrough without first understanding the history and background of the current situation.

Drawing from a shared vocabulary of precedent works sets up a dialogue with the past which helps to contextualise a new creation. The jazz influence in trip-hop, for example, is a clear reference to the spirit of spontaneous creativity that characterises jazz music. Just as the great jazz bands of the past and present are collectives of individual musicians often engaging in improvisational playing, much of trip-hop recalls the spontaneity of jazz, in terms of the way in which a mix is open to any instrumentation that can spontaneously enter and drop out of the mix. By comparing to a known past, we may find it easier to understand the cultural situation that gave rise to the current interpretation of jazz – that is, arguably, trip-hop.

The cultural heritage of jazz may be traced back to the African-American slave culture. Jazz was the result of the superimposition of African traditional tribal drum rhythms, gospel music and field hollers, which seems to indicate that jazz is essentially an expression of life. The hardship endured by the African-American slaves in early America resulted in the birth of a music that is essentially a celebration of human life. Its proponents claim that trip-hop is a similar celebration of humanity opposed to the dehumanisation and increasing mechanisation of modern life. A greater reliance on technology has desensitised us to our emotions, and techno music – which is heavily reliant on audio technology – is possibly a good indicator of the desensitisation of the modern world.

Techno music pre-dates trip-hop but also falls under the same all-encompassing umbrella of electronic music. Techno music is much more programmatic than trip-hop, concentrating more on maintaining a monotonous progression of beats to facilitate dancing. It also places less emphasis on melody, tone and lyrics than trip-hop does. Although the advent of trip-hop was largely intuitive, rather than a coherent movement with a deliberate manifesto, it could be proposed that one of the driving forces of trip-hop was the need to inject a level of human emotion into the mechanical world of electronic music, hence the references that trip-hop makes to jazz and the richness of emotional expression associated with that particular genre.

While trip-hop makes references to jazz, it is in itself an entirely new and different sound. In the case of trip-hop, contrary to Plato's suggestion that "surely no craftsman makes the idea itself", mimicry has become the generator of a totally new art form. As we all know, out of mimicry may occasionally rise originality. At the time of its birth in the late '80s, trip-hop had no precedent body of works and critics, but the style of music was so refreshingly different that the music industry had to coin a new term to describe a musical style that eluded classification into standard categories of pop, rock and electronic.

Trip-hop is a genre that elevates mimicry to an art form, but there is a fine line between creative sampling and mere plagiarism. As mentioned earlier, with its complex polyphonic nature, trip-hop can, with some legitimate argument, be considered as a musical genre in its own right, as it requires its own array of technical and musical skill, while its rich emotional content is another factor that validates it as a worthy genre of music. Although it corresponds to what Plato terms as "mimetic art", it surpasses mere plagiarism and elevates sampling to an intellectual art form through the creativity injected by personal interpretation.

Trip-hop and drum and bass tend to replace the usual four-to-the-floor beats of house with breakbeats, the more cut up the better. The slow dub bass lines are still there but are more accentuated, with echo and reverb and a bit of sub-bass applied. If you want a genuine trip-hop sound, go lo-fi. Don't worry too much, as almost anything goes here.

In the UK, trip-hop has seen an astonishingly quick ascension to widespread popularity, rivalled perhaps only by jungle, and even then exceeding it in terms of audience. Once-fledgling labels such as Mo'Wax, Ninja Tune and Wall Of Sound have since grown into release-a-week powerhouses, often prepping artists for major-label success. The music continues to evolve, as well, with its early laziness proving little more than a blueprint for artists who have taken the style in any number of directions, fusing it with electro, techno, live funk, jazz, soul and drum and bass. Now dabbled in by any number of Brit-pop and indie-rock artists, from Stereolab and Blur to Arab Strap and Day Behavior, the music has also broken well beyond the clubs, although it continues to thrive there as well.

# graphic sampler

If you want to cultivate a catholic taste but still hold a healthy abhorrence for crap, have an ear-browse through some of the following:

- Hip-Hop – Public Enemy, Boogie Down Productions, Run-DMC, A Tribe Called Quest, Eric B And Rakim, De La Soul;

- Electro – Grandmaster Flash, Afrika Bambaataa, Herbie Hancock, The Egyptian Lover, Man Parrish;

- Trip-Hop – Massive Attack, Portishead, Tricky, DJ Shadow, Wagon Christ, DJ Krush, Coldcut.

## over-generous on the genres?

OK, so we've not covered everyone's favourite dance genre in as much detail as everyone – including us – would have liked. Dance music loves labels, and in many ways this is perhaps a good example of how the term *genre* can be applied badly. As mentioned in the introduction, in many respects dance is a great example of how the word can be little more than pompous, inauthentic and downright misleading jargon designed to exclude and intimidate all but a smug bunch of initiates. However, if you're interested in a particular dance genre and you want to delve into what you will undoubtedly find to be an overly self-indulgent display of omphalescence, there are numerous individual books devoted to single genres and styles in which you can immerse yourself to your heart's content…or at least until it begins to arrest.

# it's only rock 'n' roll but we like it

*"Wanted: Narcissistic Fender rhythm guitarist for up-and-coming rock band. Minimal technique OK."*
– Ad in The Village Voice, *New York*

There must be something in that old saying "rock 'n' roll is here to stay", since certain pundits claim that its generic roots actually go back farther than two centuries and they're as integral to Western culture as 'The Marseillaise', 'The Hucklebuck' and '(I Can't Get No) Satisfaction'. As DJ Alan Freed once said, rock 'n' roll is bigger than all of us. And since he coined the phrase, he ought to know.

## give me that old-time rock 'n' roll

Back in mid 1949, *Billboard* magazine began a chart listing for "Rhythm And Blues". If the term had been around then, the magazine could have just as easily listed this as "Rock 'n' Roll", because within six years much of rhythm and blues was what we now know as rock 'n' roll. Blues, gospel, swing, boogie-woogie and rhythm and blues in every imaginable permutation merged in a kind of blending, a transition, a hybridisation or maybe even a genetic modification. The '40s and early '50s set the scene for rock 'n' roll, and the rhythm and blues of the period was the melting pot for all earlier musical forms. Until then, all of those musical forms were thrown into a pot, spiced up by the artists of the day and mixed up like a good gumbo. And if rhythm and blues was the gumbo, rock 'n' roll was what boiled out of the pot.

Rhythm and blues developed in urban America during the '40s because the money was there; war-production paycheques and post-war prosperity reaching even into the ghettos set people to buying. In those days, R&B *was* rhythm and blues, not like what tries to pass itself off as R&B today, which is nothing more than "recycled and boring" and sounds more like over-produced lounge music. In the early days, people bought radios and they bought record players. They fed juke boxes and they bought records and they went to concerts at the Apollo and at the Hollywood Bowl. They made rhythm and blues profitable.

The electric guitar upped the stakes and expanded the musical options for blues players like Lightnin' Hopkins, Muddy Waters, Elmore James, Howlin' Wolf, T-Bone Walker and, a bit later, Bo Diddley, almost all of whom conceded some influence to the earlier and brightest of guitar novae, Charlie Christian. During 1954-55, Sam Phillips and his Sun Records studio in Memphis began to record Elvis Presley, and one of Elvis' first cuts was 'Mystery Train', a rhythm and blues tune co-written by Phillips and Little Junior Parker. Although Sun Records probably entered the musical consciousness with the emergence of Elvis, it's worth noting that, way before "the King", Sam Phillips had already produced Muddy Waters, Ray Charles and BB King.

Another change to the way in which music was played and produced was the shift from big bands to small combos, and Lionel Hampton was a major figure in that transition during the late '40s. It's also worth remembering that

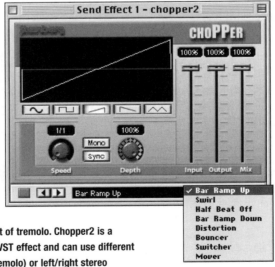

Traditional rock 'n' roll uses a lot of tremolo. Chopper2 is a combined tremolo and autopan VST effect and can use different waveforms to modulate level (tremolo) or left/right stereo position (pan) by using either tempo sync or manual modulation speed settings. It can also be used to produce '50s-style tremolo effects and can produce autopan effects when set to stereo

nurtured within his combo for two years was Ruth Jones, better known as Dinah Washington, a future icon of rhythm and blues and, later, rock 'n' roll. Music was now being shaped by the venues in which it was performed. Singers sang louder, amps were cranked up and the feet kept stomping.

Interestingly enough, names familiar in the '40s still thread through our music 50 years later. The recently deceased John Lee Hooker was a popular R&B artist back then, cutting his first big hit in 1949. On the West Coast, he recorded for LA-based Modern Records, along with Etta James and Jimmie Witherspoon, among others. Meanwhile, Ike Turner, the somewhat infamous ex-husband of Tina Turner, arranged BB King's first recording contract. 'The Thrill Is Gone' was a huge hit for King 20 years after it was written and originally recorded in 1951 by Ray Hawkins for the rhythm and blues market.

The covering of black R&B tunes by white artists became rampant in the mid '50s, notably between 1954 and 1956. Not that this hadn't happened before, of course; even clean-cut white boys like Pat Boone built their careers on covers of rhythm and blues tracks, and in 1954 Bill Haley And The Comets covered the Big Joe Turner tune 'Shake, Rattle And Roll'. Dinah Washington brought along the gospel-flavoured side of rhythm and blues, while Ray Charles provided the blend of blues and gospel that hop-skipped popular music to become soul as we identify it now.

As a genre, rock 'n' roll is probably too limiting and too restrictive, yet it's often used as an all-inclusive (although slightly leaky) umbrella. Within the rock genre, countless sub-genres and styles have emerged and blended and are constantly recycled, even today, and it's easy to hive off sections like heavy metal, glam rock, folk rock, '60s soul, stadium rock, punk, etc. However, taking all of that into account, it's still safe to say that the popular music we listen to today is as much shaped by influences from the past as by our expectations for today. Since it's impossible to detail all rock genres in a single book, we've picked out a few acknowledged "signifiers" to provide you with a bit of interesting generic background. As for what you do with it or how you might reference it to your own music...well, that's up to you.

# metal

Heavy metal supposedly got its name from a line in Steppenwolf's famous biker anthem 'Born To Be Wild'. Originally, it emerged in the mid '70s as a sort of back-to-basics rock 'n' roll, featuring ear-bleeding volume, screaming lead guitars and trebly vocals backed by a blunt blues rhythm with all the subtlety of a lead pipe. As a genre, the songs broke new ground

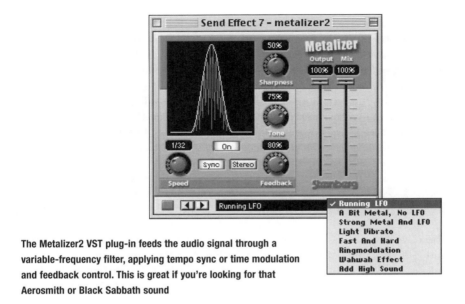

**The Metalizer2 VST plug-in feeds the audio signal through a variable-frequency filter, applying tempo sync or time modulation and feedback control. This is great if you're looking for that Aerosmith or Black Sabbath sound**

in the overall human experience by exploring themes involving fast cars, large-chested women, Norse gods and handfuls of amphetamines. In a twisted testosterone haze of male misogyny, heavy metal was taken to heart by pasty-faced and sexually anxious adolescents around the globe. Bands revelled in names like Saxon, Judas Priest, Motörhead, Deep Purple, Iron Maiden, Def Leppard and, of course, Black Sabbath. As a generic trait, each metal album had to include one really shmaltzy ballad, ("for the ladies") among the rest of the Marshall stack-driven tracks that, even if played at relatively low volume, made standing behind a revving 747 sound like a quiet night in. Like all rock genres, heavy metal soon fractured into sub-genres, such as death, thrash and even funk metal. Nowadays, a whole new generation can listen to bands like Limp Bizkit and break things to their hearts' content. The formula isn't rocket science – just randomly mix a lot of ear-bleedingly loud thrash guitars, bass and drums together with either a satanic growl or a near-falsetto whiny vocal.

# prog and glam rock

We all knew that rock 'n' roll was getting far too silly when bands started to book airline seats for their guitars. During the so-called prog rock era, pretentiousness reached biblical proportions and a lot of the fun went out of the music as musicians – or *artists*, as they then preferred to be called – began to take themselves far too seriously. Stage acts became hugely theatrical and concept albums became all the rage. Prog rock bands included the likes of Pink Floyd, Yes, Camel, The Moody Blues, King Crimson and, weirdly enough (according to some critics, at least), Jethro Tull. Although somewhere at the folky end of prog rock, Jethro Tull became famous for their twisted stage antics and piss-takes on the whole concept-album idea. They also almost single-handedly toppled General Noriega when the US troops surrounding his sanctuary in the Vatican Embassy blasted out Jethro Tull tracks 24 hours a day until he finally came out. Bands like Pink Floyd and The Moody Blues owed much of their success to large quantities of LSD, but both of these bands also pushed the boundaries of studio production techniques and acoustic presence. In many respects, they also pioneered electronica technique and probably indulged in some of the first use of samples.

As a genre, we tend to think of glam rock as a nasty aberration of platform shoes and some of the ugliest performers to ever take to the rock stage. Bands that we normally associate with this genre include T-Rex, Slade, The Sweet, The Bay City Rollers, Alice Cooper (perhaps) and – although we try to forget – Gary Glitter. But hey, if you really feel that you want to make this sort of music, don't panic; it's nothing that can't be cured with a little Prozac and a polo mallet. Then, when you get out of rehab, just blame the whole mess on David Bowie and try to move on.

# punk

Like any musical genre, it's hard to pinpoint where and when it actually began. However, unlike any other musical genre, punk rock was supposedly started as a deliberate reaction to the mass commercialism of music – or, at least, that's how popular mythology has it. A more cynical view might be that punk was just a lot of raw, lo-fi, recycled rock 'n' roll with a particularly bad dress sense that was commercialised and exploited just like any other popular musical genre. Interestingly enough, in the year 2000, it's still common to see someone trying to be *a* punk rather than seeing someone be punk.

In the late '60s and early '70s, the music industry rang eerily familiar in its method of promoting trends over music. The public was spoonfed music from which corporations simply intended to make a profit. The backlash to this came to be known internationally as *punk rock*. In New York during the early 1970s, young and virtually unknown artists like Patti Smith, The Velvet Underground and The Dolls Of New York (later changed to The New York Dolls) introduced a new style of "alternative bohemian" entertainment rooted in a do-it-yourself attitude – short, frenetic songs; aggressive, sometimes confrontational stage presences; and angry messages against consumerism

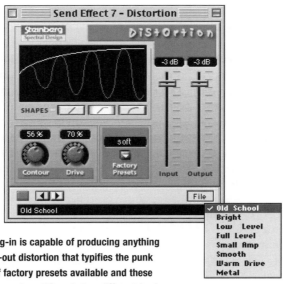

The distortion VST effect plug-in is capable of producing anything from a soft crunch to the all-out distortion that typifies the punk sound. There's a selection of factory presets available and these presets are stored not as parameter settings but as different basic distortion algorithms. The basic characters of the distortion preset models are indicated by their names

hit the stages at venues like New York's CBGB's, starting, for all practical purposes, the movement that would eventually be known as punk.

Bands like The Ramones and Talking Heads evolved out of the punk rock movement and became influences for those who shared a similar distaste of what was occurring in the music industry. Some say that the underlying roots of punk were the frustration and anger many felt from being treated as sheep, while others say that punk stemmed from the "politics of boredom". It was probably a combination of both...and neither. Meanwhile, good old Malcolm McLaren – both loved and hated for his managerial skills – played an indelible role in the history of punk rock. In February 1975, The New York Dolls – once forerunners of punk – tried to revive a lagging career by hiring McLaren as their new manager. Understanding the value of shock, McLaren took the band and re-introduced them as born-again communists. They draped themselves in communist flags and spouted catchy phrases such as "better red than dead". Unfortunately for the band, their career went down the toilet. Fortunately for McLaren, their career went down the toilet.

After his aborted attempt with The New York Dolls, McLaren returned to England and teamed up with his mate Bernie Rhodes to nurture a band that was arguably their greatest success. That band was The Sex Pistols, and McLaren and the Pistols adopted an anarchistic view of the world that made them instant celebrities. With spiked hair, tattered clothes and safety pins as jewellery, they frequented talkshows and publicly badmouthed fellow artists, bands and musicians. They spoke harshly of the British class system and the subjugation of the working class. They made news for their concert violence and for fighting with their fans. The Sex Pistols were probably as notorious for their brashness as they were for their inability to play their instruments. Their unfocused shock value not only brought them fame but also made them the single most recognisable punk band. That's why there's this mistaken (and particularly British) notion that punk rock began with the Pistols. Quite a few others believe that it made punk into a boring novelty and signified the beginning of the end.

Despite the internal turmoil of the punk movement, punk rock made several things clear to international audiences. Punk Rock, in its subculture, managed to break down many barriers of expression and language. It made an indentation in the commercial music industry. It provided a fresh alternative to a boring, stagnant music scene. But most of all, punk's legacy lies in its introduction of self-employment and activism. It illustrated that anyone can do it themselves, without reliance on the commercial media or the luxury of having financial abundance. Against the backdrop of mass consumer conformity, the punk rock movement made a kind of statement of individuality that has recently been recycled in the hype about DIY digital desktop studios and distributing music over the Internet.

In many ways, punk was nothing more than a noisy aberration, like the Reagan-Thatcher years, although much less destructive. As far as changing the attitudes and sharp practices of the record industry... Well, as the preponderance of boy-band and Britney-like bollocks clogging the airwaves suggests, some things never change. As Bill Hicks said, these people are the spawn of Satan...but the wider unwashed public still laps it up.

# post-punk, grunge, etc

Punk rock began as a response to the big-budget, over-produced music of the 1970s and was, to some extent, a reaction to disco and stadium rock. So what is post-punk? The etymology of the word points to it being...well, after punk, but generically speaking that's not the real meaning, because punk music of sorts is still being made today. To shine a light on the subject of post-punk, an interesting analogy can be made with literature. Modern literature didn't cease to be written after the advent of post-modern literature; the two exist simultaneously as movements in literature. Thus punk and post-punk somehow both exist as musical movements or genres. Post-punk is almost a catch-all genre for underground, indie or lo-fi guitar rock. It's also the music most representative of the slacker traditions of Gen X.

So how did post-punk begin? It's a hard question to answer, but many think that it began as a reaction to the nihilism of punk rock. Punk music was defined by its aggressive vocals and often sloppy, simple instrumentation. Moreover, the punks were marked by their attitude, whereas most post-punk musicians can be marked by their lack of attitude. Punk music wanted to create a revolution but wasn't bright enough to understand what a revolution was all about, while post-punk music wanted to create art. The DIY ethic of punk was perhaps the genre's greatest influence on post-punk, as post-punk bands initially avoided major record labels in the pursuit of artistic freedom and out of an "us against them" stance towards the corporate rock world. The movement probably began with Sonic Youth, an avant-garde noise band from New York, although there were many other bands that influenced the movement, such as The Velvet Underground, MC5, Joy Division and Talking Heads.

Sonic Youth came together in the New York punk scene of the early '80s. They clearly had a lot of punk influence, but their obsession with avant-garde art and pop culture distanced them from the punks. They appealed to the artsy crowd and to the college crowd. In other words, post-punk appealed to the people who were slightly brighter and more sophisticated, which was quite different than the elements appealed to by the punks. It also came to appeal to the weird kids, the ones who never quite found their place. Sonic Youth created walls of sound and noise with lyrics resembling beat poetry or the lyrics of Jim Morrison, often expressing the nihilism of the punks but in a slightly more intelligent way. Their worldview may have been skewed towards the negative, but out of the darkness their sounds would often find a sense of beauty – like saying that the world is bad but something out there *does* exist to make it worthwhile, and that's what's important. Not exactly Sartre or Camus, but you get the idea.

Like a Grolsch beer, the music needed time to grow and mature, and it wasn't until the early '90s that post-punk was "ready" and broke out into mainstream music with Nirvana. In the meantime, the music spread west over college station airwaves, small clubs, fanzines and independent record stores. Bands like Minor Threat, The Minutemen, fIREHOSE and Hüsker Dü began to delve into the sonic fields to harvest the post-punk flower. 1986 saw the arrival of The Pixies, a band that skirted the edge of fame and would prove to be very influential in the '90s.

There are many names that re-occur in post-punk because often, after one band collapsed, its members would move onto new projects. A good example of this would be Ian MacKaye from Minor Threat, who formed Fugazi after the former band's break-up. In many cases, the changes of name and line-up would produce better bands. Fugazi started from where Minor Threat left off and were able to further distance themselves from punk and move towards a more experimental sound. Similarly, The Pixies later went on to become The Breeders, The Amps and Frank Black And The Catholics, while Dinosaur Jr lost its bass player, Lou Barlow, who eventually started Sebadoh and The Folk Implosion. Another example of a re-occurring name would be Big Black's Steve Albini, who went on to be a producer on many of the best post-punk albums – including most of The Pixies' albums and Nirvana's *In Utero* – after his stint as a musician.

In 1989, Nirvana's first album, *Bleach*, was released virtually unnoticed. Three years later, they became major stars after the release of their second album, *Nevermind*, with its hit single 'Smells Like Teen Spirit' and accompanying video. Drawing from influences like Sonic Youth and The Pixies, Nirvana were able to create a sound that was popular to both mainstream and underground audiences. At this time, rock actually began to replace pop as the preferred format for radio and MTV, but this didn't last long, and post-punk went underground again after its brief sortie into the world of popular culture. One of the factors involved in this was the music industry's ability to copy the post-punk sound and package it in the likes of The Smashing Pumpkins and Weezer. Many would argue that, whatever this post-punk genre is, it's better off underground. At least there its artists might be better able to keep the music pure and uncorrupted by the entropic evils of corporate rock and reptilian record companies.

One of the most important aspects of post-punk music is its ability to combine diverse elements and genres. A great example of this can be found in the bands The Flaming Lips and Pavement, which include elements of psychedelic, country, jazz, blues and rock music in their songs. In a way, post-punk groups can be seen as the true heirs of the great bands of the '60s. The music strives to avoid being pinned down as one thing, and it's this that has helped it to survive and thrive in the jaded underground music scene. Some bands, like Sonic Youth and The Flaming Lips, have been together long enough to garner major-label contracts purely on artistic merit and strong credentials. According to the bands in question, the big deals haven't changed their attitudes towards the music but rather have given them enough money to experiment with new sounds and new ideas. Well, that's their story and they're sticking to it.

Overdrive is a distortion-type effect that emulates the sound of a guitar amplifier to replicate that post-punk sound. There's a selection of factory styles available and none of these are stored as parameter settings but instead as different basic overdrive algorithms. Like the distortion plug-in, the characteristics of these are indicated by the style names. This is a great effect for Smashing Pumpkins impressions

# rock production

### Electric Guitar

Rock music in any of its guises is about electric guitars, and to create it you need to start with a good instrument and, preferably, a good player. Studios used to use close dynamic mics to mic up guitar amps. In your digital desktop studio, you may find that, with the various modelling preamps, pods and plug-ins you have available, you can get practically any guitar sound in a convenient DI-able format. Contrary to popular belief, some of the most powerful and aggressive lead-guitar sounds are achieved with very little distortion. Excessive or gratuitous overdrive and distortion can result in a muddy, unfocused sound with poor definition. Whichever way you mic or record your guitars, you'll need to add a bit of reverb to get that authentic rock sound. You can EQ a clean, DI'd guitar effectively up to 6-7kHz, since the guitar sound contains a lot of harmonics, and you should concentrate on the 150Hz-3kHz range. Both bass and electric guitar can usually benefit from fairly aggressive EQ'ing, since – let's face it – they were never meant to sound like natural instruments in the first place.

Incidentally, unintentional digital distortion can be nasty, so you should do your best to minimise any distortion other than what's created intentionally within your effects units. The input-level meters will help you to avoid input overload, but they may not tell you about the output level. For example, a highly resonant filter sound such as wah-wah can increase the signal level internally so that, even if the original signal doesn't exceed the unit's input headroom, it can nonetheless exceed the available headroom elsewhere. Some multi-effects meters can monitor the post-processed signal, but this isn't always the case. If the distortion starts to splatter and your meters don't indicate any overload, try reducing the input level.

## Bass Guitar

Bass guitars can be a bit tricky to record. You can always use a straight DI to produce a fairly clean sound, but on rockier numbers there's a risk that it will get lost in the mix. An external bass pre-amp can give the impression of a properly miked amp and can give you a sound that will cut through the mix better. While bass guitars generate a lot of low frequencies, the actual definition of their sound comes mostly from the mid range, so try boosting at around 2-4kHz to give your sound more of an edge. Bass guitars, drums and any other low-frequency instruments should usually be panned to the centre.

If you don't actually have a bass guitar, there's a VST plug-in called VB-1 that might give you enough of a rocky sound. Although it's not a 1962 pre-

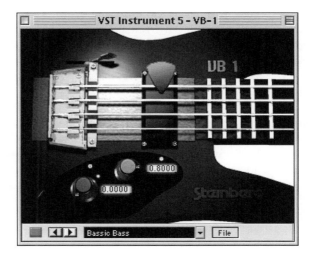

**Steinberg's VB-1 VST bass-guitar plug-in**

CBS Fender Jazz bass, VB-1 looks like a fairly funky virtual bass and is built on real-time physical modelling principles. However, with this plug-in, it's probably a case of "nice interface, pity about the sound". VB-1 is polyphonic, with up to four voices, and receives MIDI in Omni mode (ie on all MIDI channels). Like a physical electric bass, the Volume control regulates the VB-1 volume and the Damper switch controls the length of time that the strings vibrate after being "plucked". You can adjust the pick-up position, and by dragging the "mic" left or right you can also change the tone. Positioning the mic towards the bridge position produces a hollow sound that emphasises the upper harmonics of the plucked string, and when it's placed towards the neck position the tone is fuller and warmer. The position of the pick-up determines where, along the length of the string, the initial pluck is made and controls the "roundness" of the tone, just like on a real guitar, while the Wave Morph control selects the basic waveform used to drive the plucked-string model. (Be aware that this parameter can drastically change the character of the sound.) This control smoothly morphs through the waves, so if you're not careful it's possible to create sounds that have no relation to a bass guitar. But then again, there might be times when you'd want to do this.

You may need a bit of compression for the bass guitar, so start with a ratio of 3:1 and lower the threshold until there's almost always gain reduction occurring, as this will ensure that the loudest parts of the signal will be affected and the quietest parts won't, which will keep your signals a few decibels hotter and preserve some dynamics. You can then increase the ratio until you get between 3dB and 6dB of gain reduction. The attack should be fast enough to catch peaks but not so fast that it cuts down the attack of the pick, while the release should be fast enough to let go of the signal before the next note can cross the threshold. However, if your release is too fast, you'll either hear the compression taking place or you'll hear the bass-guitar signal distort. Try starting with an attack of 10ms and a release of 250ms.

## Drums

Miking real drums can be an onerous task. As with most instruments, the first step in recording a great drum sound is proper tuning, which can reduce or eliminate the amount of EQ you'll need to apply later.

First of all, start with a good kick-drum sound. For a punchy sound with a lot of attack, tune the rear head as loose as possible without it wrinkling, as this will eliminate most of the unwanted overtones and ringing. Then, removing the front head will further reduce unwanted sounds. By now, the kick drum should sound very punchy. However, you'll probably want more attack, and this can be achieved with the use of a wooden or plastic beater. Careful kick-drum tuning really makes a difference, since the drum is almost always close miked.

Next, work on the snare. You can usually loosen the snare head quite a bit, and this will give you a heavier sound. If you prefer a snare that cuts through the mix a bit more, you can tune it up a bit. In either case, you'll probably have to tune the bottom snare head tighter than the top batter head in order to reduce sympathetic buzzing and overtones. The snare is also a very important element to a good drum sound.

Next, tune the toms. To keep that heavy sound, tune them as loose as possible without having the tone die on you. If you tune the bottom heads to the same pitch, you'll get more ringing, which can make the toms sound very powerful.

The most efficient way to record drums with limited resources is a technique called *triangular miking*. In this technique, a microphone is placed on the kick drum and a stereo pair of mics is placed in front of the kit. There are other placements for the stereo pair, but most people prefer to put theirs in front of the kit. Feel free to experiment. Start with the kick-drum mic placed halfway into the drum, on a 30° angle and aimed at the beater. By placing the microphone inside the drum, you'll eliminate the most microphone bleed and capture the most thud. (The reason why the mic should be angled is so that air doesn't hit the mic head-on, causing audible woofs.) Finally, aim the mic at the beater, because the beater is what gives the attack of the drum.

Next, set up your room mics. Try placing an X-Y stereo pair placed at the drummer's chest level about three feet in front of the kit. (Some people use a spaced pair for this, but these arrangements tend to capture an unnatural sound. The X-Y pair has less stereo spread but sounds more like the kit does in the room.) Place the mics at chest level to pick up the entire kit evenly – kick drum, toms, snare, hi-hat and cymbals. Also, you'll want to place the mics far enough back to capture everything evenly but not so far back that you pick up too much room sound. When getting your levels for these microphones, make sure that the snare appears in the centre of the stereo spread, as this will make it much more effective in the final mix.

If you don't have the space or mics for a full drum kit, in most instances you can use the MIDI drum sounds found on a sequencer. Most mixes are built around the rhythm section of a song, so it's best start with those parts, usually the bass drum first. It's a good idea to separate each different rhythm sound onto its own track within your sequencer. As mentioned earlier, with most multitimbral synths the drum kit is usually on track 10 (MIDI channel 10), but that doesn't mean that you can't have as many tracks as you like on MIDI channel 10. Putting each drum on a separate track makes life that little bit easier. If you have several drum sounds all playing from the same track, try splitting them up like this:

- Bass drum – track 1, MIDI channel 10;
- Closed hi-hat – track 2, MIDI channel 10;
- Open hi-hat – track 3, MIDI channel 10;
- Snare drum – track 4, MIDI channel 10.

Incidentally, although it's tempting to record 16th-note hi-hat lines in step time by drawing the notes into the piano-roll editor, just…don't. You'll end up with something that sounds like a machine gun crossed with a roulette wheel. If you want to get realistic hi-hat lines, record them in real time by using two fingers alternately on the hi-hat key. It's really quite easy. Oh, and don't record a good bar of hi-hats and copy it; record all of the hi-hat parts live and individually to retain variety and a natural feel.

Again, VST plug-ins like the LM-9 can provide some pretty convincing drum sounds. The LM-9 is a simple polyphonic drum machine with up to nine voices. It receives MIDI in Omni mode (ie on all MIDI channels), and you

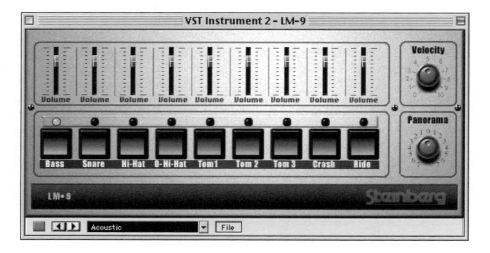

Steinberg's LM-9 VST drum plug-in

82

don't need to select a MIDI channel to direct MIDI to it. The LM-9 responds to MIDI Note On/Note Off MIDI messages and Velocity data governs volume. The plug-in comes complete with two sets of drum sounds: "Acoustic" and "Beat Box". The Acoustic setting features samples of an acoustic drum kit, while Beat Box features classic analogue drum-machine sounds, and the mapping is compatible with General MIDI. You can use the Program button to switch between the two supplied drum sets, just like you can switch between effects programs. The Velocity setting determines the global velocity sensitivity for the LM-9, and the higher the value, the more sensitive it will be to incoming Velocity data. If set to 0, the sounds will play back with a fixed velocity value. The volume sliders are used to adjust the volume for each individual drum sound, while the pads are used to audition the individual drum sounds and to select a sound for adjusting pan. The Panorama option is used to position an individual sound in the stereo image, and whatever setting you choose will apply to the currently selected sound indicated by a yellow LED over the Pad button.

On most keyboards, the LM-9 drum-sound note values are as follows:

- Bass – C1
- Snare – D1
- Hi-Hat – F1
- Open Hi-Hat – A1
- Tom 1 – D2
- Tom 2 – B1
- Tom 3 – A1
- Crash – C2
- Ride – D2

# considerations

Recording rock music is generically similar to recording any other music that uses primarily guitars, bass, keyboards, drums and vocals. It's the spice of the various effects and the nature of the mix that creates that special generic sound and feel. However, it's sometimes a glitch in the equipment that really makes the difference. They say that Phil Spector's famous Motown sound was only partly to do with his clever production techniques and his legendary "wall of sound". As it happened, there was something not quite right with the desk, and without that synchronistic glitch they never would have created that famous sound. Like any creative process, synchronicity and serendipity should never be underestimated.

## chapter 5

# songs from the wood

*"Let me bring you songs from the wood/To make you feel much better, better than you could know."*
  *– Jethro Tull, 'Songs From The Wood'*

**A**lthough a huge amount of the music being produced at home on digital desktop studios these days is the thumping silicon heart of the dance culture, it's worth noting that some scientists have proven that a regular cocktail of repetitive beats and cheap drugs can make you depressed, psychotic and downright boring. But don't panic – at the opposite end of the spectrum of the painting-by-numbers thunder of pre-programmed beats is good old acoustic music, full of heart and soul. (Well, at least half full.) And, despite the fact that current proponents and practitioners of acoustic music also take drugs, rumour has it that this kind of music is actually good for you. Broadly speaking, this genre includes all the melodic and soulful stuff that stretches back to the likes of Bob Dylan, Paul Simon, James Taylor and runs through to the likes of Dave Matthews, Ben Harper, David Gray and Badly Drawn Boy.

As a matter of fact, when you start exploring folk and country music as genres, the lineage stretches back even further. Acoustic music covers a multitude of options and overlaps a number of traditional and modern genres, including folk, country and ethnic. However, in more contemporary, popular parlance, it's generally thought of as music that uses guitar and other stringed instruments generally in conjunction with or as an accompaniment to vocal performances. Although guitars are probably the most ubiquitous instruments used in studio and home recording, acoustic music as a genre may also include violins, cellos, double-basses, banjos, mandolins, dulcimers and non-amplified instruments such as pianos, accordions, flutes and whistles. Actually, as a singer friend of mine once commented over a microphone, his acoustic guitar with built-in pick-up plugged into a Mackie PA desk with loads of effects, there's no such thing as acoustic music. These days, for live performance or recording, even traditional instruments have to come into the digital cold. As a genre, however, acoustic music in all of its permutations requires some very similar production techniques and considerations. Since most of this sort of music involves a singer, we'll also look at some of the best ways of getting good vocal recordings.

# country

*"Oh, we got both kinds of music here, country and western."*
*– barmaid to Jake in* The Blues Brothers

OK, as a genre, country music has had some pretty bad press over the years. For a lot of people, it's just a load of redneck sentimental mush about dying hound dogs, bad whisky, insatiable inbred infidelity and a honky-tonk lifestyle driven down dusty roads in old pill-poppin' pick-up trucks. Not only that but it also spawned that unforgivably twisted line-dancing craze in the early '90s, which has gained disturbing popularity, even in the UK. On a more serious note, country music has also been blighted by its appropriation by conservative middle America, right-wing bigots and white racists. But leaving all of that aside for the moment, it's also important to recognise the fundamental role that country music has played in the development of the popular song and the myriad influences it has had on all kinds of music, from rock to dance. And, like it or not, country music is still probably the largest-selling genre in the world.

Country music – as we know it, at least – found its humble beginnings in the early 1920s, when folk music was taken one step further. In the first quarter of the 20th century, those who claimed to have introduced folk music in the USA (mostly people from the Appalachians) began to introduce a slightly more sophisticated styling of the "hillbilly sound" that was already popular. In the 80-plus years of country music history, the sound and style of the music has changed dramatically, at least in some respects.

During the '20s, a boppin' playboy named Bob Wills popularised "country and western" music, which he later dubbed "western swing". At the same time, another party animal named Bill Monroe became known as the father of bluegrass music, that folky banjo/fiddle dance music born out of down-home hillbilly string bands. Mandolin player Monroe left Kentucky and teamed up with master guitarist Lester Flatt and shit-kickin' banjo picker

Earl Scruggs to form The Bluegrass Boys. Although they went on to inspire a lot of hippy longhairs and covered songs by Dylan and psychedelic bands, Flatt and Scruggs are probably best remembered for jangly get-away music like 'Foggy Mountain Breakdown'.

In its earliest years, it was the honky-tonk sound of the likes of Ernest Tubb and Hank Williams that made up the genre of country music. Roadside bars and meeting houses throughout Oklahoma and Texas were packed every Friday and Saturday evening with fans and curiosity seekers alike anxious to listen to the fast-rising sounds of steel guitars and drums. However, those roadhouses were popular for more than just the latest craze in American music; the repeal of prohibition in 1933 also relaxed the minds of many when it came to public drinking, and the audiences could now enjoy their favourite music and their favourite alcoholic beverages at the same time.

Storytelling is also a massive part of country music, and its practitioners literally sang their lives. Although Tubb and Williams had their share of popularity with the honky-tonk sound, it was Al Dexter who cut the first record that included the actual words "honky tonk", in 1936. Tubb's single 'Walking The Floor Over You', released in 1941, went on to sell more than a million copies, which in those days was quite a feat in any form of music. Meanwhile, Hank Williams' 1953 cut 'Your Cheatin' Heart' is perhaps one of the best-known records of the honky-tonk era. And it wasn't his only hit; throughout his lifetime, Williams recorded more than 100 songs.

Another form of the country music style is known as *Western country*. While honky-tonks were filled with fans of country, theatres were filled with fans of the cowboy songs made popular again in Texas and Oklahoma. The often-romanticised life of the cowboy – heroic but lonely, drifting – fit in perfectly with this style of music, which took its sound from the hills of Tennessee and the bayous of Louisiana. More often than not, at least one part of the Western song would include a lonesome whistle from the flute or some other mellow-sounding wind instrument. The lyrics to the Western sound centred directly on the pains and sorrows of life on the frontier.

Some of those famous for this style were Gene Autry – America's singing cowboy – and Roy Rogers, who later teamed up with his wife, Dale Evans, to form a famous duet of the genre. Rogers had also been a part of The Sons Of The Pioneers, a band that brought the frontier sound to over 80 Western films between 1935 and 1948.

In the early 1950s, country music morphed once again into a sound that became known as *rockabilly*, a mix of the Southern hills music and the blues. This sound was made popular by many performers who developed staying power in the country music industry, including The Everly Brothers, Jerry Lee Lewis, Conway Twitty, Carl Perkins and, of course, the King himself, Elvis Presley. With its faster-paced sound and constant rhythm, this form of country quickly worked its way up the record charts as Americans in general found themselves living a lifestyle that was also at a much quicker pace than that of their parents' generation.

# Nashville cats

It's in this town in the state of Tennessee that country music found its permanent home. It's here that the sound of country and all its variations have been produced since 1925, when the Nashville Barn Dance was established. By 1935, when it became known as the Grand Ole Opry, national broadcasting had begun in America, and soon after this a huge influx of country star wannabes drew to Nashville in the hopes of making the big time.

Among the first of those who flocked to Nashville were Ernest Tubb, Patsy Cline, Buddy Holly and Kitty Wells, otherwise known as "the queen of country music". By the 1960s, these artists and others had acquired a new sound created for their vocal talents when Owen Bradley and Chet Atkins moulded them into producing what became known as the Nashville sound.

In the 1930s, country music was beginning to spread further, thanks to the invention of the radio, which became a popular source of entertainment in a time of an impoverished economy. Radio was entertaining and it was virtually free. At this time, Gene Autry, Tex Ritter and The Carter Family were all making their ways in the expanding world of music.

WSM's *The Grand Ole Opry* – which began its long-running history in Nashville, Tennessee – started out as a radio show in the 1930s. Because of its large roster of popular country singing stars, record companies and wannabe singers from all over the United States were drawn to Nashville, which soon became known as "Music City, USA". Every singer had a nickname which pertained to their prominence in the world of country music, and Roy Acuff was no exception. Known to his fans as "the king of country music", Acuff and his band, The Smoky Mountain Boys, joined the Opry in the late 1930s. Acuff's Opry fame lasted many years, until he passed away in 1992.

*The Grand Ole Opry* went on to showcase many more singers, ladies and gentlemen alike, with the addition of Bill Monroe, Flatt And Scruggs and

Little Jimmy Dickens, to name just a few. In later years, singers who made their marks in the music world would also grace the stage, including big names like George Jones, Dolly Parton, Elvis Presley, Hank Williams, Loretta Lynn and Porter Wagoner.

In the 1950s, The Carter Family was a maternally directed group that consisted of Maybelle and her three daughters: Anita, June and Helen. This group joined *The Grand Ole Opry* and was known as "the first family of country music". In the years to come, June would gain further public exposure when she changed her name to June Carter Cash by wedding another country singer by the name of Johnny Cash. Even though Cash's early career was plagued by drug and alcohol problems, he pulled through it all and went on to become a popular country star. He was known as "the man in black" because…wait for it… his outfits always comprised solid-black shirt, slacks, coat and boots.

The '60s saw more than steel guitars and drums in the Nashville sound, and even "rock" bands like The Byrds, Buffalo Springfield, Poco and The Eagles – as well as solo artists like Neil Young and Kris Kristofferson – started to bring country music to a new and younger audience. Back in Nashville, complete orchestras were brought in to add a lushness or softness to the country sound. Also at this time, the ever-popular use of synthesisers, studio effects and overdubbing were used to create a rich, full sound that no steel guitar and drum kit could ever hope to create. This era of country was the beginning of the age of contemporary country music, and it was this sound – made popular in the '60s and '70s – that would enable artists from many different genres to come into the fold of the country music industry. Crossovers from the pop genre included Kenny Rogers, Dolly Parton and Conway Twitty, all of whom enjoyed great success when they recorded in the new style of the Nashville sound.

Even though they played basically the same instruments, which most always included guitars and drums, some of the singers and groups that took to the stage in the '80s had their own sounds. While Reba McEntire and Randy Travis had the traditional country sound, a group known as Alabama hit the scene with a country rock sound. People loved their music, though, and bought their albums as soon as they hit the stores. Finally, in the 1990s, things changed again when Garth Brooks hit the scene. He successfully attracted young people – or, at least, America's dumbed-down, post-literate majority – back into country music by crooning heartfelt ballads. At this time, other singers came onto the scene, such as The Dixie Chicks, Faith Hill, Shania Twain and several other groups, and the audiences applauded their talents. It was also at this time that the controversy about what was and what wasn't real country music arose. Shania Twain, for example, was said to have crossed the line over to pop music, even though her music was called country by many.

Over the years, country music has changed and evolved into the billion-dollar industry that it is today. The direction it will later take or the sub-genres that it might spawn will undoubtedly be directed by the massive listening audience that buys and listens to the songs that come out of country music land.

# alt country

*"Alternative (awl-tur-na-tiv) – adj. Available in place of something else. Doesn't suck. Not corrupted by the commercial formulas of the established market."*

*"Country music (kun-tree myoo-zik) – n. Simple music originated in the southern US, based on folk and cowboy songs, spirituals and gospel. Sort of all that, and doesn't suck."*

Not all performers were into the glitzy, rehabilitated trailer-trash scene out in Nashville, and before too long the bad boys of country circled up in Texas and hatched what has become known as *outlaw country*. What they did was probably more real and to the point, and the decidedly lo-fi production definitely wasn't as slick. This is the music pioneered by Willie Nelson and Waylon Jennings and expanded on by Gram Parsons, The Byrds and Neil Young. In 1969, even Dylan went country in a collaboration with Johnny Cash on *Nashville Skyline*, and Kris Kristofferson wrote some of the best songs of the time.

Today, amongst disillusioned, dance-weary youth, alternative country – or no depression, insurgent country, son of outlaw or the twangname du jour – has become relatively big stuff. It would be wonderfully romantic if this alt-country uprising spontaneously erupted as a reaction to dissatisfaction with the crap music generally being played on commercial country radio stations, but in real life that's not what happened. As is usually the situation with the birth of a new genre, the music writers and other fans are the ones who identified and named the movement – several times over, in this case. A fairly recent lead paragraph from *Billboard* is typical of pronouncements that have lately appeared in a number of music publications: "There's a new musical tent under which are gathering all the performers the big top doesn't have room for these days. The big top shelters mainstream country music; the side tent is harbouring those performers going by the name 'alternative country', 'insurgent country' or 'progressive country', and it's starting to draw a crowd."

What's most interesting about alt country is that it's a movement that isn't really a movement, so it may not even become a genre, if you follow. Basically, what makes it cool is that anything goes – for now, at least – and all influences are welcome.

# folk

Particularly in the UK, the term *folk music* often conjures up unpleasant pictures of swarthy-faced people holding pewter tankards in one hand and sticking their finger in their ear with the other while droning on interminably through 30-odd verses about some bloke picking turnips. Alternatively, there's the picture of the swarthy-faced singer who's already had several too many Guinnesses doing yet another rousing chorus of 'Whisky In The Jar'. The term *folk music* was invented by 19-century scholars to describe the musical genre of peasantry, which – theoretically – is age-old and anonymous. Nowadays, the term covers a multitude of sins and, apart from being a good way of winding up dance producers (telling them that their music shows definite folk influences always provokes a reaction), as a genre it's almost meaningless. To many, it simply means home-made music played mainly by ear that – as Pete Seeger once said – arises out of older traditions but has a meaning for today. Outside the traditional folk world, it's only used for lack of a better word, and even within the so-called "folk world" the label *folk singer* is often less accurate than, say, "a professional singer of amateur music" might be. But there are dozens of contemporary singer/songwriters that, like it or not, fit neatly into the folk genre and are consciously or unconsciously continuing a long tradition. Probably since that famous concert at which Bob Dylan outraged purists by playing electric guitar, and probably since a lot earlier than that, when it comes to folk as a genre, anything goes and all influences are welcome.

If people were to be introduced to the "folk music" of today by having had the music of a number of different artists played to them, they would be very confused indeed – some would hear pop, others country, rock, blues and other varied musical styles. So how could they all possibly be identified as folk? If folk music does indeed arise out of older traditions but still means something today, what people want to hear today is different from what they wanted to hear ten, 20 and 50 years ago. Styles change and artists evolve. Some can point to folk influences and some cannot.

According to music scholars, folk music has been with us since the dawn of history. However, it wasn't until the early 1900s that scholars began to consider folk music as a legitimate facet to be studied as a part of a culture. That's why the actual definition of folk music has undergone debate for many years. A broad general definition of folk music is that it is music of "the folk", or the people. These folk are sometimes identified as the rural or peasant people of a country. Some musicologists believed that folk music exists in all classes of society. Sometimes the folk are considered a particular ethnic group or nationality.

However, whatever its definition, folk music is part of a folk culture, and part of the culture's lore – including its ballads and stories – is passed down by word of mouth from generation to generation. Different folk cultures – sometimes referred to as folk communities (literally geographic communities) – developed in isolated areas where there was limited outside contact, and the people within these communities worked to preserve their traditional cultural values. Some other definitions and descriptions of folk music include the following:

- The music must be very old; it is a particular style of music; the author is not known;

- It is passed on in the oral tradition rather than in written form, unlike art music, which is written by a trained composer and passed on in written form;

- It is music that has been submitted to the process of oral transmission; it is the product of oral transmission; it is the product of evolution and is dependent on the circumstances of continuity, variation and selection. The music may change and evolve as it passes from person to person;

- It has a simple melody and has the ability to express the most profound of human values.

Traditionally, the folk singer's art is that of storytelling, and the performer's largest responsibility lies in telling the story rather than entertaining the audience. Because the oral-transmission definition of folk music is obsolete and today much of the music is transmitted by the mass media, some music scholars now put folk music into two basic categories: traditional folk songs and modern urban folk songs. They've also come up with eight generalisations by which one may define folk music:

- Folk songs represent the musical expressions of the common people;

- Folk songs are not composed, in that they are not the works of skilled, tutored musicians. It's more accurate to say that they have been created rather than composed;

- Folk songs are ordinarily the products of unknown people or groups of people. The credits of these songs often read along the lines of "Anonymous", "American Folk Song", "Traditional" or "Southern Mountain Song". However, there are folk-like songs that exist where the author *is* known, but these songs are patterned to fit the mould of what typical folk songs should sound like;

- The words or lyrics of folk songs are usually colloquial in nature to reflect the speech patterns and expressions of a particular people or region;

- Folk songs are highly singable, primarily because they were first presented with the singing voice rather than first written down in musical notation;

- Folk songs are simply structured both musically and verbally. It is their naïveté that gives them their charm;

- Folk songs can be effectively performed without instrumental accompaniment. When they are accompanied, a less formal instrument – such as a guitar, banjo, accordion, dulcimer or autoharp – is considered appropriate;

- Folk songs are indigenous to a particular region or people because they reflect the musical/verbal preferences of that people or region in their materials.

The definition of folk music today varies depending on who's talking and in what context. There's quite a lively scene in the UK of artists producing traditional English and Irish/Celtic music, as well as a lot of "traditionally influenced" original work. In an editorial for *Sing Out!* magazine, editor Mark D Moss noted that the folk magazine had wrestled with a definition of folk music for years: "Our community vehemently refuses to take responsibility for defining folk music." That's not such a bad thing. Moss prefers to think of folk music as an umbrella which covers blues, Cajun music, ballads and "rooted" music from around the world, along with the music of contemporary singer/songwriters – or what we've generally referred to in this book as acoustic music.

Some artists in this genre specifically consider themselves to be folk artists, while other artists don't like to be labelled. Some feel that they shouldn't have to fit into any one musical style, because that would be too confining for the expression of their art. Many see themselves as acoustic singer/songwriters using rock, jazz and other influences, and folk is simply the community to which they belong.

The definition of the term *folk* is an ongoing debate, and it can get ugly. In the 1960s, when folk music was experiencing one of its 20th-century revivals, some folklorists and musicologists refused to accept the worthiness of studying the modern folk music as true folk, because their definitions were strict and inflexible. But, as we've stressed throughout this book, the meanings of words and genres change over time, as do definitions. What is generally agreed nowadays is that the definition should not become so narrow that it excludes a vast repertoire of songs in which people express themselves, and that the definition should change to fit the current social environment.

These days, a broad interpretation of folk as a genre can include such diverse acts as Dave Matthews, Liza Carthy, Kate Rusby, Beth Orton, Neil Young, Jeff Buckley, Bob Dylan, Sarah McLachlan, The Chieftains, Dervish and Temple Bar, etc, etc, etc. Also, although it appears in the section about acoustic music, like country, folk – or what during the '60s became known as folk rock – can and certainly does use electric instruments. Groups as diverse as The Byrds, Fairport Convention and Steeleye Span transformed both traditional and contemporary folk music and gave it a serious rock edge. Folk music is a vital, living art, not an archaeological antiquity. It continues to be a medium through which the people express their thoughts, feelings and interests, just as the folk did in the past. The subject matter and the musical style have changed with the changing times, but the fundamental principle of folksong and its relation to the people have remained the same.

Many different kinds of music have folk music roots or are related to folk music, such as indigenous American country music – hillbilly, rockabilly, country and western, Negro spirituals and bluegrass – and the blues. What is important is to recognise that the music is created by individuals. So, if folk music, in all of its abundance, is as diverse as its many creators, then like it or not we're all folkies now.

# acoustic production

Unless you're using samples, acoustic music usually means using real instruments, which also means recording real audio. Although working with audio can be slightly trickier than working exclusively with MIDI, modern sequencers like Cubase are generally powerful enough to allow you to make some stunning recordings of acoustic music. However, there are some things that you'll need to consider.

First, the acoustic guitar is a rather difficult instrument to record well. The subtle quality of the overtones and suchlike make it a very complex sound to capture. Most musicians and good producers tend to agree that you should never record the piezo pick-ups mounted in some guitars. You're right, it *has* been done on major-label productions, but it still sounds thuddy, thin and metallic. Even particularly good electro-acoustic models should probably be miked for recording purposes. Your best bet is to use a good condenser mic or two, but if all you have is a choice between an SM-57 or the pick-up, you should use the SM-57 every time.

Avoid aiming the mic directly at the sound hole, as this tends to produce an overly boomy sound. Position the mic eight to twelve inches away and aim it at around the point at which the neck and body meet (usually around the 14th fret). It's normally best to use just one mic, but for a larger-than-life sound try placing one mic as discussed above and a second mic an equal distance away aimed at the bridge. This will pick up more of the mid range and bite, and the two signals can be blended to taste in the mix. This tends to work for things like mandolins, banjos, etc, although with banjos you really need to watch your levels and make sure that the sound isn't too tinny. Listen to some of the earlier album collaborations of John Renbourne and Stefan Grossman if you're looking for examples of a really natural acoustic guitar sound and an excellent example of how not to over-produce.

As with any style, the quality of the recording starts with the instrument itself, and no amount of EQ or effects will inject life into strings that are old and dull, so it's best to put new strings on your guitar before gigging or recording. Also, there's no way to totally disguise fret buzz, and while a certain amount of fret and finger noise will add to the "organic" sound, too much can spoil the performance. If you're a singer/guitarist and you want to record both bits in one take, you'll get a certain amount of spill between the guitar and vocal mics. You can minimise this by using a good directional cardioid mic placed as close to the guitar as possible and positioning a directional vocal mic with a pop shield in front of it no more than twelve inches from your mouth. Although there will still be some spill, it won't be all that serious, and if you pan the guitar to one side and the vocal mic to the other it can even create an illusion of stereo.

For something a bit more exotic, such as an acoustic bass guitar, place your mic six inches above the bridge and aim it slightly towards the sound hole.

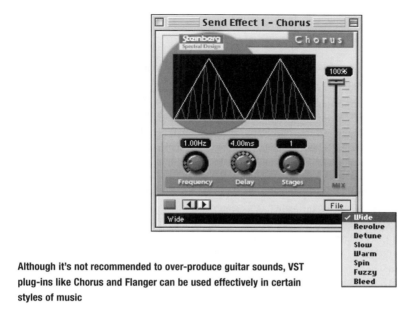

**Although it's not recommended to over-produce guitar sounds, VST plug-ins like Chorus and Flanger can be used effectively in certain styles of music**

For an upright bass, an Audio Technica ATM25 placed just outside the f-hole along with a large- or small-diaphragm condenser just above the bridge works well when recorded on two separate tracks. The bridge mic can then be blended to taste in the mix to achieve the desired amount of attack, string vibration, etc. Keep the mics within twelve inches of the instrument or you're likely to pick up phase cancellations from the reflections of the sound on the floor. You don't really want a lot of room ambience on a bass track, anyway, and even if you decided to put some outboard reverb on a bass track just for fun, the mix would instantly turn to mush.

With other instruments, such as violins, banjos, flutes, whistles, etc, start with the mic position at around six inches from the sound source and then adjust accordingly. Even moving the mic a few inches can affect the sound quite considerably. The acoustic environment in which you're recording can also play a considerable part in giving your recorded sound particular characteristics. Acoustic sound changes constantly, and the level of recording difficulty is increased when you use more than one mic. As with everything, don't be afraid to experiment until you get the mic placement and sound right. Don't be afraid to use EQ, compression, etc, but don't overuse it. Try to set EQ within the ambient range of the instrument – for example, guitars and vocals are usually mid range while bass is mid to low – and always try to record acoustic instruments clean. If you want reverb, you can add it later, but again don't overdo it, and don't expect to fix an atrociously bad sound in the mix. Always try to get the best and cleanest recording possible at source.

Since you can't (unfortunately) tune a singer, the place to start is his or her environment. For example, although it may sound a bit new age, a room with dim lighting can relax a singer about to perform a song in a mellower mood. Conversely, a brightly lit room can support a high-energy song. Temperature also affects a vocalist's performance – a cold room can cause his vocal chords to tense up, so you'll want to make sure that the room in which you'll be recording is at a comfortable temperature. The standard mic position for recording vocals is about nine inches from and slightly above the singer's mouth. (OK, recommendations vary, but usually try for a range of six to twelve inches for solo recording.) In this way, you'll have to angle the mic down a bit in order to avoid picking up pops, and in this respect a pop filter is a very useful tool. If you don't have one, they're very easy to make. I know that, throughout this book, we tend to get a bit repetitious about mics, but that's because they're important. That's why we've included an appendix devoted to microphones as well (Appendix 4), so do check it out.

Vocals will almost always benefit from having a little compression applied to them. Even well-disciplined vocalists tend to sound uneven against the very controlled dynamics of a pop mix, so it helps to apply a little compression while recording. Err on the side of caution and use less compression than you think you'll finally need, starting with a threshold of -10dB, a ratio of 3:1, a fast attack time and a moderately fast release time. Bring the threshold down until the reduction meters are almost always lit and adjust the ratio until you get about 6dB of reduction. This will be a good place to start. Meanwhile, EQ is usually helpful to pull the sound of a vocalist out of the mix. If possible, using narrow bandwidths will reduce the chance of boosting the same frequency as that produced by another instrument.

On the subject of microphones, large-diaphragm capacitor mics tend to be more flattering for recording vocals than small-diaphragm types. Since it's now possible to buy a good capacitor mic at a reasonably affordable price, there's no point in spoiling your recording with an unsuitable cheap mic. As mentioned in Chapter 1, you can now pick up an Audio Technica AT3035 capacitor mic for around £200, and these mics give all vocals a nice balance between accuracy and flattery, producing a convincingly natural sound. The AT3035 is particularly good for more sensitive, ballad-style recording, for which it will give excellent results.

One of the benefits of desktop digital recording is that there are a variety of programs and plug-ins available that to some extent can remodel recordings so that they sound as though they were made with a different microphone. However, to be perfectly honest, it's still better to start with the best microphone you can afford and get the best possible performance out of the singer.

Always try to record vocals dry and add any desired effects later in the mix. Singers usually feel more comfortable with a bit of reverb while recording, so make sure that they've got a bit on the foldback coming over their headphones. Apart from eating memory and CPU power, reverb is notorious for masking pitch problems, although there's a good assortment of VST plug-ins that you can use inside the virtual audio mixer of your sequencer. (The chances are that the "keeper" vocal track will be done as an overdub after the basic tracks or guide vocals are cut.) You'll find that the ability to "punch in" on a vocal track is helpful when fixing phrasing and bum notes. Also, you'll want to use a limiter on the vocal on the way down set at the highest possible ratio, the fastest attack and with a threshold setting that just grabs the peaks.

When the performance is in the can, you can try both subtle and heavy

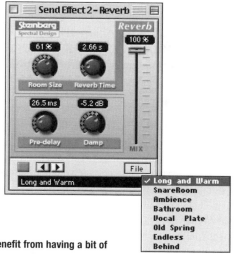

Like guitars, close-miked vocals usually benefit from having a bit of reverb adding "space" to a mix. Remember, however, that you don't need as much as you'd think. Too much reverb can unfocus the vocals, and if you listen to artists you like you'll probably find that they use relatively little vocal reverb. If you don't have rack effects, VST plug-ins work quite well, but be sure to use a lot of CPU power and memory compression to see which works best with the track, although if you're using a lot of compression you may need to gate the vocal track first, which will prevent noise build-up in the pauses between phrases. It's at the mixing stage that a compressor with an obvious character can be used to make a vocal seem larger than life. However, don't gate the vocal while recording – a poorly set-up gate can ruin an otherwise perfect take, so save gating until the mixing stage. Use the gate before any further compression, but don't gate so hard that you remove all of the breath noises preceding words, as these are part of the character of a vocal performance and the recording will sound unnatural without them.

Also, don't run amok with EQ. Mid-range boosting usually results in a nasal or phasey sound, so use as little as you can. If you've picked the right mic and taken the time to fine-tune its position during recording, you shouldn't need much corrective EQ, anyway. Of course, there are times when EQ is used for creative purposes.

Use reverb sparingly. Vocals recorded in a dry acoustic environment need reverb to give them a sense of space and reality, but don't use more than the song really needs. As a general rule, busy songs need less reverb and slower ballads with lots of space in their arrangements can afford to use more. If the vocals are very brightly recorded, they may cause any added reverb to sound sibilant. In this case, instead of de-essing the vocals (which often sounds unnatural), try instead de-essing just the feed to the reverb unit. You can also experiment with the type and tonality of the reverb to minimise sibilance and spitting.

## considerations

Although acoustic music, like folk and country, usually suggests acoustic instruments, there are effective MIDI alternatives. While most MIDI instrument sounds don't have the richness or dynamics of genuine acoustic instruments, they can still be used effectively in the recording process. Better still, however, is the use of samples. Time & Space offer a number of excellent acoustic sample CDs, and one called *American Heartland* offers an impressive assortment of country fiddle, mandolin, banjo and beefy Martin guitar. When using samples or MIDI instruments, try to remember how the real instrument is played and do your best to match what you're doing on the keyboard with the intonation a real player would get from the real instrument – to use a familiar example, don't play chords on a flute sound. With MIDI or sampled acoustic guitars, you can even add fret squeaks and slides to make the sound more authentic and "live".

# folk dance...and don't call us Morris

Just as a footnote, it's worth noting that folk music has been assimilated into the "chill-out" end of the dance music scene, and a number of folky artists such as Sarah McLachlan have even been remixed into lushy-rushy dance tracks. Meanwhile, artists like Beth Orton, Ben Harper and David Gray have done particularly well on the club scene, and there's bound to be a lot more convergence and crossover taking place in the future, particularly with some of the more interesting dance producers using acoustic instruments with programmed beats. And fortunately for all of the trendy folky-phobics, all of those scary bells, handkerchiefs and knobkerries are now well and truly confined to remote village greens and occasional seasonal festivals.

## chapter 6

# jazz...nice...

*"We're always searching. I think that now we're on the point of finding."*
*– John Coltrane*

As a musical genre, jazz music originated solely in the United States, and it's safe to say that it's a distinct and unique style of music. In a sense, it's a sort of musical collision of American and African cultures that evolved out of three centuries of cultural and racial conflict. The result was an ultra-hip clash of a more subdued dominant culture and a creatively more powerful subculture. Jazz is composed primarily of four musical elements: melody, harmony, rhythm and tone colour. However, harmony doesn't play such a powerful role in the evolution of the music itself; it's the melody, rhythm and tone colour that make up the primary elements of jazz.

Since its beginnings, jazz has branched out into so many styles that no single description fits all of them with total accuracy. However, a few generalisations can be made – bearing in mind that, for all of them, exceptions can be cited. Jazz is all about improvisation, and performers of jazz improvise within the conventions of their chosen style. Typically, the improvisation is accompanied by the repeated chord progression of a popular song or an original composition. Instrumentalists emulate black vocal styles, including the use of glissandi and slides, nuances of pitch – including *blue notes*, the microtonally flattened tones in the blues scale – and tonal effects such as growls and wails.

In striving to develop a personal sound or tone colour, an idiosyncratic sense of rhythm and form and an individual style of execution, performers create rhythms characterised by constant syncopation (ie accents in unexpected places) and also by *swing*, a sensation of pull and momentum that arises as the melody is heard alternately together with, and then slightly at variance with, the expected pulse or division of a pulse. Written scores – if there are any – are used merely as guides, providing structure within which improvisation occurs. The typical instrumentation begins with a rhythm section consisting of piano, string bass, drums and optional guitar, to which may be added any number of wind instruments. In big bands, the winds are grouped into three sections: saxophones, trombones and trumpets.

Although exceptions occur in some styles, most jazz is based on the principle that an infinite number of melodies can fit the chord progressions of any song. The musician improvises new melodies that fit the chord progression, which is repeated again and again, as each soloist is featured, for as many choruses as is desired.

Although pieces with many different formal patterns are used for jazz improvisation, two formal patterns in particular are frequently found in songs used for jazz. One is the A A B A form of popular song chorus, which typically consists of 32 bars divided into four eight-bar sections: section A; section A repeated; section B – the bridge, or release, which often begins in a new key; and a repeat of section A.

The second form is the twelve-bar blues form, which has its roots deep in black-American folk music. Unlike the 32-bar A A B A form, blues songs have a fairly standardised chord progression and are often played in the keys of E or A.

# origins of the species

As mentioned earlier, jazz is rooted in the mingled musical traditions of American blacks. These include traits surviving from west African music, black folk music forms developed in the New World, European popular and light classical music of the 18th and 19th centuries and later popular music forms influenced by black music or produced by black composers.

Among the African survivals are vocal styles that include great freedom of vocal colour, a tradition of improvisation and call-and-response patterns. These also contain a rhythmic complexity that incorporates both syncopation of individual melodic lines and conflicting rhythms played by different members of an ensemble. Black folk music forms include field hollers, rowing chants, lullabies and, later, spirituals and blues. European music contributed specific styles and forms – hymns, marches, waltzes, quadrilles and other dance music, light theatrical music and Italian operatic music – and also theoretical elements, in particular harmony, both as a vocabulary of chords and as a concept related to musical form. Much of the European influence was absorbed through specific training in European music, even when the musicians so trained could only find work in low-life entertainment districts and on Mississippi riverboats.

Black-influenced elements of popular music that contributed to jazz include the banjo music of the minstrel shows (derived from the banjo music of the slaves), the syncopated rhythmic patterns of black-influenced Latin American music heard in Southern US cities, the barrelhouse piano styles of tavern musicians in the Midwest and the marches and hymns as they were played by black brass bands in the late 19th century.

Near the end of the 19th century, another influential genre emerged called *ragtime*, which was a composed music that combined many elements, including syncopated rhythms, from banjo music and other black sources and the harmonic contrasts and formal patterns of European marches. After 1910, the bandleader WC Handy took another influential form, the blues, beyond its previously strictly oral tradition by publishing his original blues songs. Favoured by jazz musicians, his songs found perhaps their greatest interpreter later, in the 1920s, in the blues singer Bessie Smith, who recorded many of them.

Most early jazz was played by small marching bands or solo pianists, whose repertoires – besides ragtime and marches – also included hymns, spirituals and blues. The bands played this music – modified frequently by syncopation and acceleration – at picnics, weddings, parades and funerals. Characteristically, they played dirges on the way to funerals and lively marches on the way back. Although blues and ragtime had arisen independently of jazz and continued to exist alongside it, these genres influenced the styles and forms of jazz and provided important vehicles for jazz improvisation.

# New Orleans jazz

At around the turn of the 20th century, the earliest fully documented jazz style emerged, centred in New Orleans. In this style, the cornet or trumpet carried the melody, the clarinet played florid counter-melodies and the trombone played rhythmic slides and sounded the root notes of chords or a simple harmony. Below this basic trio, the tuba or string bass provided a bass line and drums played the rhythmic accompaniment. Exuberance and volume were more important than finesse and improvisation was focused on the ensemble sound.

Although some jazz influences can be heard on a few early phonograph records, a proper jazz band didn't record until 1917. This band, a group of white New Orleans musicians called The Original Dixieland Jazz Band, created a sensation overseas and in the United States. (The term *Dixieland jazz* eventually came to mean the New Orleans style as played by white musicians.) Two groups – one white and one black – followed, The New Orleans Rhythm Kings in 1922 and The Creole Jazz Band in 1923, the latter led by the cornet player King Oliver, an influential stylist. The series of recordings made by Oliver's group are the most significant recordings in the New Orleans style.

Other leading New Orleans musicians included the trumpeters Bunk Johnson and Freddie Keppard, the soprano saxophonist Sidney Bechet, the drummer Warren "Baby" Dodds and the pianist and composer "Jelly Roll" Morton. The most influential musician nurtured in New Orleans, however, was King Oliver's second trumpeter, Louis Armstrong.

The first true virtuoso soloist of jazz, Louis "Satchmo" Armstrong was a dazzling improviser technically, emotionally, and intellectually. He changed the format of jazz by bringing the soloist to the forefront, and in his recording groups The Hot Five and The Hot Seven he demonstrated that jazz improvisation could go far beyond simply ornamenting the melody by creating new melodies based on the chords of the initial tune. He also set standards for all later jazz singers, not only by the way he altered the words and melodies of songs but also by improvising without words, like an instrument, which was commonly known as *scat singing*.

# Chicago and New York

For jazz, the 1920s was a decade of great experimentation and discovery. Many New Orleans musicians, including Armstrong, migrated to Chicago, where they influenced local musicians and stimulated the evolution of the Chicago style, which was derived from the New Orleans style but emphasised the playing of soloists, often adding saxophone to the instrumentation and usually producing tenser rhythms and more complicated textures. Instrumentalists working in Chicago or influenced by the Chicago style included the trombonist Jack Teagarden, the banjoist Eddie Condon, the drummer Gene Krupa and the clarinettist Benny Goodman. Also active in Chicago was Bix Beiderbecke, whose lyrical approach to the cornet provided an alternative to Armstrong's trumpet style. Many Chicago musicians eventually settled in New York City, another major centre for jazz in the 1920s.

# jazz piano

Another vehicle for jazz development in the 1920s was piano music. The Harlem district of New York City became the centre of a highly technical, hard-driving solo style known as *stride piano*, and the master of this approach in the early part of the decade was James P Johnson, whose protégé, a similarly talented vocalist and entertainer by the name of Fats Waller, became by far the most popular performer in this idiom.

A second piano style to develop in the 1920s was *boogie-woogie*. A form of blues played on the piano, boogie-woogie consists of a short, sharply accented bass pattern played over and over by the left hand while the right hand plays freely over the top, using a variety of rhythms. Boogie-woogie became especially popular in the 1930s and 1940s, and leading boogie-woogie pianists included Meade Lux Lewis, Albert Ammons, Pete Johnson and "Pine-Top" Smith. TV presenter Jools Holland is another fan of this style.

However, the most innovative pianist of the 1920s – comparable to Armstrong and present on some of his best recordings – was Earl "Fatha" Hines, a Chicago-nurtured virtuoso considered to possess a wild, unpredictable imagination. His style, combined with the smoother approach of Waller, influenced most pianists of the next generation, notably Teddy Wilson – who was featured with Goodman's band in the 1930s – and Art Tatum, who performed mostly as a soloist and who was regarded with awe for his complex virtuosity.

# the big-band era

Also during the 1920s, large groups of jazz musicians began to play together, after the model of society dance bands, forming the so-called big bands that became so popular in the 1930s and early 1940s that the period became known as the *swing era*. One major development in the emergence of the swing era was a rhythmic change that smoothed the two-beat rhythms of the New Orleans style into a more flowing four beats to the bar. Musicians also developed the use of short melodic patterns called *riffs* in call-and-response patterns. To facilitate this procedure, orchestras were divided into instrumental sections, each with their own riffs, and opportunities were provided for musicians to play extended solos.

The development of the big band as a jazz medium was largely the achievement of Duke Ellington and Fletcher Henderson. Henderson and his arranger, Don Redman, helped to introduce written scores into jazz music, but they also attempted to capture the quality of improvisation that characterised the music of smaller ensembles. In the latter aim, they were aided by gifted soloists such as the tenor saxophonist Coleman Hawkins. During the 1920s, Ellington led a band at the Cotton Club in New York City. Continuing to direct his orchestra until his death in 1974, he composed colourful experimental concert pieces ranging in length from the three-minute 'Koko' (1940) to the hour-long 'Black, Brown And Beige' (1943), as well as songs such as 'Solitude' and 'Sophisticated Lady'. More complex than Henderson's, Ellington's music turned his orchestra into a cohesive ensemble, with solos written for the unique qualities of specific instruments and players. Other bands in the tradition of Ellington and Henderson were led by Jimmie Lunceford, Chick Webb and Cab Calloway.

In the mid 1930s, a different style of big-band jazz was developed in Kansas City and was epitomised by the band of Count Basie. Originally assembled in Kansas City, Basie's band reflected the southwestern emphasis on improvisation by keeping the written or simply memorised passages relatively short and simple. The wind instruments in his band exchanged ensemble riffs in a free, strongly rhythmical interplay, with pauses to accommodate extended instrumental solos. Basie's tenor saxophonist, Lester Young, played with a particular rhythmic freedom that was rarely apparent in the improvisations of soloists from other bands. Young's delicate tone and long, flowing melodies, laced with an occasional avant-garde honk or gurgle, opened up a whole new approach, just as Armstrong's playing had done in the 1920s.

Other trendsetters of the late 1930s were the trumpeter Roy Eldridge, the electric guitarist Charlie Christian, the drummer Kenny Clarke and the vibraphonist Lionel Hampton. Meanwhile, jazz singing in the 1930s became increasingly flexible and stylised, and during the time Ivie Anderson, Mildred Bailey, Ella Fitzgerald and, above all, Billie Holiday were the leading singers.

# popular and classical musical influences

The pioneering efforts of Armstrong, Ellington, Henderson and others made jazz a dominant influence on American music during the 1920s and 1930s. Such popular musicians as bandleader Paul Whiteman used some of the more obvious rhythmic and melodic devices of jazz, although with less improvisational freedom and skill than were displayed in the music of the major jazz players. Attempting to fuse jazz with light classical music, Whiteman's orchestra also premièred jazzy symphonic pieces by American composers such as George Gershwin. Meanwhile, closer to the authentic jazz tradition of improvisation and solo virtuosity was the music played by the bands of Benny Goodman, who used many of Henderson's arrangements, along with Gene Krupa and Harry James.

Jazz composers had admired classical music since the days of ragtime. A number of swing-era musicians jazzed the classics in recordings such as 'Bach Goes To Town' (Benny Goodman) and 'Bony Rhapsody' (Ellington and others). In turn, composers of concert music paid tribute to jazz in works such as *Contrasts* (1938, commissioned by Goodman) by the Hungarian Béla Bartók, and the "Ebony" concerto (1945, commissioned by the orchestra led by Woody Herman, 1913-87) by the Russian-born composer Igor Stravinsky. Other composers, such as the American Aaron Copland and Darius Milhaud, from France, also acknowledged the spirit of jazz in their works.

# the post-war decades

The pre-eminently influential jazz musician of the 1940s was Charlie Parker, who became the leader of a new style known as *bebop*, *rebop*, or just *bop*. Like Lester Young, Charlie Christian and other outstanding soloists, Parker had once played with big bands. During World War II, however, the wartime economy and changes in audience tastes had driven many big bands out of business. Their decline, combined with the radically new bebop style, amounted to a revolution in the jazz world. Bebop was still based on the principle of improvisation over a chord progression, but the tempo was faster, the phrases were longer and more complex and the emotional range was expanded to include more unpleasant feelings than before. Jazz musicians became aware of themselves as artists and made little effort to sell their wares by adding vocals, dancing and including comedy, as their predecessors had.

At the centre of the ferment stood Parker, who could do anything on the saxophone, in any tempo and in any key. He created beautiful melodies that were related in advanced ways to the underlying chords and his music possessed endless rhythmic variety. Parker's frequent collaborators were the trumpeter Dizzy Gillespie – known for his formidable speed and range and daring harmonic sense – and the pianist Earl Bud Powell and drummer Max Roach, the latter of whom were both bandleaders in their own right. Also highly regarded were the pianist/composer Thelonious Monk and the trumpeter Fats Navarro. The jazz singer Sarah Vaughan was also associated early in her career with bop musicians, particularly Gillespie and Parker.

The late 1940s brought forth an explosion of experimentation in jazz. Modernised big bands led by Gillespie and Stan Kenton flourished alongside small groups containing innovative musicians such as the pianist Lennie Tristano. Most of these groups drew ideas from 20th-century pieces by such masters as Bartók and Stravinsky. However, most musicians – particularly on the East Coast – continued to expand on the hotter, more driving bebop tradition. Major exponents of the hard-bop or East Coast style included the trumpeter Clifford Brown, the drummer Art Blakey and the tenor saxophonist Sonny Rollins, whose unique approach made him one of the major talents of his generation. Another derivative of the Parker style was *soul jazz*, played by the pianist Horace Silver, the alto saxophonist Cannonball Adderley and his brother, cornet-playing Nat.

# the late '50s, '60s and '70s

Several new approaches characterised jazz in the third quarter of the century. The years around 1960 ranked with the late 1920s and the late 1940s as one of the most fertile periods in the history of jazz.

### Modal Jazz

In 1955, Miles Davis organised a quintet that featured the tenor saxophonist John Coltrane, whose approach produced a striking contrast to Davis' rich-toned, unhurried, expressive melodic lines. Coltrane poured out streams of notes with velocity and passion, exploring every melodic idea, no matter how exotic, and yet he could still play slow ballads with poise and serenity. In his solos, he revealed an exceptional sense of form and pacing. In 1959, he appeared on the landmark Miles Davis album *Kind Of Blue*. Along with the pianist Bill Evans, Davis devised for this album a set of pieces that remain in one key, chord and mode for as long as 16 bars at a time (leading to the term *modal jazz*), allowing much freedom for the improviser. Striking out on his own, Coltrane first pushed the complexity of bop to its limits on *Giant Steps* (1959) before settling on the other extreme: modal jazz. The latter style dominated his repertoire after 1960, when he recorded 'My Favourite Things' using an open-ended arrangement in which each soloist stayed in one mode for as long as he wished. Coltrane's quartet included the pianist McCoy Tyner and the drummer Elvin Jones, two musicians who, because of their dramatic musical qualities, were widely imitated.

### Avant-Garde Movements

Another product of the experimentation of the late 1950s and 1960s was the attempt made by the composer Gunther Schuller – together with the pianist John Lewis and his Modern Jazz Quartet – to fuse jazz and classical music into a third stream by bringing together musicians from both worlds in a repertoire that drew heavily on the techniques of both kinds of music. Also active during those years was the composer, bassist and bandleader Charlie Mingus, who imbued his chord-progression-based improvisations with a wild, raw excitement. Most controversial was the work of the alto saxophonist Ornette Coleman, whose at times almost atonal improvisations did away with chord progressions altogether while retaining the steady, rhythmic swing so characteristic of jazz. Although Coleman's wailing sound and rough technique shocked many critics, others recognised the wit, sincerity and rare sense of form that characterised his solos. He inspired a whole school of avant-garde jazz that flourished in the 1960s and 1970s and included The Art Ensemble of Chicago, the clarinettist Jimmy Giuffre, the pianist Cecil Taylor and even Coltrane himself, who ventured into avant-garde improvisation shortly before his death in 1967.

## Developing The Mainstream

Meanwhile, the mainstream of jazz, although incorporating many of Coltrane's melodic ideas and even some modal jazz pieces, continued to build improvisations largely on the chord progressions of popular songs. In the 1960s, Brazilian songs – especially those in the bossa nova style – were added to the repertoire. Their Latin rhythms and fresh chord progressions appealed to jazz musicians of several generations, notably Stan Getz and flautist Herbie Mann. Even after the bossa nova style declined, the sambas that gave rise to it remained staples of the jazz repertoire and many groups augmented their regular drum sets with Caribbean percussion. The trio formed by the pianist Bill Evans treated popular songs with depth, the musicians constantly interacting instead of simply taking turns for solos. This interactive approach was carried even further by the rhythm section of Miles Davis' quintet of 1963 and later, which included the drummer Tony Williams, the bassist Ron Carter, the pianist Herbie Hancock and, later, the highly original tenor saxophonist Wayne Shorter.

## Fusion

Jazz underwent an economic crisis in the late 1960s. Younger audiences favoured soul music and rock, while older aficionados turned away from the abstractness and emotional rawness of much of the modern style. Jazz musicians realised that, in order to regain their audiences, they had to draw ideas from popular music. Some of these ideas came from rock, but most were drawn from the dance rhythms and chord progressions of soul musicians such as James Brown. Some groups also added elements of music from other cultures. The initial examples of this new *jazz fusion* met with varying success, but in 1969 Davis recorded *Bitches Brew*, a highly successful album that combined soul rhythms and electronically amplified instruments with uncompromising, highly dissonant jazz. Not surprisingly, alumni of Davis' groups created some of the most musically successful fusion recordings of the 1970s, including Herbie Hancock; Wayne Shorter and the Austrian-born pianist Joe Zawinul, co-leaders of the ensemble Weather Report; English electric guitarist John McLaughlin; and the brilliant pianist Chick Corea and his group Return To Forever. Some rock groups, in turn, began to feature jazz phrasings and solos over rock-based rhythms. These groups included Chase, Chicago and Blood, Sweat And Tears.

During this same period, another Davis alumnus, the iconoclastic pianist Keith Jarrett, succeeded commercially while eschewing electronic instruments and popular styles. His performances of popular standards and original songs with a quartet, as well as his improvisations alone at the keyboard, marked him as a major contemporary jazz pianist.

# the '80s

In the mid 1980s, jazz artists were once again performing in a variety of styles to sizable audiences, and there was renewed interest in serious (as opposed to pop-oriented) jazz. Associated with this interest was the trumpeter Wynton Marsalis, who was also acclaimed for his performances of classical music. Although jazz remained essentially the province of American musicians, its international audience flourished to the extent that non-American musicians formed an increasingly significant subgroup within jazz in the 1970s and 1980s, just as their predecessors – including the Belgian guitarist Django Reinhardt – had done in the 1930s and later.

# jazz production

The relationship between jazz and sound recording is of paramount importance. In the case of many other genres, whether musical or not, the recording effectively immortalises a completed, even perfected statement, and such statements remain essentially the same whenever they are recorded or performed. Most jazz, however, has the property of spontaneity, its creativity being concentrated in the act of improvisation, a form of impromptu composition. As a result, any recording of improvised or partly improvised jazz acts as a snapshot, freezing a single creative moment that can never be recreated without unconscious change. Because it's impossible for such a performance to be repeated exactly, each recording acquires a unique value, and it's this that has made the recording of jazz so vitally important.

No other genre rivals jazz in its preoccupation with issues of alternative and multiple takes of individual titles, so be sure to record everything.

Among the varying styles of jazz, one style is the *work song*, which is mainly a rhythmic song that could be described as a song that makes hard work easier and be done more quickly. Work songs are usually unaccompanied, upbeat-rhythm songs that are usually repeated over and over in a sort of chanting designed to make worktime go by faster.

Another style is the New Orleans style, which is famous for the driving beat that is considered to be the epitome of the swing feel. This style of jazz still exists today and is normally referred to as the original style of jazz. This style is also considered to be ensemble jazz and is known for its polyphonic texture.

The Chicago style of jazz music evolved after unemployed musicians moved to the Chicago area, played their new sounds and sought for places to perform this new, exciting style of jazz. With this style, the musicians play popular songs with a more homophonic sound. This is the era in which the piano was introduced into background accompaniments.

When recording these three styles, try a lo-fi approach and even experiment with mono recording to capture the authentic feel of 1940s and 1950s recording techniques. Often, the mono mixes turn out to be radically different from the stereo mixes, and sometimes they sound even better. Keep your use of effects to a bare minimum and don't be afraid to experiment.

If you don't actually play all of the usual jazz instruments, there are some great sample CDs available. Just remember that, when you're playing a sax or trumpet from a keyboard, you should try to emulate the phrasing and dynamics of the natural instrument. Again, don't play chords on instruments that were designed to play only single notes. In bebop and fusion or more modern experimental jazz, use electric instruments in a similar fashion to the way in which they're used on rock recordings. There is a school of thought that suggests that dance is the new jazz, so programming in beats with jazz-structured riffs can produce some truly inspired results.

As a genre, jazz music has and always will reflect the artist of the time through the different styles that the form has taken. Over the years, the genre of jazz has changed to meet the needs of changing times and people's changing tastes in music, introducing new sounds and styles to stay afloat in the ever-changing modern world. However, the core of jazz music hasn't really changed all that much since it began all those years ago – the framework is still there and always will be. However, the surface *will* change, as illustrated by the different styles that have evolved over the years. Deep down, it's the earthy tones, melody and rhythm that have made jazz music what it is today and that carry the memories of what it used to be.

# blues

The blues came originally from unwritten folk tradition and probably got its first generic recognition in around 1912, mainly because several tunes were published with the word "blues" in their titles. Of course, many musicians had been playing this stuff for years before any of it saw publication. Lyrically, early blues used a sort of two-line structure and repetitive guitar style that eventually evolved into the more familiar three-line form comprising a basic one-line statement, a repeat to provide emphasis and a third line answering, commenting on or completing the thought.

The actual blues singer was probably a later phenomenon that evolved out of a fusion of songs and styles. Most musicians threw in a lot of other kinds of songs, some of which were a great deal older than the blues and, although there are African influences, nothing resembling the blues has ever been found in the parts of Africa from which slaves originated.

By the '20s, local heroes like Blind Willie McTell, Blind Lemon Jefferson and Robert Hicks (professionally known as "Barbecue Bob") started to become known. Unlike country music, blues doesn't have the same sense of place, and artists evolved in both rural and urban environments. Stylistically, Hicks accompanied himself on twelve-string guitar, which gave a rich and resonant clarity on the relatively new electrical recordings. However, in general, the twelve-string never really caught on in the Deep South, although it was extremely popular with a group of artists working around Atlanta. Barbecue Bob had a brother called Charley Lincoln who was known mainly for his uproarious laugh, which he used to punctuate his singing. In contrast, Blind Willie McTell had a much more subtle approach to the blues, and his steel-bar/bottle-neck style was said to make his strings shimmer like dew on the grass at dawn. Atlanta was the main recording centre for the blues in the '20s, and these early songs set the agenda for much that came after.

At around this time, there was a lot of movement in American society and many Southern blacks moved north to find better work. As cities grew, people had more money in their pockets at the same time that more records began appearing in the shops. In the North, the blues began to boom in cities like Harlem, Chicago and St Louis, although down South a lot of shops still hadn't become accustomed to "coloured business". However, blues continued to capture the hearts and imaginations of its black audience, because blues seemed to be about the here and now. Women singers achieved a lot of notoriety in the mid to late '20s as well, and Ma Rainey was so popular that she had her picture on the label of one of her records. However, in a few years' time, even she had to yield to a younger rival called Bessie Smith.

Bessie Smith spent her ten-year career with Columbia, the first company to adopt electrical recording equipment, in 1925. Most of her records give a reasonably accurate impression of her majestic and heartfelt singing. They also showed her accompanists in a particularly good light, including leading jazz players of the day such as Louis Armstrong and pianist James P Johnson. The blues of the vaudeville age found its finest exponent in Smith, and as a singer her voice instilled a deep blues feeling, even before her words made their mark. Songs such as 'St Louis Blues', 'Nobody Knows You When You're Down And Out' and 'Young Woman's Blues' are perfect in their own way and widely acknowledged as masterpieces.

The subject matter of blues as a genre has always been daily life and its trials, tribulations and triumphs, and even the most innovative guitarists, such as T-Bone Walker, started off singing basic blues numbers. Walker was one of the most influential bluesmen and changed blues guitar playing forever, inspiring greats like BB King and others. It has been said that blues is a story, but not a conventional narrative with a beginning, middle and end. In some ways, the blues is more like a soliloquy or a monologue of the mind. In the blues, thoughts don't have to come out in a chronological or even logical sequence. The mind broods on some while pushing others out impatiently. Sometimes, it may run through a series of thoughts that have no apparent visible connecting thread, and often no conclusion is reached – or, at least, not by the end of three minutes. Often a blues song will start with some locating phrase, establishing a "who", "when" or "where" – ie the often clichéd "Well, I woke up this morning…". Similarly, there will often be a hook or some memorable phrase or specific reference to a person, thing or place (as in T-Bone Walker's famous 'Wichita Falls') that provides the song with a distinctive title. And since nearly every title includes the word *blues*, this can be quite important. Apart from these few structural markers, however, the song can go anywhere it likes.

As the blues grew in popularity, it was easy enough for record companies to gather material to put on disc. As it happened, the music was waiting for them in most parts of the USA because it had already been transported all over the country by itinerant musicians. Guitarists evolved picking, strumming and bottle-neck styles, and the harmonica became an integral part of the blues scene, and it's been said that the harmonica is to blues what the saxophone is to jazz. One of the best proponents of the harmonica is Junior Wells, a post-bebop legend and one of the better players of the blues. Along with James

Cotton, he's the last of a generation that grew out of Chicago in the late '40s and early '50s, when the blues scene featured such notables as John Lee Williamson and Rice Miller, Little Walter and Walter Horton. In 1952, at the age of 19, Junior replaced Little Walter in Muddy Waters' band, after first performing when he was 14 with Tampa Red, Big Maceo and Johnnie Jones in south-side Chicago clubs. Before joining Waters, he was a member of the famous Four Aces, an innovative, hard-driving blues ensemble consisting of Louis and Dave Myers and former jazz drummer Fred Below. In his late teens and early 20s, he recorded for States Records, recording with Elmore James, Otis Spann, Willie Dixon, Johnnie Jones and Muddy Waters, among others.

In the late '50s, Wells left the Waters band to pursue his own sound, and was the featured act for many years at Theresa's, a south-side basement blues club. In 1965 he recorded his first album, the famous *Hoodoo Man Blues*, on Delmark Records. This became the first album ever by a Chicago blues artist and one of the first records to capture the raw sound of the period. Then, after the success of the *Paul Butterfield Blues Band* album in the same year, Wells' went on to perform for white audiences in colleges, music halls and on tour. 1970 saw him teaming up with Buddy Guy, opening for The Rolling Stones and recording *Drinkin' TNT, Smokin' Dynamite* at the Montreal Jazz Festival, now hailed as one of the classic live albums of all time and in 1974 as one of the ten best albums. Over the years, he has recorded numerous albums and his hard-edged style has caused him to be dubbed "the godfather of the blues", in the manner of James Brown's approach to soul. After his 1990 album, *Harp Attack* – a *tour de force* ensemble concept for Alligator, which also featured James Cotton, Carey Bell and Billy Branch – his newest album for Telarc, *Better Off With The Blues*, includes performance from artists like Bonnie Raitt and Carlos Santana.

The catalogue of blues greats is huge. Some, like John Lee Hooker, Robert Johnson, T-Bone Walker, Muddy Waters, etc, were in at the beginning, some 50 years ago. Others, like John Mayall, Canned Heat, Eric Clapton, Buddy Guy and Bo Diddley, were driving forces in the major blues revival of the '60s and '70s. One of the things that makes blues so magical and enduring is that there is an unbroken line and fusion in the music that has led to some amazing collaborative performances featuring new and established artists. The blues has influenced rock, jazz, dance, folk and a variety of other musical genres over the years. And, as the films *The Blues Brothers* and *Blues Brothers 2000* proved, there's always a new audience for blues out there somewhere.

So, generically, is the blues inconsistent and contradictory? Possibly. But so are emotions. So is life. And everyday life, shared emotions and our confused reactions to all these things, are the legitimate raw material of the blues.

## chapter 7

# epilogue

*"I'm sort of out there in the middle somewhere without any category."*
  *– Emmylou Harris*

*"I accept chaos. I wonder if it accepts me."*
  *– Bob Dylan*

As Patti Smith once said, "As far as I'm concerned, being any gender is a drag." Perhaps being any genre is a drag as well, particularly in the world of music. However, out there in the real world (or, at least, somewhere reasonably close by), despite what MTV, the recording industry or even musicologists might say, you'll probably find that, when it comes to genre – or anything else, for that matter – essentially all statements are true in some sense, false in some sense, meaningless in some sense, true and false in some sense, true and meaningless in some sense, false and meaningless in some sense and…well…true and false and meaningless in some sense. Don't worry, a grasshopper is always wrong in an argument with a chicken, and in the world of genre common sense (or, more likely, popular culture) is what tells you that the world is flat.

Musical interest is usually stimulated either emotionally or intellectually, and in an ideal world it should include both. Listeners or practitioners with no formal knowledge of musical technique, no acquaintance with form or musical history and no familiarity with the more scientific aspects of music may still have emotions profoundly stirred when listening or creating. On the other hand, it's also possible to derive considerable intellectual pleasure from knowing something about the roots, structure and technical side of the art. In some genres, the emotional appeal is so strong that the intellectual features are hardly noticed, unless pointed out, while in others the appeal to the intellect is much stronger than the appeal to the emotions, although these two aspects don't necessarily exclude each other. However, to follow a generic line of thought, it's necessary to have some knowledge of the principles underlying musical development – transformation and combination of themes, tonality, tone colour, etc. Like it or not, the concept of genre gives us an assortment of convenient boxes in which to contain our recognition. Bewilderment is one of the least pleasurable emotions, so we try to conquer it with familiarity. And, as psychologists have observed, the feeling of satisfaction one derives from recognising a familiar object can be one of the strongest of pleasurable emotions.

Out there in music land, the real problem with thinking about the future isn't so much that it might fail but that it might actually succeed. According to pundits, projection assumes that a sign of the times can be posited and not simply read, while its spirit may be conjured and not merely captured. This means that extrapolation is merely an attempt to expand the jurisdiction of the *zeitgeist* and extend its value beyond the point at which we may merely wish to grasp it to the point at which it can become manufactured to satisfy a need or desire.

According to Wagner, nothing but the "artwork of the future" could "close the last link in the bond of holy necessity". That's probably why Disney built Tomorrowland, too – as an attempt to advertise the future and to allow us to consume it now. To some extent, such impatience has spelled the demise of "the buzz" – the relatively slow, unstructured, uncertain word of mouth that disseminates culture. These days, buzz has been usurped by hype – the pre-emptive disseminator whose attempt to minimise the risk and impact of rejection by means of enforced value is heavily backed by speculation in both the financial and the predictive senses, not to mention the proliferation of sub-literate email and text messaging. In the glow of hype, the uncertainty of what the future holds sheds the interrogative in favour of the imperative. The question remaining shrivels to that of middle management and the allocation of resources. In attempting to guide us into the future by guiding the activity of others, a cynic might say that the visionary invariably leads from behind and that the future is nothing more than a program for the misuse of authority. But then, Frank Zappa had it right when he said that cynicism is a positive value. In a digital and over-commercialised age, you *have* to be cynical, and the more people that can be encouraged to be cynical the better.

So a cynic might say that somehow the whole exercise of defining musical genre and style displays the same sort of noisy metaphoric futility of a woodpecker endlessly banging away at a tree hoping to find a small morsel of sustenance. The question is, how come a woodpecker doesn't bash its brains out? Well, to be honest, despite all of the pseudo-scholarship and hip-posturing, the simple answer is that…well, nobody has ever explained why. In some cultures, it's believed that, if you know the true name of something, you have magical power over it and can make it do your bidding. Perhaps the same applies to a musical genre. If we understand where it's been and what it's been called in the past, perhaps we'll have a better understanding of where it might be going and what it might be called in the future.

Regardless of genre, creating really great music should be like pulling yourself up by your bootstraps, throwing away the bootstraps and still managing to stay suspended in mid-air. In a world of increasingly ubiquitous desktop digital studios, the role of engineer, producer and performer are more often than not played by the same person, and if you're reading this book, that person is probably you. However, while this amalgamation may stimulate creativity and eliminate a lot of the traditional communication problems that arise in commercial studios, unless you're a practised schizophrenic you may find it difficult to maintain your objectivity and sense of balance. When you compose, play or record, the best advice that anyone can give you is simply to trust your ears. Instinct is what makes genius, and if you really know what you're trying to create then you'll certainly know it when you hear it, and believe me, that's definitely more important than what you or anyone else decides to call it. A great deal of creative harm is done by people who profess that the narrow little sphere of music in which they are specialists is the only form of art that matters. An equal amout of harm is done by those who pretend to like a particular type of music merely because they're told by peers or the media that they ought to. Tolerating really poor music is the mark of a bad musician and a lazy listener. In its true sense, music is about holy necessity, and as a musician – unless you're part of some sad, commercially manufactured package trying to sell even more recycled pap to an increasingly pre-teen market – you already know that, no matter how experienced or proficient you are, artistically there's always something more to learn. So be like the *South Park* kids and learn something today. Learn the names and take the power, but don't lose the essence. And always remember that music creates genres; genres never create music.

There's an old Sufi parable about the great sage Nasrudin, who once invented a magic wand. Wishing to patent this extremely valuable device, he waved the wand and created a patent office which immediately appeared in full 3D Technicolor. Nasrudin walked into the office, walked up to the clerk and said, "I want to patent this. It's called a magic wand." The clerk looked up at him and said, "Don't be stupid. There's no such thing as a magic wand. You can't do that." So Nasrudin simply shrugged his shoulders, waved the wand again and the patent office and clerk disappeared.

# sectional forms and structures

irst, some basic definitions.

Form – The overall structure of a composition.

Forms – Pre-existing structural (formal) schemes used to compose new music.

Function – Extra-musical purpose for the music (ie dancing, wedding, funeral, military, etc).

Genre – A classification of music by form, function, medium or idiom, normally in some combination.

Idiom – A device used to explore the capabilities of a medium (ie Alberti bass).

Medium – The instrument(s) for which a composition is written.

## short forms

These forms have traditionally been used to compose short pieces.

### Binary, Simple

This form comprises two sections, labelled A and B, usually with repeats – ie ||: A :|: B :||. Each section commonly divides into two parts, with the second part of ||: A :|| focusing on the dominant, if the first part is in a major key, or focusing on the relative major if the first part is in a minor key. The second part of ||: B :|| returns to the tonic. In very short binary pieces, a modulation or motion away from the tonic may not occur. Many classical dances are in simple binary form, such as Beethoven's German dances.

### Binary, Rounded

This form also comprises two sections, labelled A and B, usually with repeats – ie ||: A :|: B :||. Again, each section commonly divides into two parts, with the second part of ||: A :|| focusing on the dominant, if the first part is in a major key, or focusing on the relative major if the first part is in a minor key. As with simple binary form, the second part of ||: B :|| returns to the tonic. Additionally, the rounded binary form brings back the first or second part (usually the second part) of the ||: A :|| section at the end of ||: B :|| . In very short binary pieces, a modulation may not occur. Most classical dances are in rounded binary form.

### Strophic

Strophic is a vocal form in which the same music is repeated with different verses, ie the text changes but the music doesn't. Thus it is musically expressed as A A A A A A, etc. Most folk songs are in strophic form.

### Strophic Binary

This form is a combination of strophic and binary forms and is sometimes called *refrain form*.

||: verse A | B :||
...............................refrain or chorus 1
||: verse A | B :||
...............................refrain or chorus 2
||: verse A | B :||
...............................refrain or chorus 3

A refrain is sung after each verse. It contains the same music and text every time it repeats, while the ||: A | B :|| section changes the words and repeats the same music every time it's sung. Many popular songs are written in strophic-binary form.

### Ternary

Ternary form is a three-section form comprising an A B A layout. Each section commonly has repeats. Each also begins and ends in the same key, although the B section is normally in a different key to that of A. Additionally, each section normally subdivides into binary form. Examples include classical minuets and scherzi, including the third movement of Beethoven's piano sonata number 15 in D major, Op 28.

# large or long forms

These forms are normally used to compose large traditional or classical works.

### Arch

(Modern) An arch form is vaguely defined as one in which the music starts with a soft and thin texture, comes to a climax in the middle and returns to a soft and thin texture again at the end. This is normally combined with one of the other large forms. An example of this form can be found in the first movement of Bartók's *Music For Strings, Percussion And Celesta*.

### Chaconne

(Baroque) This is a special type of theme and variations and is normally written in triple time, often in a minor key and with a slow tempo. The theme occurs as a bass or harmonic progression, often with an accent on the second beat, and is usually four to eight bars long. The chaconne is similar to the passacaglia. For an example of this form, see JS Bach's chaconne in D minor for solo violin from the second sonata (partita) for solo violin or the last movement of Brahms' symphony number four in E minor.

### Ground Bass

A form of theme and variations based on a repeating bass line. See JS Bach's *Goldberg Variations*.

### Passacaglia

(Baroque) A special type of ground-bass theme and variations, normally written in triple time, in a minor key and with a slow tempo. In this form, the theme recurs as a bass line usually four to eight bars long. The passacaglia is similar to the chaconne. For an example, see JS Bach's passacaglia and fugue in C minor for organ.

### Rondo

(Classical) Rondo form is essentially an extended ternary form that follows the plan A B A C A D A...B A. The basic principle is a repeating A section that alternates with new material any number of times. See the rondos in Beethoven's sonatas for examples of rondo form.

### Sonata

(Classical) A large instrumental work, usually in three or four movements, in which one or more of the movements is in sonata form. The Classical sonata has a standard design, in which the third movement is optional:

| MOVEMENT | I | II | III | IV |
|---|---|---|---|---|
| KEY | tonic | related | tonic | tonic |
| TEMPO | fast | slow | moderate | very fast |
| FORM(S) | sonata | sonata or ternary | ternary (minuet or scherzo) | sonata, rondo or theme and variations |

### Sonata Form

(Classical) An elaborate rounded binary form in which the first section (the *exposition*) contains two contrasting themes in first the tonic and then the dominant key (or tonic and relative major, if written in a minor key), which are sometimes called *masculine* and *feminine*. The second section is divided into two parts called the *development* and *recapitulation*. The development contains themes from the exposition manipulated in various ways – commonly fragmented, transposed, inverted, retrograded, etc. This section also contains rapid modulation and a contrapuntal treatment of thematic material focused on the dominant or relative major. The recapitulation is a repeat of the material from the exposition, although in this case both of the themes are presented in the tonic key. The first movement of a sonata is normally written in this form.

### Theme And Variations

(Baroque-Classical) A set of variations based on a theme that is stated at the beginning – ie A A1 A2 A3 A4...A. The theme itself is often in rounded binary form. Examples include JS Bach's *Goldberg Variations*, the third movement of Mozart's piano sonata in D, K 284, the first movement Beethoven's piano sonata number 12 in A flat major, Op 26, or any of his variations.

# contrapuntal forms

### Canon

(Renaissance) Music composed in continuous imitative counterpoint. An example of a canon can be found in JS Bach's *The Art Of Fugue*.

### Fugato

(Baroque-Classical) A fugue that is contained in a larger work – ie a symphony. See the B section in the second movement (*"Marche Funèbre"*) of Beethoven's symphony number three in E flat major, "Eroica".

### Fugue

(Renaissance) A complex, strictly composed form that employs imitative counterpoint. The fugue (literally meaning "flight") is a monothematic composition derived from one subject, which is stated at the outset in all of the voice parts in turn in a specific tonal scheme, alternating between tonic and dominant. The subject is then manipulated in a variety of ways, including transposition, fragmentation, inversion, retrograde, etc. A fugue employs certain specific sectional types, including an exposition, stretto, counter-exposition, episodes, etc. With the exception of the exposition, these sectional types are not required to be in any specific order. Examples of fugues can be found in JS Bach's *The Well-Tempered Clavier*.

### Round

(Renaissance) A circular (repeating) canon. The song 'Frère Jacques' is an example of a round.

# traditional/historical genres

### Aria

(Baroque-Romantic) A self-contained song with instrumental accompaniment within a larger, dramatic or narrative genre, such as an opera, cantata or oratorio. Arias are often (at least, those composed in the 17th century and later) in triple meter or with a ground bass, especially in laments. The "*da capo* aria" (A B A) became common by the late 17th century. In opera, the function of an aria is to express a character's emotional response to a dramatic action. For examples, see Mozart's arias from his operas.

### Arioso

(Romantic) Similar to an aria but sung between an aria and a recitative in idiom. For examples of ariosos, see Wagner's operas.

### Art Song

(Romantic) A song set to a poem. See Schubert's lieder.

### Ballad

A strophic narrative form of song used in English folk ballads, for example.

### Ballet

(Romantic) A highly stylised dance that pantomimes a dramatic narrative, normally with an orchestral accompaniment. Examples of ballets include Tchaikovsky's *The Nutcracker Suite* and Stravinsky's *The Rite Of Spring*.

### Cantata

(Baroque) Literally a "sung piece". A cantata comprises vocal narrative, yet is part of a non-dramatic work – ie without action or staging. It is similar to an oratorio but is shorter and more allegorical in nature. See JS Bach's cantata number four, 'Christ Lag In Todesbanden'.

### Canzona

(Italian Renaissance) Originally (in Italy in the late 16th century) described a song transcribed for instruments. Later, in the 17th century, the term signified an independent instrumental genre, particularly the works of Frescobaldi.

### Chamber Music

(Classical) Music written for small ensembles with one instrument per part, originally intended to be performed with friends – usually without an audience – in someone's parlour. Haydn's string quartets are chamber music.

### Chorale

(Renaissance-Baroque) A metrical and somewhat homorhythmic hymn, German Protestant in origin, with more or less symmetrical phrases punctuated by *fermata* cadences. See JS Bach's chorales.

### Concerto

(Classical) A sonata for a solo instrument and orchestra. For examples, see Mozart's piano concerti or Beethoven's "Emperor" piano concerto.

### Dirge

(Ancient) Funeral music, a lament for the dead. See the second movement ("*Marche Funèbre*") of Chopin's piano sonata in B flat minor, Op 35.

### Étude

An exercise or study used to build technical skill on an instrument. See Czerny's or Paganini's études.

### Divertimento

(Classical) A light, free suite of dances.

### Fantasy

(Romantic) An instrumental composition in a free, quasi-improvisational style.

### Gigue

(Baroque) A lively dance, usually in compound duple or quadruple time with a skipping, syncopated rhythm and sometimes fugal form. The last dances in Baroque suites are usually gigues. For an example, see JS Bach's *Fugue À La Gigue* in G major for organ, S 577.

### Hymn

(Ancient) A song in praise of God or a hero.

### Impromptu

(Romantic) A short instrumental piece in an extemporaneous style, often in ternary form. For examples, see Schubert's impromptus.

### Intermezzo

(Baroque vocal) A light dramatic musical entertainment inserted between the acts of *opera seria* (serious or tragic opera), which later became *opera comique* or *opera buffa*. In the Romantic period, the intermezzo became a short, independent instrumental piece of a light, lyrical character. For an example, see Brahms' A major intermezzo, Op 118, number two.

### Invention

(Renaissance) A short, contrapuntal instrumental piece based on a motif and constructed with strict rules. For examples, see JS Bach's two-part inventions.

### Lullaby

A song used to lull one to sleep. See Brahms' lullaby.

### Madrigal

(Italian Renaissance) Vocal *a cappella* contrapuntal composition, often with five voice parts. See Monteverdi's madrigals.

### March

(Renaissance-Romantic) An instrumental piece with a pronounced repetitive rhythm in duple or quadruple time, punctuated by drum beats. Marches were originally played to keep troops in line. Examples include Sousa's marches.

### Mass

(Medieval-Renaissance) A musical setting of the Roman Catholic Mass. For an example, see Josquin des Prez's *Missa Hercules D'Este*.

### Mazurka

(Romantic) A Polish folk dance from Mazovia composed in triple time with accents falling off the first beat – ie syncopated. See Chopin's Mazurkas.

### Minuet

(Classical) A stately court dance in triple time, with a moderate tempo and in ternary form. Baroque minuets were most often in binary form.

## Motet

(Renaissance) A normally sacred *a cappella* vocal composition featuring imitative counterpoint. Examples include Victoria's 'O Magnum Mysterium' and JS Bach's 'Singet Dem Herrn Ein Neues Lied'.

## Nocturne

(Romantic) Instrumental music about the night or to be heard at night. For an example of a nocturne, see Chopin's nocturne in C sharp minor, Op 27, number one.

## Opera

(Baroque-Romantic) A drama set to music with action, staging, singers and an orchestra. Mozart wrote many operas, including *Don Giovanni*.

## Oratorio

(Baroque) A sacred story set to music with no action or staging, unlike opera, but still with singers and an orchestra. Handel's *Messiah* is an example of an oratorio.

## Overture

(Baroque-Romantic) Instrumental introduction to a large dramatic work, such as an opera. See the overtures to Rossini's operas.

## Polonaise

(Romantic) A Polish dance in triple time and a moderate tempo. Although the polonaise is known as a Renaissance folk dance, it is the later courtly version that has passed on to us via Chopin's examples. Its characteristic rhythm is that of an eighth note followed by two 16th notes and then four more eighth notes (ie a quaver followed by two semiquavers and four more quavers), often with an accent on the second beat and a cadence on the weak third beat. For an example, see Chopin's polonaise in F sharp minor, Op 44.

## Prelude

(Baroque-Romantic) An introductory instrumental piece that conventionally precedes the main fare. Both JS Bach and Chopin wrote many preludes.

### Programme Music

See *tone/symphonic poem*.

### Recitative

(Baroque) A vocal idiom used in dramatic and narrative works, such as an opera, oratorio or cantata. The music is subservient to the text, with the vocal rhythm conforming to textual rather than metrical rhythm. The instrumental accompaniment is simple, often just sparse block chords.

### Rhapsody

(Romantic) A series of melodies strung together with no dependence on or connection with each other. For examples, see Liszt's Hungarian Rhapsodies.

### Ricercare

(Renaissance) An instrumental "motet" with more than one subject, treated as in a fugue.

### Romance

(Romantic) A short instrumental or vocal piece expressing a sentiment.

### Sarabande

(Baroque) A slow dance in triple time, often with an accented dotted rhythm on the second beat and cadencing on the third beat. Sarabandes are normally in binary form.

### Serenade

(Renaissance onwards) An evening piece addressed to a lover, friend or person of rank. For an example, see Mozart's 'Deh, Vieni Alla Finestra' from *Don Giovanni*.

### Sinfonia

(Baroque) A Baroque proto-symphonic form that also applied to the sonata and canzona.

**Song**

(Romantic) A short composition for voice with text, normally accompanied. See Schubert's lieder.

**String Quartet**

(Classical) A sonata for two violins, viola and cello. For examples, see Beethoven's string quartets.

**Suite**

(Baroque) A set of dances. See JS Bach's partita number two for clavier.

**Symphony**

A sonata for orchestra. For an example, see Beethoven's symphony number five in C minor.

**Toccata**

(Baroque) Literally a "touch piece" – a brilliant, virtuoso keyboard work intended to show off the ability of a performer. For an example, see Bach's toccata and fugue in D minor for organ.

**Tone/Symphonic Poem**

(Romantic) An orchestral work written to narrative prose or a poem. Examples include Liszt's *Les Preludes* and his *Faust Symphony*.

**Waltz**

(Romantic) A couple-dance in triple time and at a moderate tempo. For examples, see Johann Strauss' waltzes.

# Mac or Windows?

*"In terms of multitracking actual audio, I've only ever used Macs. I had
more problems just trying to use a PC."*
  *– Guy Fixsen, Music Producer*

## Apple Macintosh

While there are arguments for and against both Macs and PCs in terms of
them being used for producing music, most serious musicians wouldn't
use anything but a Macintosh. The Macintosh has been the computer of
choice of creative types for over 15 years and most major recording
studios and record companies still use Macs to control their digital audio
installations. The Mac OS (Operating System) is user friendly and
Macintosh computers are relatively easy to upgrade and maintain.
Although you'll read nearly everywhere that Macs are always more
expensive than PCs, when you start adding all the extras that you'll need
to make your PC usable for music production you'll find that there's really
not all that much in it.

If you decide to base your desktop digital studio around a Mac, you'll
want to get something like a PCI-bus Power Mac, especially if you intend
to get into digital audio editing or CD mastering. The PowerPC 604, 750
(G3) or the new G4 processors are preferred over the 603e. An older,
used, PowerPC 601 processor-based Power Mac would still be usable for
a starter/budget set-up, especially if the computer has PCI expansion
slots rather than NuBus slots, while a used Power Mac 9500 or 9600 in
good condition can still make a good computer for your home studio, as
long as you don't mind using older software. In some cases, you can
upgrade an older Power Mac with a G3 or G4 processor upgrade.

Always get as much RAM installed as you can afford. The absolute minimum that you should have for running Mac OS 8.x or higher is 64MB, although 128MB or more will make things run much more smoothly. There's no reason to play around with older, pre-PowerPC Macintoshes; sound editors and MP3 encoders rely heavily on a fast FPU for processing their data, and while all Power Mac's have excellent FPUs integrated into their main processors, some older Macintosh computers don't have any FPU at all. Power Macs all come with usable 16-bit audio capabilities.

The iMac and G4 are the newest Mac OS computers. They come standard with an IDE hard drive and CD-ROM drive and decent quality 16-bit audio built in. The iMac/G4s' major selling points are their speed, easy Internet connectivity, ease of use and the fact that they're very nicely styled. The trade-off is that these new iMacs and G4s have no modem or printer ports for connecting typical serial-port MIDI interfaces or Mac-compatible printers. Instead, the new Macs are fitted with USB and FireWire (IEEE1394) ports. This means that iMac/G4 owners will have to buy either brand-new USB MIDI interfaces or USB-to-serial adaptors, which isn't guaranteed to work with all serial-port MIDI interfaces. Some recent magazine articles and reviews have pointed out that there are ongoing problems with using USB devices on the iMac DV or G4 running MacOS 9.x, and several manufacturers of USB MIDI interfaces have acknowledged this problem and are claiming that installing the recent USB driver updates from Apple Computers and the latest MIDI interface drivers will remedy the situation, and so iMac and G4 owners are advised to do their homework before buying a MIDI interface. Mark Of The Unicorn recently released the first commercially available FireWire digital audio interface, the MOTU 828, which can be used with any G4 or iMac with a FireWire port, including the iBook.

The Apple G4 also lacks the familiar Mac SCSI port, so if you already have a SCSI hard drive, CD burner and/or scanner you'll need to buy and install a PCI SCSI accelerator card to make use of them. However, the iMac, iBook and G4 Power Macs do come with a FireWire interface, which is said to be the interface of the future. It can be used for hard drives and CD-Recordable drives, and there are now audio interfaces that connect via FireWire, too. FireWire allows for hot-swappable connection of up to 64 devices and allows for a theoretical maximum throughput of around 40MB per second. There are some FireWire hard drives in the *Mac Warehouse* and *Mac Connection* catalogues, but these are pretty expensive and are actually UltraATA hard drives in an enclosure with a FireWire interface built in. These new FireWire hard drives are advertised as having a throughput of 15MB per second, which is about as fast as Ultra SCSI but not nearly as fast as Ultra2Wide or Ultra160 SCSI.

Apple has recently launched its new operating system, OS X (OS 10). OS X is radically different from previous versions of the Mac OS and it's way too early to tell how easily music equipment manufacturers will be able to update their drivers and applications. For now, you should stay with Mac OS 9.x, at least until your favourite music hardware and software companies announce full support for OS X.

You'll also need a big SCSI or FireWire hard drive of at least 4.5GB, although 9.1GB or more is better. If you have a SCSI-equipped Mac, getting an internal SCSI hard drive will save a good chunk of money, as long as you're willing to open up your computer and install it yourself. However, you can't open up an iMac DV, so you'll need an external FireWire drive for these. (Older, non-DV iMac owners are out of luck on this one.) The internal WideSCSI bus is faster than the external SCSI bus on the older beige G3s. If the thought of opening your Mac's case makes you shake with fear, you'll probably be better off spending the extra £75-£150 on an external hard drive. (Incidentally, there is no such thing as a "Macintosh-only" SCSI or FireWire hard drive. SCSI is SCSI and FireWire is FireWire, whether in a Mac, in a PC or in an SGI or Sun SPARC workstation.)

Some software can be more expensive on the Macintosh platform, but most of what's available is as good as it gets, like Cubase VST, Mark Of The Unicorn's Digital Performer, TCWorks' SparkXL and BIAS Peak, for example. Nowadays, prices are usually the same for Mac software as they are for PC programs. There is some Mac music shareware available, although not nearly as much as exists for Windows. It should also be noted that most of the "heavy hitters" in music software developed their applications for the Mac long before they started coding for Windows.

# Windows PC

For the more budget conscious, there's the Wintel or PC platform. It used to be that IBM PCs were an artistically inclined person's worst nightmare, and to be honest they're still not brilliant. Even though Windows 95 and plug and play made PCs much easier to use, they're still more of a challenge to use than Macs. However, if you're willing to become a bit of a computer nerd, here's what you'll need to get started.

First of all, make sure that you buy a machine equipped with Pentium MMX, Pentium II or Pentium III or a compatible computer. The Intel Pentium III and Celeron (with 128kB L2 cache) processors work well for audio work and are the most widely compatible with all of the various soundcards and other peripherals for use with PCs, while the AMD Athlon ("Thunderbird" version) is a really fast processor (it works faster than a Pentium 4 at some tasks) and seems to work quite well for audio. Meanwhile, the new AMD Duron is every bit as fast as a Pentium III and kicks Celeron's butt all over the place. The AMD K6-II and K6-III chips (Pentium clones) manufactured after November 1997 are OK, too, although they're now pretty much obsolete and not widely supported by soundcard manufacturers. It's best to avoid the IBM/Cyrix 6x86, MII and MIII chips, as many have found them to be liabilities when used in a music computer. Using anything slower than a Pentium 166 MMX will make it very hard to work on stereo digital audio files for CD mastering.

In general, it's best to use a PC that's built onto a motherboard (the big circuit board inside the case) made by a well-known, reputable manufacturer. Each motherboard is built around a *core logic chipset* that functions as the heart of the computer system. You'll want to choose a motherboard based on a chipset that's compatible with all of your hardware and software, and typically the Intel chipsets are the most compatible because all of the software and soundcard manufacturers originally design their products to work on Intel hardware first before they check their products on the other chipsets. Names of motherboard manufacturers to look for include Intel, ASUS, Gigabyte, MSI, Soyo, FIC and Abit, where ASUS is recommended for best performance and Intel for widest compatibility. For the latest Pentium 4 and Celeron processors, the best choices of chipsets are the Intel i850 or the i815e. It's best to avoid the Intel i810, i820 and i840 chipsets, as these are buggy and won't be around for much longer now that the i815e chipset has hit the streets. For Pentium II and Pentium III processors, the Intel i440BX is the best bet, while for older Pentium and Pentium MMX processors the best core logic chipsets are the Intel i430HX and i430TX, with the ALi Aladdin V and VIA Apollo chipsets as second choices, although these aren't always supported by audio hardware manufacturers. Dell and Gateway computers using Intel processors are usually built on Intel motherboards, which always use Intel chipsets, and computers made by these manufacturers are usually safe bets, although you should check to see which chipset they're using before you buy. One of the best chipsets for use with the latest AMD Athlon/Duron CPUs is the VIA KT133A, and the ASUS A7V133 looks like the best motherboard for Athlon/Duron that uses this chipset. The Abit KT7A is also popular, but it has problems.

There are now several companies that will custom build you a PC optimised for music production. These often include your choice of CPU, RAM, operating system, audio and MIDI interfaces and software. Some large music stores are also custom building music computer systems. If you're building your own PC or upgrading, always use high-quality parts, as systems can malfunction because of weak power supplies, substandard RAM or lousy motherboard design, so stick with well-known brands and you should be OK. For RAM, Crucial, Corsair and Micron are all good bets, and LCS, Hitachi and Samsung aren't bad, either. For IDE hard drives, look at IBM DeskStar drives, while Maxtor DiamondMax and Western Digital are said to be good, too, and Fujitsu drives are supposed to be very reliable, if a bit slow. For SCSI hard drives, check out IBM UltraStar LVD or Ultra160 drives. For CD-R, you're pretty safe with Yamaha, Plextor and Panasonic. Some have reported good results from using Sony, Ricoh and Hewlett-Packard CD-Rs.

A frequently overlooked piece of hardware is the power supply, which is usually supplied with the case. A cheap or under-powered power supply will often cause instability, so it's always a good idea to get a good case and power supply from a quality manufacturer like Enlight, Inwin or SuperMicro. Also, be sure to install adequate cooling fans in your case and watch out for compatibility issues between peripherals. If you're really set on a particular soundcard or audio interface, check the manufacturer's website for links to user forums or newsgroups where you can read about users' experiences with various types of peripherals and software. You may find that advanced features of a particular soundcard won't work in your favourite audio program or that a certain video card will cause problems in your particular system. This is the price of the PC's so-called open architecture – you're provided with many possibilities, but hidden and not-so-hidden pitfalls abound.

If you're scrounging around for a freebie starter PC, avoid older-model Pentium 60MHz, 66MHz or 90MHz PCs, as these often have ISA, VLB (Vesa Local Bus) and PCI slots all on the same motherboard. These first-generation Pentium machines had a lot of problems and aren't compatible with most modern hardware, such as the latest soundcards, video cards or RAM chips. At this point, trying to limp along with an old 486 would be too frustrating for most people, and your best bet for a back-of-the-lorry special is an old PC based around a Pentium 133MHz or 166MHz. A Pentium 200 or 233 with MMX or an AMD K6-2 would be better yet. It's best to avoid the AMD K5 and Cyrix 6x86 processors for audio work.

For the operating system, you'll probably want to be running either Microsoft Windows 98 Second Edition or Windows Millennium Edition (Windows ME). For the more hardcore, Windows NT Workstation 4.0 with Service Pack 6 is more industrial strength. If you want to run Windows 2000 with Service Pack 1 (essentially Windows NT version 5.0), you'll need at least a Pentium II 300 with 128MB of RAM, although 256MB or more is recommended.

Windows 95 OSR2 (Windows 95B) is a good choice if:

• You have an older PC that would get bogged down running all the bells and whistles that get installed with Windows 98. A Pentium 133 with only 32MB of RAM will run much better using Windows 95B than it will with Windows 98;

• You're not using any USB or FireWire devices. These technologies are not well supported in Windows 95. You'd be better off using Windows 98 Second Edition or Windows 2000 with these devices;

• You're doing extensive MIDI work and can't tolerate sloppy MIDI timing. While Windows 98 is essentially the same as Windows 95, it tends to get bogged down running all of its extra gimmicks. Windows 95B gives you most of the advantages of Windows 98, including support for large hard drives using the FAT32 file system, without some of its disadvantages (ie the higher load on the system). With less stuff running in the background, MIDI timing on Windows 95B tends to be very good.

Windows 98 Second Edition is a good choice if:

• You have a computer that will work well with it, such as a typical Pentium 166 MMX or faster loaded up with at least 64MB of RAM, while 128MB or more is highly recommended. DON'T use a Pentium 75 with 16MB of RAM;

• You're using an ATA-100 hard drive, USB, FireWire devices and/or you intend to attach DV (Digital Video) cameras to your computer. All of these technologies are supported better in Windows 98 Second Edition than in Windows 95, NT or Windows 2000;

• You're doing extensive MIDI work and must have good MIDI timing and lots of MIDI channels at your disposal. By turning off the extra doodads that Windows 98 installs by default, you can usually get very good MIDI timing in your sequencer applications under Windows 98. Also, check out Windows 98 Lite for a cool way to strip down Windows 98 to its bare essentials;

• You must use a PC but you don't want to spend time learning about computers. While the Macintosh is a better choice for this type of user, these days most people are buying PCs, and Windows 98 is definitely the easiest to use and configure of all the various PC operating systems. It also has by far the widest compatibility with hardware and software.

Windows ME is a good choice if:

- You have a computer that will work well with it – a typical Pentium II 233 or faster – loaded up with at least 64MB system RAM, while again 128MB or more is recommended;

- You're buying all new hardware and are into having all of the latest USB and FireWire gadgets;

- You never need to run a DOS prompt;

- You don't mind scouring the Internet for all of the latest drivers.

Windows NT 4.0 Workstation is a good choice if:

- You're very good with PCs and you don't mind being the system administrator for your set-up. If you don't know what this means, NT is definitely not for you;

- You have a computer that will work with it – such as a typical Pentium 133 or faster – loaded up with at least 128MB of RAM, while 256MB or more is highly recommended. (DON'T use a 486 DX2-66 with 16MB of RAM.) A WideSCSI controller and hard drive(s) are also highly recommended for NT;

- You have software that will work with it, such as SoundForge, CoolEdit Pro or Cakewalk 7.02 – NOT Nemesys GigaSampler or Emagic Logic Audio.

  (Note that software that requires Microsoft DirectX 5.0 or later to work probably won't work in Windows NT. This includes software synths like GigaSampler, Seer Systems' Reality, FruityLoops or Roland's Virtual SoundCanvas. There is an unofficial, unsupported patch that installs DirectX 5.0 in NT, but there are absolutely no guarantees with these kinds of "hacks". However, if this sounds like something you want to try, search on the Internet for a file named "NT4DX5.zip".)

- You have music hardware with drivers that will work with NT, like Lynx Studios' LynxONE, DAL's CardDeluxe, Creative Labs' Sound Blaster Live! or RME's DIGI96/8-series soundcards, or a MidiMan BiPort 2X4s, Opcode Studio 64X or Roland MPU-401 or compatible MIDI interface. DON'T use Digidesign's Digi001, Aardvark's multitrack audio/MIDI interfaces or MidiMan's 1x1 or 2x2 MIDI interfaces, as these are for Windows 95 or 98 only. Long-time NT users know that they have to choose their hardware carefully for compatibility;

• You're mostly doing audio work rather than memory-intensive MIDI-sequencing work. This is because MIDI timing is generally worse in NT than in Windows 95/98 due to NT's fully protected-mode, 32-bit architecture. Since Windows 95, 98 and ME allow 16-bit real-mode access to the hardware, MIDI can be made to run much more smoothly. The downside is that, because of this, Windows 95, 98 and ME are less stable. Note that this does not affect audio timing.

Also note that this becomes less of a problem with a faster processor and hard-disk subsystem. Cakewalk recommends at least a Celeron 400MHz processor for use with Pro Audio 8 in Windows NT, and this should be less of a problem now that Pentium III 733MHz and faster processors are becoming commonplace.

Windows 2000 Professional is a good choice if:

• You're very good with PCs and you don't mind being the system administrator for your set-up. Again, if you don't know what this means, Windows 2000 is not for you;

• You have a computer that will work well with it, like a Pentium II 300MHz model or faster, loaded up with at least 128MB of RAM (although again 256MB or more is highly recommended), NOT a Pentium 200 with 32MB of RAM. An Ultra2Wide SCSI controller and hard drive(s) are also highly recommended for Windows 2000;

• You have software that will work with it, like SoundForge 4.5, CoolEdit 2000 or Cakewalk Pro Audio 9.02, NOT Digidesign Pro Tools LE or Logic Audio;

(Note that software requiring Microsoft DirectX 5.0 or later is supposed to work in Windows 2000, since it comes with DirectX 7.0 built in. Software synths like Nemesys' GigaSampler and Seer Systems' Reality are DirectSound-accelerated applications that rely on DirectX to work. Unfortunately, it seems that life in Windows 2000 isn't as simple as that, as these applications have proved problematic in Windows 2000. As usual, check with the manufacturer of your favourite software before you upgrade.)

• You have music hardware that will work with it. While most audio hardware will work in Windows 2000 using Windows NT 4.0 drivers, not all hardware that works in Windows 98 or ME will work in Windows 2000.

Check with the manufacturer(s) of your hardware to see if it's compatible with Windows 2000 before you upgrade. Also note that there are severe audio latency (delay) problems with the native Windows 2000 WDM driver architecture. One of the only professional soundcard manufacturers that claims to offer full support for its products in Windows 2000 is RME Audio. (Speaking of hardware, please note that, even though Microsoft promises support for all of the latest digital video, FireWire and USB gadgets in Windows 2000, this doesn't mean that your particular gear is guaranteed to work with it. Once again, check with the manufacturer of your hardware before you upgrade);

• You're doing mostly audio work, rather than intensive MIDI sequencing work. This is because MIDI timing is generally worse in Windows 2000 than it is in Windows 95, 98 and ME due to Win2000's fully protected-mode, 32-bit architecture. Since Windows 98 and ME allow 16-bit real-mode access to the hardware, MIDI can be made to run much more smoothly. The downside is that Windows 98 and ME are less stable because of this, although this doesn't affect audio timing. Again, this becomes less of a problem with a faster processor and hard-disk subsystem.

Although it's not much of an issue any more, you should steer well clear of IBM OS/2 Warp. There's almost no useful music software available for it and most good audio and MIDI hardware has no OS/2 driver support available. This is too bad, because OS/2 had some useful features and capabilities that Windows will probably never have.

Linux is not for the non-technical. However, it is fast becoming a more viable alternative to Windows, and there's a lot of work going on that's aimed at making Linux a workable OS for the masses – Corel's WordPerfect Suite is available for Linux, Netscape has had a Linux version of Navigator available for a while now and more programs are sure to follow. A few soundcards are currently supported in Linux, including the Sonorus STUDI/O, SEK'D Prodif Gold, Zefiro Acoustics ZA-2, Aureal Vortex 2 (Turtle Beach Montego II and Diamond MX-300) and the Ensoniq AudioPCI (audio only), while the venerable Roland MPU-401 is supported for MIDI i/o. Musicians who are interested in Linux should check out Open Sound System and the Linux "MIDI And Sound Applications" website.

# considerations

PCs don't always come with built in-sound, so a soundcard may have to be purchased and installed. Soundcard marketing is a morass of false advertising and hyperbole, but there are many really good products available. Suffice it to say that it pays to do your homework before you spend your money.

You'll need to have a big IDE or SCSI hard drive with at least 4.5GB available, and preferably 9.1GB or bigger. You'll also have to decide if you want to use the typical PC's IDE (or ATA) hard drive and CD-ROM or if you want to invest in a SCSI adaptor to connect your PC to the higher-performance SCSI hard drives and CD-ROM/CD-R drives.

Adaptec has recently announced the release of its new Ultra160 SCSI controllers. When used with the appropriate Ultra160 SCSI hard drives (the prices of which have recently fallen dramatically), Adaptec claims that burst rates of up to 160MB per second should be achievable. Now that's fast! There are now 9.1GB Ultra2 SCSI (LVD) drives available for less than £200. The IBM UltraStar drives, for example, are excellent.

There's a lot of fine-quality Windows music shareware available on the Internet, and you shouldn't be afraid to try these programs out, as some of them are excellent. Two great shareware stereo sound editors are Cool Edit 2000 and GoldWave. Of course, there are also tremendous commercial Windows sound editors available, such as SoundForge, CoolEdit Pro, Samplitude, Steinberg WaveLab and SAW, as well as MIDI/audio sequencers such as Cakewalk Sonar, Steinberg Cubase VST and Emagic Logic Audio on the high end and PG Music Power Tracks Pro Audio and FASoft n-Track Studio bringing up the low end.

Speaking of software, there are a number of things that can really screw up a PC's ability to play and record clean-sounding digital audio. Resource-greedy device drivers, overly intrusive anti-virus programs and fancy fax software are examples of just a few. Excessive "feature bloat" is the kiss of death for good audio performance from a PC. If your first priority is music production, it's essential that you fine-tune your system for your musical uses as opposed to playing games or viewing multimedia on the web.

# samplers, the universe and everything

## how to save memory

Although not quite the issue it was five years ago, sampler memory is still a problem. The irritation of not having enough room for the last cymbal lick is beyond words, so here are some basic tips that will hopefully help you to avoid premature baldness.

• At a full audio bandwidth of 20kHz, using a 44.1kHz sampling rate, one minute of stereo sound takes up around 10MB of RAM. If you can make do with mono samples, this immediately doubles the amount of sampling time available.

• If you can tolerate a lower audio bandwidth, setting a lower sampling rate can extend your sampling time by a factor of two or more.

• When sampling sustained musical sounds such as strings or flutes, another time-saving strategy is looping the sample (not to be confused with sampling the loop). Most sustained sounds have a distinctive attack portion, but then, as they start to decay, the sound becomes more consistent. Listen to something like a flute or a string section playing a sustained note and you'll notice that very little about the sound changes after the initial attack. This being the case, there's no reason to sample the whole sound being played. Simply sample the first few seconds and then use your sampler's editing facilities to create a loop so that the middle part of the sample repeats itself continually until you release the key. Obviously, there's little point in trying to loop short or percussive sounds – they probably wouldn't sound right, anyway – but you can loop long percussive sounds, such as the decay of a cymbal.

NB: There's another good reason for looping sounds, and that's to get around the fact that the length of a sample changes as you play higher or lower on the keyboard. And besides, the length of this original sound will probably be too short if you want to hold down a string pad for the next 24 bars. Once a sound is looped, its level never has to decay to zero, because the same section of sound is being continuously looped.

- The use of panning can be an effective way of fooling listeners into believing that they're inhabiting a stereo world in your memory-dictated mono realm. The most obvious and straightforward panning arrangement for a mono multisample is to pan sounds to one side at the bottom of the keyboard and then to pan things through the centre and to the opposite side as you progressively play higher up the keyboard. (Some samplers have this panning "template" as an onboard option.) Simply panning sounds alternately left and right will give you an effective stereo image, and the apparent size of your multisampled instrument(s) will be doubled. However, if you're willing to venture under your sampler's bonnet and get your hands dirty, there are a number of multisample panning tricks that can open up new stereo-soundscape possibilities to you. Here is a set of maps.

|  | **NARROW** | **WIDE** |
|---|---|---|
| Low | L05/R05 | L10/R10 |
|  | L10/R10 | L20/R20 |
|  | L15/R15 | L30/R30 |
|  | L20/R20 | L40/R40 |
| High | L25/R25 | L50/R50 |

|  | **STAGGERED** | **STEREO POSITIONAL (L/R)** |
|---|---|---|
| Low | L05/R10 | L50/R10 |
|  | L15/R20 | L40/R20 |
|  | L25/R30 | L30/R30 |
|  | L35/R40 | L20/R40 |
| High | L45/R50 | L10/R50 |

"Narrow" and "wide" stereo-panning patches can also be layered on top of one another and switched between, via velocity switching or crossfading, which widens the stereo image the harder you play. Here are some rough outlines, but take into account your personal playing style for the velocity rates.

| VELOCITY SWITCH | VELOCITY CROSSFADE | PANNING |
|:---:|:---:|:---:|
| 0-90 | 0-110 | L05/R05 (soft) |
| 91-127 | 80-127 | L10/R10 (loud) |
| | | |
| 0-90 | 0-110 | L10/R10 (soft) |
| 91-127 | 80-127 | L20/R20 (loud) |
| | | |
| 0-90 | 0-110 | L15/R15 (soft) |
| 91-127 | 80-127 | L30/R20 (loud) |
| | | |
| 0-90 | 0-110 | L20/R20 (soft) |
| 91-127 | 80-127 | L40/R40 (loud) |
| | | |
| 0-90 | 0-110 | L25/R25 (soft) |
| 91-127 | 80-127 | L50/R50 (loud) |

# sample CDs

Sample CDs are a confusing phenomenon to the traditional musician stumbling into the realm of music technology, not so much in application but rather in concept. The idea of using ready-made riffs and drum loops as a basis for "original" music has had many classically trained musicians scratching their heads. Needless to say, working with some construction-based loop CDs has a lot in common with remixing. In fact, if you wish to practise remixing alien material, investing in a song-based sample CD isn't the worst thing you can do.

The concept of copyright and sample CDs is also strange. Most offer the user licence but not ownership of the samples. This means that you can use them in commercial projects but not sell them or distribute them in sample form. They come in a variety of formats, colours and concepts. Here's a brief overview.

# audio CDs

**Pros**

- They're cheap.
- There's a large number of available releases.
- They offer the quick and easy auditioning of sounds.
- They're compatible with every possible sampling format.

**Cons**

- It can be very time consuming and fiddly to sample and store large numbers of sounds.
- You need a good knowledge of your sampler's workings to get the most from an audio sample CD.

# CD-ROMs

**Pros**

- With these, it's quick and easy access to all sounds.
- You need to spend less time sampling.
- You can give your songs an instantly "professional" touch.
- They often contain more sounds than audio CDs.

**Cons**

- They're more expensive, sometimes incredibly so.
- You have no chance to audition sounds without loading them (although this depends on the format).
- They don't always encourage the user to experiment as much as they could.

# mixed-mode CDs

**Pros**

- These are often the same price as audio CDs, and sometimes even cheaper.
- They can offer the best of both worlds, both audio and ROM data.
- They're good for auditioning sounds on a regular CD player before loading up samples.

**Cons**

- Having to fit both file types on a single disc can mean fewer samples.
- Although nearly all popular sampler formats can be catered for on a mixed-mode release, WAV and AIFF are the most common these days, which isn't to everyone's tastes.

Sample CDs are available from places like Time & Space in the UK (www.timespace.com) or other similar shops.

# samples, copyright and the law

Copyright is a horribly entangled issue. Every musician has a different opinion about it, while the law tends to stick to one. As with anything legal, copyright law has an unhealthy fascination with semantics. Reams and reams of documentation deal with the subject, but some basic points are worth noting.

There are three owners of the copyright in a sample:

- The publisher of the original piece of music;

- The record company (or film company, if the sample is from a film or video) who released it and therefore own the performance of the music or speech;

- The owner of the moral rights to the copyright (which, for a piece of music, lie ultimately with the original composer).

These days, most music-related contracts have a clause which states that the composer waives the moral rights to their work. Having said that, there are two issues on which a composer – or the custodian of his copyright – can insist. One is the right of *paternity*, which means that he can insist on being fully credited in the songwriting credits. The other is the right of *integrity*, a precept as familiar to remixers as picket fences are to Klan members. Integrity means that, if an artist doesn't like the new track that uses his material, for whatever reason, he can block the use of his work. In fact, if any of the three owners of the copyright refuse permission for you to use their property, there's nothing you can do about it; two out of three isn't enough.

# how are copyright issues resolved?

These are the main types of deal you can strike with companies.

### A Buy-Out Fee

This is a one-off payment for the use of the sample. Breakbeat CDs work on this principle.

### A Percentage Deal

There are two ways in which this kind of deal works:

- The owner of the sample will become co-owner of your track and will be paid royalties directly;

- You will pay the owner of the sample an agreed royalty rate on every copy of your material that's pressed.

The difference between the two is that, in the second case, you will still own the copyright to your track, as opposed to owning only a percentage of it. This is known officially as *financial participation*.

### A Roll-Over Fee

With this kind of agreement, you pay an agreed amount of money for the number of records pressed. This saves having to calculate royalty payments. Everything is open to negotiation, including whether you need to credit the source of your sample (which is usually required). Of course, you may be able to come to some other arrangement that is agreeable to all sides – sample clearance is still in its infancy. Whatever deal you strike, get it in writing and stick to your side of the bargain.

# other information

For further information on the subject of sampling copyright, contact the MCPS's Sample Clearance Department at the address below:

Mechanical Copyright Protection Society Limited
Sample Clearance Department
Elgar House
41 Streatham High Road
London SW16 1ER

Tel: +44 (0)20 8769 7702
Fax: +44 (0)20 8664 4698

(The MCPS's main switchboard number is +44 (0)20 8664 4400 for all enquiries not to do with sample clearance.)

Thanks to *Sound On Sound* magazine for the information provided here.

# microphone magic

When it comes to serious recording, you can never over-emphasise the importance of microphones. Microphones convert the sounds that you hear into electrical signals that can be recorded, and, as mentioned earlier in the book, choosing the right mic for the musical genre at hand is critically important to getting the sound you want on your final tracks. No amount of EQ, compression or reverb can change the subtle signature that any particular microphone leaves on an audio track.

So how do you choose that perfect mic without buying and auditioning everything on the market? For a start, you could talk to other musicians and producers to find out what has worked for them in the past and what sort of mics they'd recommend, and reviews in magazines like *Sound On Sound* are always worth a look. Before you start shopping around for anything, however, make sure that you're familiar with the basic microphone "families". These include mics used for recording vocals and instrumentation.

To begin with, microphone pick-up patterns include *omnidirectional*, *cardioid*, *figure of eight* and *stereo*, while the types of pick-up themselves include *dynamic*, *condenser* and *ribbon*.

## pick-up patterns

### Omnidirectional

An omnidirectional mic picks up sound equally from all directions. Omni mics tend to have a very good bass response, without the artificial low-frequency boost provided by the proximity effect picked up by a typical cardioid mic. (The proximity effect determines that, the closer a sound source is to a cardioid mic, the more the mic will accentuate that sound source's bass-frequency output.) This can add richness and fullness to a singer's voice or to a saxophone's sound, but it can also muddy the sound of a guitar amp or acoustic bass.

Really good omnidirectional condenser mics are great at capturing a sense of open space and air, which makes them the first choice for critical reproduction of acoustic instruments – such as symphonic orchestras, vocal choirs, pianos or string quartets – in good-sounding acoustic spaces like concert halls. You can also use omnidirectional microphones to close mic an instrument or vocalist without worrying about the artificial bass boost caused by the proximity effect picked up by a directional mic.

Some of the highest-fidelity mics available are of the omnidirectional condenser variety, including models from Schoeps, DPA (B&K) and Earthworks.

## Cardioid

A cardioid mic is more sensitive to sounds directly in front of it than it is to sounds 90° off to either side and is even less sensitive to sounds directly behind it. In fact, cardioid mics practically cancel out any sounds that emanate from directly behind the mic. This makes them very useful for PA and live recording use and the most popular choice for use in the imperfect recording environments of most home digital studios. To use a cardioid mic, simply aim the mic at the instrument that you want to record and the rest of the stage sound will be at least somewhat quieter than the desired instrument's sound. Most of today's most popular microphones have a cardioid pick-up pattern.

There are also a couple of variations on the cardioid pick-up pattern. Supercardioid and hypercardioid mics are less sensitive to 90° off-axis sources than plain cardioids, which means that they'll do a better job of rejecting sounds from off to the sides. However, hypercardioids pick up some sound from directly behind the front of the mic, which makes them a little bit like figure-of-eight mics (see below), and cardioid mics in general also pick up the proximity effect.

When miking from a distance, cardioid mics have a tendency to sound somewhat thin in the bass when compared to omnidirectional mics. For this reason, cardioid mics are usually used for close miking, with the mic placed less than two feet away from the sound source, while omnidirectional or figure-of-eight mics are usually used when miking from farther away.

### Figure Of Eight

Figure-of-eight mics have the "open" sound and good bass response of omnidirectional mics with the added advantage of rejecting sounds from either side of the mic. Since figure-of-eight mics pick up sound equally well from directly behind and directly in front of the mic, you should take care that you don't capture undesirable reflections from low ceilings or nearby walls. A good place to use a figure-of-eight-pattern mic is when you need to cancel reflections from side walls in a narrowish room but you still want to capture a good sense of room ambience.

# pick-up types

### Dynamic

Dynamic mics use a moving coil to sense the changes in air pressure that make sound waves. The wire coil is suspended over a permanent magnet, and when moving air hits the coil the air causes the coil to move over the magnet, which causes a process called *electromagnetic induction* to take place. This causes an AC voltage to be formed that is electrically analogous to the original sound. The electrical signal that appears at the mic's output is a more or less faithful reproduction of the original vibrations in air, only in fluctuating AC voltages instead of air-pressure changes.

### Small-Diaphragm Dynamic

These are by far the most commonly used mics for PA and stage sound use. Dynamic microphones are typically very rugged and don't require a voltage source to work properly. Cardioid-pattern small-diaphragm dynamic mics are most often used as hand-held vocal mics (such as the ubiquitous Shure SM-58) or as instrument mics for stage use (like the equally ubiquitous Shure SM-57). There are many other similar dynamic mics available from companies like Audix, Electro-Voice, Sennheiser and many others.

### Large-Diaphragm Dynamic

While similar to their small-diaphragm siblings, large-diaphragm dynamic mics are typically used for very loud, bass-heavy instruments such as tom-

toms, kick drums and bass-amp speakers. The larger diaphragm allows these mics to withstand higher SPLs (Sound Pressure Levels) with ease, which allows low-distortion sound reproduction. However, the larger diaphragm will also weigh more and has a higher moving mass, which can limit the high-frequency response and transient response of the mic. Some popular large-diaphragm dynamic mics include the following:

- Electro-Voice RE-20 – A favourite of radio announcers and a good mic for kick drums;

- Shure SM-7 – Similar to the Electro-Voice RE-20;

- Sennheiser MD-421 – Commonly used on tom-toms and hand percussion;

- Shure SM7 – A large-diaphragm dynamic mic used for broadcasts and voice-overs as well as for miking kick drums and brass and bass instruments.

## Condenser

A condenser mic captures sound by using a conductive diaphragm with a capacitative charged plate behind it. The charge is supplied by a DC voltage source such as a battery or the 48V phantom power supply present in most mixers and mic pre-amps. Air-pressure changes meeting the conductive diaphragm cause it to move, which in turn causes an analogous AC voltage to be formed in the charged plate. These tiny AC voltages are sent to a small pre-amp built into the microphone, which brings the signal up to the level at which it can drive a typical microphone pre-amp. The signal leaves the microphone via the cable and is sent to the microphone pre-amplifier stage of the mixer. Because their diaphragms can be made very thin and light, condenser mics tend to be more accurate and "faster" than dynamic mics, especially in the mid-range and treble frequencies. However, they also tend to be more physically delicate than dynamic mics, so they're more commonly used for studio recording than for live sound and PA situations. There are a few condenser mics specially designed to withstand the rough and tumble of stage use, such as the Shure SM-87.

## Small-Diaphragm Condenser

Small-diaphragm condenser mics have the best high-frequency response and quickest transient response of all of the commonly available types of microphone. For this reason, small-diaphragm condenser mics are most often used as drum kit overhead mics to faithfully capture cymbals and stick attacks, for acoustic stringed instruments such as guitars and violins and for percussion instruments such as vibraphones, shakers and marimbas. Another common use for small-diaphragm condenser mics is as stereo pairs to pick up ambient acoustic events in good-sounding spaces. However, the one downside to small-diaphragm condensers is that they tend to be noisier than other types of microphone.

Popular small-diaphragm condenser mics include the following:

- Shure SM-81 – A mic with a very flat frequency response, commonly used on acoustic guitars and as a drum kit overhead mic;

- Audio Technica AT-3528 – A cardioid model that is a sort of a poor man's KM-84;

- AKG C 1000 S – A good all-round budget favourite;

- Neumann KM184 – A truly professional recording mic;

- Oktava MC-012 – From Russia, this is another mic designed to be similar to the KM-84 but cheaper;

- Earthworks QTC-1 – Another great professional mic with an extremely accurate response.

**Large-Diaphragm Condenser**

Since condenser mics are intrinsically more sensitive to higher frequencies, it's possible to combine the warmth and fullness of a large diaphragm with the high-frequency detail typical of a small-diaphragm condenser mic in a single microphone. These large-diaphragm condenser mics are the mainstay of recording studios everywhere, especially for recording vocals, pianos, horns and other acoustic instruments. Some older vacuum-tube-based large-diaphragm condenser mics, such as the Neumann U47 and AKG C12, are collector's items and prized for their sonic warmth and smoothly accurate reproduction of aural details. The 1960s vintage Neumann U87 is an FET-amplified large-diaphragm mic that is more of a modern classic…and well beyond the budgets of most home studios.

Popular large-diaphragm condenser mics include the following:

- AKG CS 414 ULS – an industry standard for overhead drum miking and general use, providing a choice of cardioid, hypercardioid, omni and figure-of-eight pick-up patterns;

- AKG C 3000 B – A budget mic based on the design of the venerable CS 414 (cardioid only);

- Neumann U87 – The standard by which all others are judged, providing a choice of cardioid, hypercardioid, omnidirectional and figure-of-eight pick-up patterns;

- Neumann TLM 103 – A new, lower-priced version of the famous U87 (cardioid only);

- Audio Technica AT-4033A – A fabulous microphone for the price (cardioid only, and great on saxophones).

## Ribbon

By suspending a small, wafer-thin aluminium ribbon between two mounting points inside a strong magnetic field, you get a microphone that is extraordinarily sensitive to vibrations in the air. Ribbon mics can really capture the thump of a plucked acoustic bass or the subtle dynamics of jazz drums. Unfortunately, ribbon mics tend to be extraordinarily fragile; blow on the ribbon the wrong way and you can stretch it out beyond repair. Nevertheless, ribbon mics remain a favourite amongst well-heeled recordists everywhere.

Common ribbon mics include the following:

- RCA BX-44 and BX-77 – The original classics;

- Coles 4038 – Sets the standard of modern ribbon mics;

- Beyerdynamic M-260 – a budget ribbon mic (hypercardioid only);

- Royer Labs R-121 – A new ribbon mic design that's getting a lot of attention.

## Stereo

If you combine two cardioid condenser elements in one chassis, you get a single-point stereo mic. This is usually an X-Y type, where the two cardioid elements are pointed away from each other at a 90° angle. Some stereo mics are of the mid-side type, using a combination of a forward-facing cardioid element with sideways-oriented figure-of-eight element, which allows you to remotely control adjustments of the stereo-image width.

Popular stereo mics include the following:

- Audio Technica AT-825

- Shure VP-88

- Crown SASS

# vocal versus instrument mics

### Vocal Mics

Recording the human singing or speaking voice presents some unique challenges. Most people prefer a heightened sense of presence on the human voice and will often also prefer a mild bass boost for added warmth. As a result, most microphones meant for recording or amplifying vocals have a tailored response characteristic. Dynamic vocal mics are designed to be very sturdy and to produce as little handling noise as possible. They are also designed with a very tight cardioid or hypercardioid pick-up pattern so that there is minimal bleed from other instruments on the stage. As mentioned earlier, the standard mic of this type is the Shure SM58, which can withstand very rough treatment and has very good feedback rejection, making it perfect for daily use on stages where amplified rock, pop, R&B or jazz bands play. The SM58 has a specially tailored response that reduces bass pick-up from far away, thus minimising booming from the stage sound, but it will boost the bass when the singer comes in close, creating a big, warm sound. The SM58 has a substantial peak in its response from about 2kHz up to about 12kHz, which adds a pleasant sheen and an overall brightness to the sound. This helps vocals cut through a dense mix and increases clarity and intelligibility.

You can usually tell if a microphone is designed for live sound vocal use by checking to see if it's equipped with a pop filter to protect the pick-up from blasts of air on plosive sounds. The Shure SM58 has a spherical metal screen pop filter that is lined with foam rubber on the inside.

When recording vocals, most studios use large-diaphragm condenser microphones like the Neumann U87 or AKG C12. Like stage mics, these also have a presence peak and proximity effect tailored to enhance the sound of the vocalist. However, because these large-diaphragm condenser microphones are to be used in the more controlled environment of a recording studio, they can have wider cardioid pick-up patterns, allowing for a more open sound.

When choosing a mic to record a particular musical genre, you'll need to pick your microphone like a musician picks his instrument. For example, a darker mic will help to tame a high, shrill voice, while a clearer, brighter-sounding mic will help the vocal cut through a dense mix. Unfortunately, there is no single best microphone for all situations, only a palette of good microphones from which you have to choose the right tool for the job at hand. The standard large-diaphragm vocal mic is the Neumann U87, although some prefer the vacuum-tube-based Neumann U47. These microphones have a distinctive upper-mid range to treble/presence boost and a warm, rich bass boost via their tendency to pick up the proximity effect. Similar mics to the U47 and U87 are the AKG C12 and CS 414 ULS, both of which have the crisper sound characteristic of AKG microphones in general, which some producers love and others hate. There is an increasing number of less expensive versions of these microphones on the market today, including mics like the following:

- RØDE NT1000

- Audio Technica AT-4033a, AT-4047

- AKG C2000S, C3000B

- Marshall Electronics MXL-2001-P

- Joe Meek Meekrophone

- Oktava MC-319

When you use a condenser mic to record a vocalist, it's usually a good idea to hang a pop screen between the vocalist and the microphone to keep loud "p", "b" and "k" sounds from overloading the mic's pick-up and spoiling a take. You can buy these or make them out of an old pair of tights and a tea strainer.

## Instrument Mics

When it comes to recording instruments, different priorities arise, depending on your musical genre and style. When recording acoustic instruments, the microphone should be faithful to the original sound. However, instruments used in rock and pop music can be very loud and require a mic that can withstand extremely high sound pressure levels without distorting. It's extremely difficult to make a mic that's both sensitive enough to pick up the subtle nuances of a fine acoustic instrument while also being able to capture the brute force of a rock kick drum or guitar amp without overloading. Once again, there's no single best mic for all situations, and you'll have to base your choice on what you have to record and what mics are available.

Dynamic mics are best for loud sounds such as rock drum kits, guitar amplifiers and close-miked brass instruments. There are a select few dynamic microphones around that are both rugged and have a smooth sound that's suitable for recording high-decibel musical instruments, but be aware that typically these are more expensive than dynamic vocal microphones and don't work as well as condenser types on instruments with complex high-frequency information. The Sennheisser 421 and 422 and the Beyerdynamic M88 are among the most widely used of this type of dynamic instrument microphone, while the Electro-Voice RE-20 is also popular. The Shure SM57 is frequently used on snare drums, hand percussion (congas, bongos, timbales, etc) and guitar amplifiers but not usually for bass-heavy instruments like kick drums or electric bass guitars. You'll usually see dynamic microphones used for live stage performances, while condenser mics are more often used in the recording studio.

When choosing a condenser mic, again the type must be chosen to match the sonic characteristics of the source that you want to record. Orchestral instruments, acoustic stringed instruments and classical music ensembles will usually be recorded with sensitive condenser microphones that have relatively flat frequency responses. It's generally acknowledged that small-diaphragm condenser mics such as those from DPA, Schoeps and Earthworks provide the most accurate response, while some prefer the pleasant-sounding colouration of the large-diaphragm Neumann M50 or similar.

# close-miking individual acoustic instruments

When recording an individual brass, wind or reed instrument for a pop or jazz recording, a large-diaphragm condenser microphone such as a Neumann U87 or AKG CS 414 ULS will often be used. If recording a featured solo, the instrumentalist is treated similarly to a vocalist – ie the microphone may be chosen as much for its desirable colourations as for its clarity, warmth, headroom or lack of distortion. Acoustic piano is treated in several different ways, depending on the style of music and the sound quality desired. A solo classical piano is usually miked from a considerable distance away, with careful attention paid to the quality of the room's acoustics and the degree to which the microphones pick up the ambient sound of the room compared to the more direct sound of the instrument. Often, an X-Y stereo pair of condenser mics will be used. For rock, pop or jazz piano in a group, the instrument will often be miked much closer, often with the lid closed and the piano isolated from the room sound with sound-absorbing blankets. For a robust, rich sound, choose a large-diaphragm condenser mic; for a brighter, clear sound, choose a small-diaphragm model.

## Drum Kits

For rock and pop, the individual pieces of the drum kit are usually miked individually. This allows greater freedom at the mixdown stage to alter the sound to taste. As a general guideline, try the following set-up:

* Snare drum – The most common technique is to place a Shure SM57 so that it picks up the sound from the batter (top) head. Sometimes a second microphone is placed underneath the drum to pick up the sound of the snare wires. The output from this microphone may need to be reversed in polarity so that it doesn't introduce phase cancellations with the signal from the top snare mic;

* Kick drum – Depending on the sound of the kick drum itself, a large-diaphragm dynamic mic such as an Electro-Voice RE-20 may be placed close to the centre of the front drumhead or inside the drum, if the front head has a hole in it or has been removed. Experimentation with placement will be necessary to achieve the desired sound;

* Cymbals – In most cases, a stereo pair of condenser microphones will be placed at least two feet above the kit to capture the sound of the cymbals and the overall sound of the drum kit. Where it's desired to capture the sound of the tom-toms with the overhead mic pair, it's usually best to use large-diaphragm condenser microphones. (The AKG CS 414 works well here.) If the tom-toms are close-miked, it's usually best to use small-diaphragm condenser mics so that the low mids don't build up to an unusable degree. Suitable small-diaphragm condenser mics include the AKG C1000S, the Audio Technica AT-4041, the Neumann KM-184 and the Oktava MC012;

* Tom-toms – If desired, the individual tom-toms can be close-miked with a large-diaphragm dynamic microphone such as the Sennheisser 421, while small clip-on condenser mics such as the Shure Beta 98 are also used. Take care to place the microphones so that they won't cause phase cancellations or introduce excessive bleed between tracks.

In the 1950s and 1960s, drum kits were often miked with only two microphones, one a couple of feet or so in front of the kit and the other a couple of feet overhead and pointed at the snare drum. Ribbon mics like the RCA BX-77 or Coles 4038 were often used, as well as the newer large-diaphragm condenser mics such as the Neumann U67. While you won't get a stereo spread with this set-up, it is possible to get a very accurate picture of the acoustic sound of the drum kit. This can be a very effective technique for making live recordings of jazz groups.

# glossary

*"This is exactly what we need. If our system self-organises to a state of criticality, we can construct reality from pseudo-objects and simultaneously hide them from view."*
*– Reginald Cahill*

## acoustic(al)

Having to do with sound that can be heard by the ears.

## acoustical absorption

The quality of a surface or substance that allows it to take in a sound wave rather than reflect it or pass it through, or an instance of this.

## ADAT

A trademark of Alesis for its modular digital multitrack recording system, released in early 1993.

## ADSR

Abbreviation for *attack, decay, sustain* and *release*, the various elements of volume changes in the sounding of a keyboard instruments, and also the four segments of a common type of synthesiser envelope. The controls for these four parameters determine the duration (or, in the case of sustain, the height) of the segments of the envelope.

## AIFF

Abbreviation of *audio interchange file format*, a common format for Macintosh audio files. It can be mono or stereo, and at a sampling rate of up to 48kHz. AIFF files are compatible with QuickTime.

## algorithm

A set of procedures designed to accomplish something. In the case of computer software, the procedures may appear to the user as a configuration of software components – for example, an arrangement of operators in a Yamaha DX-series synthesiser – or as an element (such as a reverb algorithm) that performs specific operations on a signal.

## algorithmic composition

A type of composition in which the large outlines of the piece, or the procedures to be used in generating it, are determined by the human composer, while some of the details, such as notes or rhythms, are created by a computer program using algorithmic processes.

## aliasing

Undesired frequencies that are produced when harmonic components within the audio signal being sampled by a digital recording device or generated within a digital sound source lie above the Nyquist frequency. Aliasing differs from some other types of noise in that its pitch changes radically when the pitch of the intended sound changes. On playback, the system will provide a signal at an incorrect frequency, called an alias frequency. Aliasing is a kind of distortion.

## All Notes Off

A MIDI command, recognised by some (but not all) synthesisers and sound modules, that causes any notes that are currently sounding to be shut off. The panic button on a synth or sequencer usually transmits All Notes Off messages on all 16 MIDI channels.

## ambience

The portion of a sound that comes from the surrounding environment, rather than directly from the sound source.

## ambient field

The same as *reverberant field*, ie the area away from the sound source where the reverberation is louder than the direct sound.

## ambient miking

Placing a microphone in the reverberant field in order to take a separate recording of the ambience or to allow the recording engineer to change the mix of direct to reverberant sound in the recording.

## amplitude

The height of a waveform above or below the zero line, or the amount of a signal. Amplitude is measured by determining the amount of fluctuation in air pressure of a sound, the voltage of an electrical signal or, in a digital application, numerical data. When the signal is in the audible range, amplitude is perceived as loudness.

## analogue

Representative, continuous changes that relate to another quantity that has a continuous change. Capable of exhibiting continuous fluctuations. In an analogue audio system, fluctuations in voltage correspond in a one-to-one fashion with (that is, are analogous to) the fluctuations in air pressure at the audio input or output. In an analogue synthesiser, parameters such as oscillator pitch and LFO speed are typically controlled by analogue control voltages, rather than by digital data, and the audio signal is also an analogue voltage.

## analogue-to-digital converter

A device which converts a quantity that has continuous changes (usually of voltage) into numbers that approximate those changes. Alternatively, a device that changes the continuous fluctuations in voltage from an analogue device (such as a microphone) into digital information that can be stored or processed in a sampler, digital signal processor or digital recording device.

## attack

The first part of the sound of a note. In a synthesiser ADSR envelope, the attack segment is the segment during which the envelope rises from its initial value (usually zero) to the attack level (often the maximum level for the envelope) at a rate determined by the attack-time parameter.

## attack

The rate at which a sound begins and increases in volume.

## attenuator

A potentiometer (pot) that is used to lower the amplitude of a signal passing through it. The amplitude can usually be set to any value between full (no attenuation) and zero (infinite attenuation). Pots can be either rotary or linear (sliders), and can be either hardware or virtual sliders on a computer screen.

## automatic gain/volume control

A compressor with a very long release time. Used to keep the volume of audio material constant.

## axis

A line around which a device operates. In a microphone, for example, this would be an imaginary line coming out of the front of the mic in the direction of the diaphragm's motion.

## baffles

Sound-absorbing panels used to prevent sound waves from entering or leaving a certain space.

## balance

1. The relative level of two or more instruments in a mix, or the relative level of audio signals in the channels of a stereo recording. 2. To even out the relative levels of audio signals in the channels of a stereo recording.

## bandwidth

1. The range of frequencies over which a tape recorder, amplifier or other audio device is useful.
2. The range of frequencies affected by an equalisation setting – ie the available "opening"

through which information can pass. In audio, the bandwidth of a device is the portion of the frequency spectrum that it can handle without significant degradation taking place. In digital communications, the bandwidth is the amount of data that can be transmitted over a given period of time.

## bank

1. A collection of sound patches (data concerned with the sequence and operating parameters of the synthesiser generators and modifiers) in computer memory. 2. A number of sound modules grouped together as a unit.

## baud rate

Informally, the number of bits of computer information transmitted each second. MIDI transmissions have a baud rate of 31,250 (31.25 kilobaud), while modems typically have a much lower rate of 2,400, 9,600 or 14,400 baud.

## bar

The same as the American term *measure*, ie the grouping of a number of beats in a music (most often four).

## barrier miking

A method of placing the head of a microphone as close as possible to a reflective surface, thus preventing phase cancellation.

## bass roll-off

An electrical network built into some microphones to reduce the amount of output at bass frequencies when close-miking.

## beat

1. A steady, even pulse in music. 2. The action of two sounds or audio signals mixing together and causing regular rises and falls in volume.

## beats per minute

The number of steady, even pulses in music occurring in one minute and therefore defining the tempo of a song.

## bi-directional pattern

A microphone pick-up pattern that has maximum pick-up directly in front and directly to the rear of the diaphragm and least pick-up at the sides.

## bit

The smallest unit of digital information, representing a single zero or one. Digital audio is encoded in words that are usually eight, twelve or 16 bits long (ie the bit resolution). Each additional bit represents a theoretical improvement of about 6dB in the signal-to-noise ratio.

## board

1. Another, less formal, term for console or desk. 2. A set of controls and their housing which control all signals necessary for recording and mixing. 3. A slang shortening of the term *keyboard instrument*.

## boom

1. A hand-held, telescoping pole used to suspend a microphone above a sound source when recording dialogue in film production. 2. A telescoping support arm attached to a microphone stand which holds the microphone. 3. Loosely, a boom stand.

## BPM

Abbreviation of *beats per minute*.

## brick-wall filter

A low-pass filter at the input of an analogue-to-digital converter. Used to prevent frequencies above the Nyquist frequency from being encoded by the converter.

## bulk dump

Short for *system-exclusive bulk dump*, a method of transmitting data, such as the internal parameters of a MIDI device to another MIDI device.

## bus(s)

A wire carrying signals somewhere. Usually fed from several sources.

## byte

A grouping of eight information bits.

## cancellation

A shortening of the term *phase cancellation*, which occurs when the energy of one waveform significantly decreases the energy of another waveform because of phase relationships at or close to 180°.

## capsule

1. The variable capacitor section of a condenser microphone. 2. In other types of microphone, the part of the microphone that includes the diaphragm and the active element.

## card

1. A plug-in memory device. RAM cards, which require an internal battery, can be used for storing user data, while ROM cards, which have no battery, can only be used for reading the data recorded on them by the manufacturer. 2. A circuit board that plugs into a slot on a computer.

## cardioid pattern

A microphone pick-up pattern which picks up most sound from the front, less from the sides and the least from the back of the diaphragm.

## CD-ROM

Abbreviation of the term *compact disc, read-only memory*, a compact disc used to store digital data, such as large programs, that can be read by a computer. Many programs, libraries of sound samples and graphics are distributed on CD-ROM, because each CD can store hundreds of megabytes of information and yet costs about the same to manufacture as a floppy disk, which only stores about 1MB.

## centre frequency

That frequency of an audio signal that is boosted or attenuated the most by an equaliser with a peak equalisation curve.

## channel

1. In multitrack tape machines, the same as *track* (ie one audio recording made on a portion of the width of a multitrack tape). 2. A single path that an audio signal travels or can travel through a device from an input to an output.

## chord

Two or more musical pitches sung or played together.

## chorus

1. The part of a song that is repeated and has the same music and lyrics each time. The chorus usually gives the point of the song. 2. A musical singing group that has many singers. 3. A delay effect that simulates a vocal chorus by adding several delays with a mild amount of feedback and a medium amount of depth. 4. A similar effect created in some synthesisers by detuning (reducing the pitch slightly) and mixing it with a signal that has regular tuning and a slight delay.

## chorusing

A type of signal processing. In chorusing, a time-delayed or detuned copy of a signal is mixed with the original signal. The mixing process changes the relative strengths and phase relationships of the overtones to create a fatter, more animated sound. The simplest way to achieve chorusing is by detuning one synthesiser oscillator from another to produce a slow beating between them.

## clangorous

Containing partials that aren't part of the natural harmonic series. Clangorous tones often sound like bells.

## clock signal

The signal put out by a circuit that generates the steady, even pulses or codes used for synchronisation.

## close miking

A technique involving placing a microphone close to (ideally within a foot of) a sound source being recorded in order to pick up primarily the direct sound and to avoid picking up leakage or ambience.

## co-ax

Twin-conductor cable consisting of one conductor surrounded by a shield.

## coincident microphones (coincident pair)

An arrangement by which the heads of two microphones are placed as close as possible to each other so that the path length from any sound source to either microphone is, for all practical purposes, the same.

## compander

1. A two-section device used in noise-reduction systems. The first section compresses the audio signal before it is recorded and the second section expands the signal after it's been recorded. 2. In Yamaha digital consoles, a signal processor that applies both compression and expansion to the same signal. Digital companding allows a device to achieve a greater apparent dynamic range with fewer bits per sample word (see *digital word*).

## compressor

A signal-processing device that allows less fluctuation in the level of the signal above a certain adjustable or fixed level.

## condenser

An old term meaning the same thing as *capacitor*, ie an electronic device that is composed of two plates separated by an insulator and can store charge. The term is still in common use when used to refer to a microphone's active element.

## condenser microphone

A microphone that converts changes in sound pressure into changes in capacitance. The capacitance changes are then converted into variations in electrical voltage (ie an audio signal).

## contact microphone

A device that senses vibrations and puts out an audio signal that is proportional to the vibrations.

## controller

1. Any device – for example, a keyboard, wind synth controller or pitch-bend lever – capable of producing a change in some aspect of a sound by altering the action of some other device. 2. Any of the defined MIDI data types used for controlling the ongoing quality of a sustaining tone. (Strictly speaking, MIDI continuous controllers are numbered from 0 to 127.) In many synthesisers, the controller-data category is more loosely defined in order to include pitch-bend and aftertouch data. 3. Any device generating a control voltage or signal fed to another device's control input.

## critical distance

The point a distance away from the sound source at which the direct sound and the reverberant sound are equal in volume.

## crossfade looping

A sample-editing feature found in many samplers and most sample-editing software in which some portion of the data at the beginning of a loop is mixed with some portion of the data at the end of the same loop in order to produce a smoother transition between the end and the beginning of the loop.

## crossover (network)

A set of filters that "split" the audio signal into two or more bands, or two or more signals, each of which have only some of the frequencies present.

## crossover frequency

1. The frequency that is the outer limit of one of the bands of a crossover. 2. In the Lexicon 480L delay/reverberation effects unit, the frequency at which the bass-frequency reverb time is in effect rather than the mid-frequency reverb time.

## cut-off frequency (turnover frequency)

1. The highest or lowest frequency in the pass band of a filter. 2. The highest or lowest frequency passed by an audio device. The cut-off frequency is usually considered to be the first frequency to be 3dB lower than a reference frequency in the middle of the bandwidth of the device.

## cut-off rate/slope

The number of decibels that a filter reduces the signal for each octave past the filter's cut-off frequency (ie outside the pass band).

## cycles per second

A unit used in the measure of frequency, equivalent to Hertz. Cycles per second is an outdated term that was replaced by Hertz in 1948.

## daisy chain

1. A hook-up of several devices where the audio signal has to pass through one device to reach the second device and through the second device to reach the third device. 2. In MIDI, a hook-up of MIDI devices where the MIDI signal has to pass though each device in order to reach the next device.

## DAT

An abbreviation of *digital audio tape* and a standard format for recording digital audio on small, specially designed cassette tapes.

## DAW

Abbreviation of *digital audio workstation*, a dedicated device that is both a recorder and mixer of digital audio.

## dB

Abbreviation of the term *decibel*, a unit used to compare signal strengths.

## DBX

A brand of noise reduction systems, dynamic processing equipment and other audio gear.

## decay

1. The rate of reduction of an audio signal generated in synthesisers from the peak level to the sustain level. (See also *ADSR*.) 2. The fade-out of the reverberation of a sound.

## decibel

A unit of measurement used to indicate audio power level. Technically, a decibel is a logarithmic ratio of two numbers, which means that there is no such thing as a decibel measurement of a single signal. In order to measure a signal in decibels, you need to know what level it's referenced to. Commonly used reference levels are indicated by such symbols as dBm, dBV and dBu.

## de-esser

1. The control circuit of an audio compressor or limiter that is made more sensitive to the sounds made by a person pronouncing the letter S. 2. Any device that will reduce the high-frequency energy present when the letter S is pronounced loudly.

## definition

1. The quality of a sound that allows it to be distinguished from other sounds. 2. In Lexicon reverb units, a parameter that sets a decrease in reverberation density in the later part of the decay.

## delay effects

Any signal processing that uses delay as its basis for processing, such as echo, reverb delay and special effects, such as flanging and chorusing.

## detune

1. A control that allows one oscillator to sound a slightly different pitch than another. 2. To change the pitch of one oscillator relative to another in order to produce a fuller sound.

## DI

Abbreviation of *direct injection* or *direct input*.

## diaphragm

The part of the microphone which moves in response to fluctuations in the sound-pressure wave.

## digital controls

1. Controls that have changing number displays when the control is changed. 2. Controls that change the digital control signal information bits to change the value of some functions.

## digital delay

A delay line or delay effects unit that converts audio signal into digital audio signal, delays it and then converts it back to analogue audio signal before sending it out of the unit.

## digital recording

The process of converting audio signals into numbers representing the waveform and then storing these numbers.

## digital signal processing (DSP)

Any signal processing done after an analogue audio signal has been converted into digital audio.

## digital-to-analogue converter (DAC)

A device that changes the sample words put out by a digital audio device into analogue fluctuations in voltage that can be sent to a mixer or amplifier. All digital synthesisers, samplers and effects devices have DACs (pronounced to rhyme with fax) at their outputs to create audio signals.

## direct box

An electronic device utilising a transformer or amplifier to change the electrical output of an electric instrument (for example, an electric guitar) to the impedance and level usually obtained from a microphone.

## direct injection

The same as *direct pick-up*.

## direct input

The same as *direct pick-up*, feeding the signal from an electrical output of an electric instrument to a recording console or tape recorder without using a microphone but instead by changing the electrical output of the instrument to the same impedance and level as a microphone.

## direct pick-up

Feeding the signal from an electrical instrument to the recording console or tape recorder without using a microphone.

## direct sound

The sound that reaches a microphone or listener without hitting or bouncing off any obstacles.

## distant miking

The technique of placing a mic far from a sound source so that reflected sound is picked up with the direct sound.

## distortion

1. The audio garble that can be heard when an audio waveform has been altered, usually by the overloading of an audio device like an amplifier. 2. The similar garbled sound that can be heard when the sound-pressure level is too loud for the waveform to be accurately reproduced by the human hearing mechanism.

## Dolby

The name and trademark of a manufacturer of noise-reduction systems and other audio systems. These systems improve the performance and fidelity of devices that record, play back and transmit audio material.

## Doppler effect

A change in frequency of a delayed signal caused by changes in the delay time while the cycle is being formed.

## drum machine

A sample playback unit or sound module with drum sounds that can be sequenced by an internal sequencer to play drum patterns.

## drum pattern

A sequence of drum sounds played by a drummer or sequenced into a drum machine, especially a short pattern used in part of a song.

## dry signal

A signal consisting entirely of the original, unprocessed sound. The output of an effects device is 100% dry when only the input signal is being heard, ie with none of the effects created by the processor itself, with no reverberation or ambience. The term is more loosely used to describe an audio signal free of signal processing.

## DSP

Abbreviation of *digital signal processing*, ie any signal processing performed after an analogue audio signal has been convened into digital audio. Broadly speaking, all changes in sound that are produced within a digital audio device – other than those caused by the simple cutting and pasting of sections of a waveform – are created via DSP. A digital reverb is a typical DSP device.

## dynamic microphone

1. A microphone in which the diaphragm moves a coil suspended in a magnetic field in order to generate an output voltage proportional to the sound-pressure level. 2. Occasionally used to mean any microphone that has a generating element which cuts magnetic lines of force in order to produce an output, such as a dynamic microphone (definition 1) or a ribbon microphone.

## dynamic (signal) processing

An automatic change in level or gain effected to change the ratio in level of the loudest audio to the softest audio.

## dynamic range

1. The level difference (in decibels) between the loudest peak and the softest level of a recording, etc. 2. The level difference between the level of clipping and the noise level in an audio device or channel.

## dynamics

1. The amount of fluctuation in level of an audio signal. 2. In music, the playing of instruments loudly or softly.

## dynamic voice allocation

A system found on many multitimbral synthesisers and samplers that allows voice channels to be reassigned automatically to play different notes (often with different sounds) whenever required by the musical input from the keyboard or MIDI.

## early reflections

1. The first echoes in a room, caused by the sound from the sound source reflecting off one surface before reaching the listener. 2. A reverb algorithm whose output consists of a number of closely spaced, discrete echoes, designed to mimic the bouncing of sound off nearby walls in an acoustic space.

## echo

1. One distinct repeat of a sound caused by the sound reflecting off a surface. 2. Loosely used to mean reverberation (ie the continuing of a sound after the source stops emitting it, caused by many discrete echoes closely spaced in time).

## echo return

An input of the console which brings back the echo (reverberation) signal from the echo chamber or other echo effects device.

## editing

1. Changing the sequence of a recording by cutting the recording tape and putting the pieces together in the new sequence with splicing tape. 2. Punching in and then punching out on one or more tracks of a multitrack tape recorder to replace previously recorded performances. 3. Changing the sequence of a digital recording's playback by using a computer program.

## electret condenser

A condenser microphone that has a permanently polarised (charged) variable capacitor as its sound-pressure-level sensor.

## envelope

1. Description of the way in which a sound or audio signal varies in intensity over time. 2. How a control voltage changes in level over time, controlling a parameter of something other than gain or audio level. The shape of a synthesiser's envelope is controlled by a set of rate (or time)

and level parameters. The envelope is a control signal that can be applied to various aspects of a synth sound, such as pitch, filter cut-off frequency and overall amplitude. Usually, each note has its own envelope(s).

## envelope generator

A device that generates an envelope. Also known as a *contour generator* or *transient generator*, because the envelope is a contour (shape) that is used to create some of the transient (changing) characteristics of the sound. (See *ADSR*.)

## envelope tracking

Also called *keyboard tracking*, *key follow* or *keyboard rate scaling*. A function that changes the length of one or more envelope segments, depending on which key on the keyboard is being pressed. Envelope tracking is most often used to give the higher notes shorter envelopes and the lower notes longer envelopes, mimicking the response characteristics of percussion-activated acoustic instruments, such as guitar and marimba.

## equalisation

Any time that the amplitudes of audio signals at specific set of frequencies are increased or decreased more than the signals at other audio frequencies.

## expansion

The opposite of compression. For example, an expander may allow the signal to increase 2dB every time the signal input increases by 1dB.

## expansion ratio

The number of decibels that the output signal will drop for every decibel that the input signal falls below the threshold.

## fade

1. A gradual reduction of the level of an audio signal. 2. A gradual change of level from one preset level to another.

## fader

A device to control the gain of a channel on a console, thereby determining the level of a signal in that channel.

## far field

The area covering the distance from three feet away from the sound source up to the critical distance.

## fat

Having more than a normal amount of signal strength at low frequencies or having more sound than normal by the use of compression or delay.

## feed

To send an audio or control signal to a device.

## feedback

1. The delayed signal sent back to the input of a delay line, used in repeat-echo effects. 2. The pick-up of the signal out of a channel by its input or the howling sound that this produces. 3. In an amplifier, the phase-reversed output signal sent back to its input, reducing gain but also causing distortion and noise.

## figure-of-eight pattern

Another name for a bi-directional pattern, a microphone design that picks up best from the front and rear of the diaphragm and not at all from the side of the diaphragm.

## FireWire

The popular name for a high-speed digital standard connection for linking up peripherals such as digital video cameras, audio components and computer devices. FireWire was originally developed by Apple Computers as a replacement for the SCSI bus. IEEE 1394 is formal name for the standard. Vendors must obtain a licence from Apple in order to use the term FireWire.

## flange

An effect caused by combining an approximately even mix of a modulated (varying) short delay with the direct signal.

## flat

1. Lower in musical pitch. 2. A slang term used to describe the sensitivity to frequency of a microphone, amplifier, etc, as being even at all frequencies (usually within 2dB).

## Fletcher Munson effect

A hearing limitation shown by Fletcher Munson equal-loudness contours that, as music is lowered in volume, it's much more difficult to hear bass frequencies and somewhat harder to hear very high frequencies.

## foldback

A European term for the signal sent to the stage monitors in a live performance.

## formant

An element in the sound of a voice or instrument that doesn't change frequency as different pitches are sounded. Can also be described as a resonant peak in a frequency spectrum. The variable formants produced by the human vocal tract are what give vowels their characteristic sound.

## FreeMIDI

A Macintosh operating system extension developed by Mark Of The Unicorn that enables different programs to share MIDI data. For example, a sequencer could communicate with a librarian program to display synthesiser patch names – rather than just numbers – in the sequencer's editing windows.

## frequency

The number of cycles of a waveform occurring in the space of a second.

## frequency range

The range of frequencies over which an electronic device is useful or over which a sound source puts out substantial energy.

## frequency response

The measure of sensitivity shown by an electronic device (microphone, amplifier, speaker, etc) to various frequencies. Often communicated via a graph.

## FSK (frequency shift key)

A simple clock signal that can be used to run a sequencer in time with an audio tape.

## full step

A change in pitch that occurs when one moves up or down two piano keys.

## fundamental

The tuned frequency and, almost always, the lowest frequency that is present in the sounding of a pitch by a musical instrument.

## gain

An increase in the strength of an audio signal, often expressed in decibels.

## gain reduction

A reduction in gain during high-level passages, effected by a limiter or compressor.

## gate

A dynamics-processing device that turns a channel off or down when a signal drops below a certain level.

## General MIDI (GM)

A set of requirements adopted by manufacturers of MIDI devices and used to ensure the consistent playback performance on all instruments bearing the GM logo. Some of the requirements include 24-voice polyphony and a standardised group and location of sounds. For example, patch 17 will always be a drawbar organ sound on all General MIDI instruments.

## glide

A function where the pitch slides smoothly from one note to the next instead of jumping over the intervening pitches. Also called *portamento*.

## golden section

A ratio of exact height to width to length of a room in order to achieve good acoustics. First recommended by the ancient Greeks. The ratio is approximately the width of a room x 1.6 times its height and its length x 2.6 times its height.

## graphic equaliser

A device equipped with several slides to control the gain of an audio signal present within one of several evenly spaced frequency bands, spaced according to octaves.

## guitar controller

An electric guitar or device played like an electric guitar that produces MIDI signals which can be used to control synthesisers and sound modules.

## guitar processor

A unit that adds effects to a direct guitar signal, including a simulated instrument amplifier sound and, often, delay and reverb effects.

## Haas effect

Simply stated, a factor in human hearing where delay has a much bigger effect on the human perception of direction than level does.

## half step

A difference in pitch present between adjacent keys on a piano.

## harmonic

A frequency that is a whole-number multiple of the fundamental frequency. For example, if the fundamental frequency of a sound is 440Hz, the first two harmonics are 880Hz and 1,320Hz (1.32kHz). Harmonics are whole-number multiples of the frequency that determines the timbre recognition of an instrument's sound.

## harmonic distortion

The presence of harmonics in the output signal of a device that weren't present in the input signal.

## headroom

1. The level difference (in decibels) between normal operating level and clipping level in an amplifier or audio device. 2. A similar level difference between normal tape-operating level and the level at which the distortion would be 3%.

## hearing limitation

An inability of the human ear to hear important characteristics of sound under certain conditions. Characteristics that can be affected include pitch, level, clarity, presence and direction.

## Hertz

The basic unit of frequency, equivalent to *cycles per second*, usually abbreviated to Hz.

## high frequencies

Audio frequencies at 6,000Hz and above.

## high impedance

Impedance of 5,000 ohms or more.

## high-impedance mic

A microphone designed to be fed into an amplifier with an input impedance greater than 20,000 ohms.

## high-pass filter

A device that rejects signals below a certain frequency (known as the *cut-off frequency*) and passes signals with frequencies that are higher than this.

## highs

Abbreviation of *high frequencies* (ie audio frequencies of 6,000Hz and higher).

## horn

A speaker or speaker enclosure where sound-pressure waves are fed through a narrow opening (by a speaker cone or driver) and where the narrow opening flares out into a larger opening.

## hum

Produced when 60Hz power-line current is accidentally induced or fed into electronic equipment.

## hypercardioid pattern

A microphone pick-up sensitivity pattern demonstrating that the least-sensitive pick-up point is more than 90° but less than 150° off axis (usually 120°).

## Hz

Abbreviation of *Hertz*, the unit of frequency.

## ID

An index signal (ie digital data that provides a machine with information concerning the starting points and selection numbers of sections, etc) on a DAT or CD.

## IM distortion

Abbreviation of *intermodulation distortion*, which is caused by one signal beating with another signal and producing frequencies that are both the sum and the difference of the original frequencies present.

## impedance

The opposition to alternating current (AC).

## impedance matching

Having or converting the output impedance of a device so that it matches the impedance of the input that it will feed.

## infinite baffle

A baffle so large that the sounds coming from one side don't reach the other.

## infinite repeat

A function on some delay lines that cause enough feedback for the repeat echo to last forever but not enough to cause a howling sound.

## in port

A jack on a MIDI device or computer that will accept an incoming data signal.

## input

1. The jack or physical location of the point at which a device receives a signal. 2. A signal being received by a device. 3. To feed a signal from one device to another.

## input impedance

The opposition to current flow exerted by the first circuits of a device.

## input overload

Sending too high a signal level into a device, so that the first amplifier of the device overloads.

## insert

1. A punch in performed on all of the tracks being recorded in a recording session. 2. On Solid State Logic consoles, to place an outboard piece of gear in a channel by patching and activating a switch.

## instrument amplifier

A device that has a power amplifier and speaker in a case (or in separate cases) to reproduce the signal put out by an electric instrument (such as an electric guitar) and to allow the instrument to be heard.

## insulator

A substance that, for all practical purposes, won't conduct electricity, such as glass, air or plastic.

## intermodulation distortion

Form of distortion caused by one signal beating with another signal and producing frequencies that are both the sum and the difference of the original frequencies.

## inverse square law

This expresses the fact that, in an unobstructed area (such as an open field), the sound-pressure level will drop to half pressure (-6dB) every time the distance to a sound source is doubled.

## I/O

Abbreviation of *input/output,* referring to: 1. an in-line console module that contains controls for the input section, output section and monitor section; 2. a module in electronic gear containing input and output amplifiers for the device; and 3. a digital port (connector) able to both receive digital data and output digital data.

## isolation

A containing of the sound wave in a certain area so that it won't leak into other areas and/or unintended mics.

## isolation booth/room

A room that prevents loud sounds produced by other instruments from leaking in.

## jack

A connector mounted on the casing of a device or on a panel.

## jam sync

A generation of new SMPTE according to the input SMPTE signal.

## k

Abbreviation of *kilo*, a prefix for 1,000.

## K

Abbreviation of *kick drum*.

## key

The control of a dynamics-processing device via an external audio signal.

## keyboard

1. Any musical instrument controlled by pressing a key. 2. The part of the computer that has the keys.

## keyboard controller

A device that has the standard music keys of piano but transmits MIDI signals.

## keyboard scaling

A function by which the sound can be altered smoothly across the range of a keyboard by using key numbers as a modulation source. Level scaling changes the loudness of the sound, while filter scaling changes its brightness.

## key note number

A number assigned to each key of a synthesiser or controller keyboard that is transmitted in the MIDI signal.

## kHz

Abbreviation of *kiloHertz* (1,000 Hertz).

## kilo

A prefix meaning 1,000.

## kilobyte (KB)

Linguistically, 1,000 bytes. In practice, a kilobyte generally contains 1,024 bytes.

## layering

The recording or playing of a musical part with several similar sound patches playing simultaneously.

## lead

The musical instrument or vocal that plays or sings the melody of a tune.

## lead sheet

A written chart showing the melody, lyrics and chords of a tune, complete with full musical notation.

## leakage

Sounds from other instruments and sources that weren't intended to be picked up by a microphone.

## LED (light-emitting diode)

A light that allows current to flow in one direction only and emits light whenever a voltage of a certain level or beyond is applied to it.

## level

The amount of signal strength (ie the amplitude, especially the average amplitude).

# LFO

Abbreviation of *low-frequency oscillator*.

# lift

To boost the gain of an audio signal at a particular band of frequencies with an equaliser.

# limiter

A device that reduces gain when the input voltage exceeds a certain level.

# linear

The condition of obtaining a change at the output of the device which is proportional to the change occurring at the input.

# line input

An input designed to take a line-level signal.

# line level

An amplified signal level put out by an amplifier and used as the normal level that runs through the interconnecting cables in a control room.

# line out(put)

Any output that sends out a line-level signal, such as the output of a console that feeds a recorder.

# link

A term used with reference to compressors and dynamic-processing units meaning to combine the control input signals of two channels of a compressor (or dynamic-processing unit) so that both channels always have the same gain and are triggered to change gain by the signal of either channel.

# live

1. Refers to the sound produced by instruments during a performance to an audience. 2. Having a large portion of reverberant or reflected sound.

# live recording

1. The practice of recording where all musicians are playing at once and no overdubbing takes place. 2. Recorded material with a lot of natural reverberation.

# load

1. The opposition to an audio output signal of a device by the input of the device being fed. 2. A resistor that would have the lowest impedance that a device was designed to feed into used during the testing of a device. 3. To copy the digital data on a storage medium into the RAM of a computer. 4. To put tape onto a tape machine and activate the computer-controlled constant-tension system.

## load impedance

The opposition to the flow of output current caused by the input that it feeds.

## Local (mode) On/Off

A switch or function in a synthesiser that connects (On) or disconnects (Off) the keyboard control of the synthesiser's sound module.

## long delay

Delay times greater than 60ms.

## loop

1. The same as *anti-node*, ie the points of maximum displacement of motion in a vibrating, stretched string. 2. A piece of material that plays over and over. In a sequencer, a loop repeats a musical phrase. In a sampler, loops are used to allow samples of finite length to be sustained indefinitely.

## loud

Causing equal volume changes at all frequency ranges, including frequency response changes at lower operating levels in order to compensate for the Fletcher Munson effect.

## loudness

A measure of how loud something sounds to the ear.

## low end

A slang term for bass-frequency signals (ie those below 250Hz).

## lower toms

Large toms that sit on the floor, mounted on metal feet, with heads up to approximately 20 inches in diameter.

## low frequencies

1. Audio or audible frequencies below 1kHz. 2. The range of bass frequencies below approximately 250Hz.

## low-frequency oscillator

An oscillator that puts out an alternating-current signal between .1Hz and 10Hz, used for a control signal. Especially devoted to applications below the audible frequency range, and typically used as a control source for modulating a sound to create vibrato, tremolo, trills and so on.

## low impedance

Impedance of 500 ohms or less.

## low-pass filter

A device that rejects signals above a certain frequency and passes those that are lower in frequency.

## mapper

A device that translates MIDI data from one form to another in real time.

## margin

The amount of decibels between the highest peak level of a program and the point at which overload occurs.

## masking

The characteristic of hearing by which loud sounds prevent the ear from hearing softer sounds of similar frequency.

## master

1. A control to set the level going out of a console, especially the stereo output to a two-track machine at mixdown. 2. A term with the same meaning as *sub-master*, ie a control that adjusts the level of a signal mixed together and sent out to one track of a multitrack recorder. 3. A term with the same meaning as *VCA master*, ie one slider that controls the control voltage sent to several VCA faders. 4. A machine used as a speed reference when synchronising two or more machines to run together. If the master tape transport changes speed, the other machines synced to it will change speed with it. 5. The original recording, used for making copies. 6. To make an original recording which will be used to make commercial copies, especially making a master lacquer (for record manufacturing) or a master CD.

## master fader

1. The fader which controls the main output(s) of a console during mixdown. 2. In some consoles, faders which control outputs to a multitrack tape recorder during recording. 3. Occasionally used to mean a VCA master (ie one slide that controls the control voltage sent to several VCA faders).

## MCI

Abbreviation of *media control interface*, a multimedia specification designed to provide control of onscreen movies and peripherals, such as CD-ROM drives.

## MDM

Abbreviation of the term *modular digital multitrack*, ie a multitrack digital recorder with (usually) eight tracks that can be run in synchronisation with other machines (of the same type) in order to attain more tracks. An example of this type of machine is the ADAT (Alesis' modular digital multitrack recording system).

## measure

The grouping of a number of beats in music.

## medium delay

Delay times of 20-60ms.

## meg(a)

1. A prefix for 1,000,000. 2. A slang abbreviation of megaHertz (1,000,000Hz) or megabytes (1,024,000 bytes).

## merger

A MIDI accessory that allows two incoming MIDI signals to be combined into one MIDI output.

## meter

A device which measures or compares electrical signals, often used to read the voltage levels of audio signals.

## mic

Abbreviation of *microphone*.

## mic gain control

A level control on a mic pre-amp that sets gain and is used to prevent the overload of that pre-amp.

## mic input

The input of a console or other device into which a microphone can be plugged.

## mic level

The very low audio voltage level that comes out of a studio microphone.

## mic/line switch

The selector switch on the input of a console channel that chooses which input jack feeds the console.

## mic pad

A device that reduces the level of a signal, placed just before a microphone pre-amplifier to prevent overloading of the pre-amplifier.

## mic pre-amp

An amplifier that boosts the low-level audio signal produced by a microphone up to line level.

## microphone

A transducer that converts sound-pressure waves into electrical signals.

## MIDI

Abbreviation of *musical instrument digital interface*, a digital signal system (ie a system of number signals) used to send and receive performance information to and from musical instruments.

## MIDI channel

A grouping of data concerning the performance of one synthesiser or device separate from the data concerning other synthesisers or devices. MIDI commands contain all of the information that a sound board needs to reproduce the desired sound.

## MIDI clock

Time data in a MIDI signal that advances one step each $1/24$ of a beat and can be used to sync two sequencers together.

## MIDI clock with song pointer

A MIDI clock that which also has a number signal for each measure or bar to indicate the number of measures or bars into the tune.

## MIDI controller

A device that can be played by a musician that transmits MIDI signals to control synthesisers or sound modules.

## MIDI echo

A function in a synthesiser that causes the output of a sequencer to send a MIDI signal out of the out port matching the MIDI signal coming in for the track being recorded.

## MIDI interface

A device that converts a MIDI signal into the digital format used by a computer so that the computer can store and use the MIDI signal.

## MIDI mode

Any of the ways in which devices respond to incoming MIDI data. While four modes – Omni Off/Poly, Omni On/Poly, Omni Off/Mono and Omni On/Mono – are defined by the MIDI specification, Omni On/Mono is never used. There are also at least two other useful modes that have been developed: Multi mode, for multitimbral instruments, and Multi-Mono mode, for guitar synthesisers.

## MIDI patch bay

A device that has several MIDI inputs and outputs and allows any input to be routed to any output.

## MIDI sample dump

The copying of a digitally recorded sample without converting it to analogue between different storage units or sound modules through a MIDI transmission.

## MIDI sequencer

A computer that can record and play back MIDI data in such a way as to control the performance of MIDI-controlled musical instruments or devices in a series of timed steps.

## MIDI Thru

There are two types of MIDI Thru. One, a simple hardware connection, is found on the back panels of many synthesisers. This Thru jack simply duplicates whatever data is arriving at the MIDI In jack. Sequencers have a second type, called Software Thru, where data arriving at the In jack is merged with data being played by the sequencer, and both sets of data appear in a single stream at the Out (rather than the Thru) jack. Software Thru is useful because it allows you to hook a master keyboard to the sequencer's MIDI In and a tone module to its Out. You can then play the keyboard and hear the tone module, and the sequencer can also send its messages directly to the tone module.

## MIDI time code

All of the information contained in SMPTE time code that has been converted into part of the MIDI signal.

## mid-range frequencies

Audio frequencies from around 250Hz through to 6,000Hz.

## milli

A prefix meaning a thousandth – for example, milliwatt.

## MiniDisc

A small, recordable compact disc that can be used by general consumers, introduced by Sony at the end of 1992.

## mix

1. To blend audio signals together into a composite signal. 2. The signal made by blending individual signals together. 3. A control or function on a delay/reverberation device that controls the amount of direct signal that is mixed into the processed signal.

## mix down

To combine the signals from the tracks of a multitrack tape onto a master tape. Reverberation and other effects may be also added.

## mixer

1. A console or other device that blends audio signals into composite signals and has a small number of outputs. 2. A section on a console that performs this function. 3. In Europe, a fader. 4. An engineer or technician who mixes, especially a live-sound mix during a live performance.

## mixing console/desk

A device that can combine several signals into one or more composite signals in any proportion.

## mixing solo

A button that turns off all other channels, thus allowing the signal to be heard in the stereo perspective and the level used at mixdown, and with reverberation also applied.

## modulation

The control of one signal by another AC signal.

## modulation noise

Noise that is present only when the audio signal is present.

## monitor

1. To listen, in the context of audio. 2. To indicate with a meter or light the conditions in a circuit, especially level and overload. 3. A device designed to listen or observe.

## monitor mixer

1. A console or other device that blends audio signals into composite signals and has a small number of outputs. 2. The section of a console that is used to complete a rough mix so that an engineer can hear what's being recorded without effecting the levels being fed to the multitrack recorder. 3. The audio technician who mixes the signals sent to the stage monitor speakers.

## monitor pot

A rotary control used to set the level of the track signal in the monitor (ie the signal to or the signal back from one track of a multitrack tape recorder).

## monitor (mixer) section

The section of a console that is used to complete a rough mix so that an engineer can hear what's being recorded without effecting the levels being fed to the multitrack recorder.

## monitor selector

1. On consoles, a switch that allows you to hear various things over the control-room monitor speakers, such as the main console outputs (for mixing purposes), the monitor mixer section (for recording and overdubbing), the disc player, tape machines and other devices. 2. On tape machines, a switch that, in one position, sends the signal from the tape to the meters and the output of the machine's electronics or, in a second position, sends the input signal being fed to the machine to the meters and the outputs of the electronic devices.

## mono

Abbreviation of *monophonic*.

## monophonic

1. More formal term for mono and meaning that there is only one sound source, or that the signal was derived from one sound source. 2. In synthesisers, a term meaning that only one pitch may be sounded at a time.

## moving-coil microphone

The same as *dynamic microphone*, ie a mic in which the diaphragm moves a coil suspended in a magnetic field in order to generate an output voltage proportional to the sound-pressure level.

## moving-fader automation

In consoles, a feature that enables an engineer to program changes in fader levels so that these changes happen automatically upon playback of a multitrack recording, because the fader positions actually change. The faders are driven by tiny motors.

## ms

Abbreviation of *milliseconds* (thousandths of a second). Not usually capitalised.

## MS miking

A method of placing stereo microphones so that one cardioid microphone points directly at the middle of the area to be miked and a bi-directional microphone is as close as possible to the first microphone, with its rejection pointing the same way as the axis of the first microphone.

## MTC

Abbreviation of *MIDI time code*, ie all of the information of SMPTE time code that has been converted into part of the MIDI signal.

## multi(jack)

Abbreviation of the term *multiple jack(s)*. 1. A jack at the output of a device which is not normalised so that plugging into the jack socket will allow the output to be sent to a different input and the output will also feed the place that it normally it feeds. 2. A set of jacks (or one of a set of jacks) with each terminal wired to a corresponding terminal of another or other jacks.

## Multi mode

A MIDI reception mode in which a multitimbral module responds to MIDI input on two or more channels and maintains musical independence between the channels, typically playing a different patch on each channel.

## multisample

The distribution of several related samples at different pitches across a keyboard. Multisampling can provide greater realism in sample playback (wavetable) synthesis, since the individual samples don't have to be transposed over a great distance.

## multitimbral

A synthesiser that is able to send out several signals of different sound patches (and often playing different parts) or has several sound modules is said to be a multitimbral instrument.

## Mute switch

A switch that turns off a channel, takes out a track signal from the monitors or turns off the entire monitor signal.

## nano

A prefix meaning one billionth.

## nanowebers per metre

The standard unit in measuring magnetic energy.

## narrow-band noise

Noise (random energy) produced over a limited range of frequencies.

## near field

The area up to one foot away from the sound source.

## negative feedback

Used to describe an out-of-phase portion of an output signal that is fed into the input of an amplifier.

## noise

1. Random energy that contains energy at all audio frequencies. 2. Any unintentional or objectionable signal added to an audio signal.

## noise filter

A filter that passes only signals with the intended audio frequencies, thus eliminating noise signals at other frequencies.

## noise floor

The level of noise below the signal, measured in decibels.

## noise gate

A gate used to turn off an audio channel when noise but no signal is present.

## noise reduction

Any device designed to remove noise in a device or system.

## non-directional

Used with microphones to mean the same thing as *omni-directional* (ie picking up sound from all directions).

## non-linear

The condition of obtaining a change at the output of the device that is not proportional to the change occurring at the input, therefore causing distortion.

## normalise

1. To provide normalised switches on a jack. 2. To reset a synthesiser, sound module or sample-playback unit to the original factory settings. 3. To adjust the level of a selection so that the highest peak is at the maximum recording level of the medium. 4. To boost the level of a waveform to its maximum amount without experiencing clipping (distortion), thus maximising resolution and minimising certain types of noise.

## normalising jacks/normals

Switches on patch jacks that connect certain jack sockets together until a patch cord is inserted.

## notch

A narrow band of audio frequencies.

## nW/m

Abbreviation of *nanowebers per meter*, the standard unit in measuring the amount of magnetic energy.

## nybble

Half a byte (ie four information bits).

## Nyquist frequency

The highest frequency that can be recorded and reproduced properly by a particular sampling rate. Theoretically, the Nyquist frequency is half of the sampling rate. For example, when a digital recording uses a sampling rate of 44.1kHz, the Nyquist frequency is 22.05kHz. If a signal being sampled contains frequency components that are above the Nyquist frequency, aliasing will be introduced in the digital representation of the signal, unless those frequencies are filtered out prior to digital encoding.

## Nyquist rate

The lowest sampling rate that can be used to record and reproduce a given audio frequency.

## octave

A difference of pitch where one tone has a frequency that is double or half that of another tone.

## off axis

1. Away from the front or axis of the mic. Measured in degrees. 2. 180° from the front.

## offset (time)

1. SMPTE time that triggers a MIDI sequencer. 2. The amount of position difference needed to get two reels to play music in time.

## omni

A prefix meaning "all".

## omni-directional

1. Used to describe microphones that pick up evenly from all directions. 2. Used to describe speakers that send out evenly in all directions.

## Omni mode

When Omni mode is activated in a MIDI device, all MIDI messages are recognising and acted on, no matter what their channel.

## OMS

Abbreviation of *open music system* (formerly *Opcode MIDI system*), a real-time MIDI operating system for Macintosh applications. OMS allows communication between different MIDI programs and hardware so that, for example, a sequencer could interface with a librarian program to display synthesiser patch names in the sequencer's editing windows, rather than just numbers.

## on axis

The position directly in front of the diaphragm of a mic, in line with its direction of movement.

## oscillator

1. A device that puts out test tones at various frequencies in order to align a tape machine or for other testing purposes. 2. In a digital synth, an oscillator more typically plays back a complex waveform by reading the numbers in a wave table.

## out of phase

1. Being similar to another signal in amplitude, frequency and wave shape but being offset in time by part of a cycle. 2. Having the opposite polarity (ie being 180° out of phase).

## out port

A jack that sends out digital data from a computer or digital device.

## output

1. The jack or physical location at which a device sends out a signal. 2. The signal put out by a device.

## output impedance

The opposition to current flow by the output circuits of an amplifier or some other device.

## output level

The signal level at the output of a device.

## output selector

The switch on a tape machine which, when activated, allows the VU meter and audio output of the circuits of a tape machine to monitor and send out either the input signal to the tape machine, the playback of what was being recorded or the level of bias currently being fed to the record head.

## overdub

To record additional parts alongside or merged with previous tracks. Overdubbing enables "one-man band" productions, as multiple synchronised performances are recorded sequentially.

## Over-Easy

DBX's trademark term for the gradual change of compression ratio around the threshold, thus making it difficult to detect when compression is taking place.

## overload

To put out too much signal level, thereby causing distortion.

## overload indicator

An LED on a console channel that lights up when the input or some other part of the circuit is receiving an overload.

## oversampling

A process where the analogue audio (or the digital audio, for playback) is sampled many times more than the minimum sampling rate.

## overtones

The harmonics of an instrument's sound minus the fundamental frequency.

## pad

1. An attenuator usually used to prevent the overloading of the amplifier that follows it. 2. A device with a surface that can be hit by a drum stick, whereby hitting the pad produces an output signal pulse (or MIDI command) which causes a drum machine or synthesiser to produce a drum sound.

## pan pot

An electrical device that distributes one audio signal to two or more channels or speakers.

## parallel

1. A circuit interconnection where the source feeds several branched circuit components and where interrupting the current flow in one component doesn't stop current flow in another. 2. A method of sending data where each digit of a digital word is sent at the same time over separate connections.

## parallel jacks

Several jacks that are wired together so that each connection is wired to the corresponding connection of other jacks.

## parallel port

A jack that sends out or receives digital data where several bits are being sent or received at the same time through different pins.

## parameter

A user-adjustable quantity that governs an aspect of a device's performance. Normally, the settings of all of the parameters that make up a synthesiser patch can be changed by the user and stored in memory, but the parameters themselves are defined by the operating system and cannot be altered.

## parametric EQ

An equaliser in which all of the parameters of equalisation can be adjusted to any amount, including centre frequency, the amount of boost or cut in gain and bandwidth.

## partial

1. In acoustic instruments, a term with the same meaning as *overtone*. 2. In synthesisers, the term means literally "part of a sound patch", ie circuitry in the synthesiser that generates and/or modifies elements of a sound in order to provide a particular tone with timbre. 3. The sound element generated by definition 2.

## pass band

The frequency range of signals that will be passed by a filter, rather than reduced by it.

## patch

To connect together – as in the inputs and outputs of various modules – generally with patch cords. Also applied to the configuration of hook-ups and settings that results from the process of patching and, by extension, the sound that such a configuration creates. Often used to denote a single tone colour or the contents of a memory location that contains parameter settings for such a tone colour, even on an instrument that requires no physical patching.

## patch bay

A series of jacks with connections for most of the inputs and outputs of a console, the console sections, tape machines and other pieces of equipment.

## patch editor

A computer program that allows the creation or the changing of sound patch parameters, thereby creating or modifying a specific synthesised sound outside a synthesiser.

## patch librarian

A computer program that allows the storing of sound patches outside a synthesiser.

## patch map

A map with which any incoming MIDI Program Change message can be assigned to call up any of an instrument's patches (sounds).

## patch panel

A series of jacks with connections for most of the inputs and outputs of the console, console sections, tape machines and other pieces of equipment.

## peak

1. The highest point in an audio waveform. 2. Short for *peak detecting* (ie responding to a peak) or *peak indicating* (ie showing a peak). 3. Having a frequency response that would draw something similar to a mountain peak on a frequency response graph.

## peak detecting

Recognising and responding to peak values of a waveform, rather than average values.

## peak indicating meter

A meter that reads the absolute peak level of a waveform.

## peaking filter

An EQ circuit which exhibits a peak response.

## peak level

The same as *peak value*, ie the maximum positive or negative instantaneous value of a waveform.

## peak responding

Recognising and responding to (or indicating) a peak value, rather than the average or effective value.

## peak response

1. The same as *peak*. 2. A raising or lowering of the amplitude of signals at the centre frequency more than signals at any other frequency.

## peak-to-peak value

The difference in amplitude between positive and negative peaks. Equal to twice the peak value for a sine wave.

## peak value

The maximum positive or negative instantaneous value of a waveform.

## percentage quantisation

A method of quantisation by which notes recorded into a sequencer with uneven rhythms aren't shifted all the way to their theoretically perfect timings but are instead shifted part of the way, with the degree of shift being dependent on a user-selected percentage (quantisation strength). (See *quantise*.)

## phase

A measurement (expressed in degrees) of the time difference between two similar waveforms.

## phase addition

Phase addition occurs when the energy of one waveform increases the energy of another waveform because the two waveforms have similar phase relationships.

## phase cancellation

Phase cancellation occurs when the energy of one waveform decreases the energy of another waveform because of phase relationships at or close to 180°.

## phase distortion

A change in a sound because of a phase shift in the signal.

## phase-distortion synthesis

A method of altering a wave shape in order to add harmonics by phase-shifting while a cycle is being formed.

## phase lock

1. A method of keeping tape machines synced together by sensing phase differences in the playback of pilot tunes by the two machines and adjusting their speeds to eliminate the phase difference. 2. In synthesisers, the control of one tone generator so that it begins its waveform in phase with the signal from another tone generator.

## phase reversal

A change in a circuit effected in order to cause a waveform to shift by 180°.

## phase shift

A delay introduced into an audio signal, measured in degrees delayed.

## phasing

An effect sound created by the variable phase-shifting of an audio signal mixed with the direct signal.

## phon

1. A unit of equal loudness for all audio frequencies. 2. The phon is numerically equal to dBSPL (Sound-Pressure Level) at 1,000Hz but varies at other frequencies according to ear sensitivity.

## phone plug (jack)

A plug (or its mating jack) with a diameter of a quarter of an inch and a length of one and a quarter inches used for interconnecting audio devices.

## pick-up

1. A device on an electric guitar (or other instrument) that puts out an audio signal according to the motion of the strings on the instrument. 2. A device that puts out an audio signal according to the vibration of something. This term means the same thing as *contact microphone*.

## pick-up pattern

The shape of the area from which a microphone will evenly pick up sound, giving similar but less detailed information than a polar pattern.

## pink noise

Noise that has equal energy per octave or portion of an octave.

## pitch

1. The ear's perception of frequency (ie music sounding higher or lower). 2. A control on a tape machine which increases or decreases speed slightly, thus changing the pitch and time of the music. 3. The spacing of the grooves on a phonographic record.

## pitch bend

1. In a synthesiser, the pitch-bend control makes the pitch smoothly glide upwards slightly. 2. The wheel controller or MIDI command used to bring this about.

## pitch change

1. A characteristic of human hearing where bass frequencies sound lower in pitch at high levels of sound pressure, often as much as 10% lower. 2. A function of a delay device where the pitch of the output signal is different to that of the input signal.

## pitch ratio

The percentage of pitch change in a delay line's pitch-change program.

## pitch shift

To change the pitch of a sound without changing its duration, as opposed to *pitch transpose*, which changes both. Some people use the two terms interchangeably.

## pitch-to-MIDI converter

A device that converts audio signals into MIDI information.

## pitch-to-voltage converter

A device that converts the frequency changes of audio signals into proportional voltage changes.

## plate

1. A type of reverb device in which a large metal sheet is suspended on spring clips and driven like a speaker cone. 2. An electrode in a tube that receives electrons.

## plate program

A setting in a digital delay/reverb device that simulates the sound of plate reverberation.

## playback level

1. The same as *reproduction level*. 2. A control that determines the output levels of signals played back from recorded tracks.

## plug-in

A software program that acts as an extension to a larger program, adding new features.

## point source

A design in speaker systems where separate speakers are made, reproducing different frequency ranges, so that the sound appears to come from one place.

## polarising voltage

Voltage applied to the plates of the variable capacitor in a condenser microphone capsule.

## polar pattern

1. A graphic display of the audio output levels caused by sound waves arriving at a microphone from different directions. 2. A graphic display of a speaker's dispersion pattern.

## Pole mode

A MIDI mode that allows voices of controlled synth to be assigned polyphonically by incoming key-note numbers. The more poles a filter has, the more abrupt its cut-off slope. Each pole causes a slope of 6dB per octave. Typical configurations are two-pole and four-pole (12dB and 24dB per octave).

## polyphonic

Used to describe a device capable of producing more than one note at a time. All synthesisers place a limit on how many voices of polyphony are available. General-MIDI-compliant synthesisers are required to provide 24 voices of polyphony.

## polyphony

The number of voices (notes) that a device can produce at once.

## poly(phonic) pressure

Also called key pressure. A type of MIDI channel message by which each key senses and transmits pressure data independently.

## pop shield/filter

A device that is placed over a microphone or between the microphone and the singer to prevent loud popping sounds – caused by breath on the microphone – from being picked up.

## port

1. An opening in a speaker case or just behind the diaphragm in a microphone casing. 2. A jack that accepts or sends digital data.

## portamento

1. A pitch change that glides smoothly from one pitch to another. 2. The synthesiser mode or MIDI command that allows or causes this to happen.

## ported-case microphone

A microphone with at least one port (opening behind the diaphragm) in its casing.

## post-echo

The positioning of an echo send control after the main channel fader in the signal path.

## pot

Abbreviation of *potentiometer*, a device that outputs part of the input voltage according to the position of the control's knob.

## power

1. Measurement of the ability of an electrical current to produce light, produce heat or do other work. 2. Similar measurement of another form of energy to perform work. 3. The name of the switch which turns on a device.

## pre-amp

A low-noise amplifier designed to take a low-level signal and bring it up to normal operating line level.

## precedence effect

A factor in human hearing where delay has a much bigger effect on the human perception of the location of the sound source than level does.

## pre-delay

Delay circuits at the input of a reverb device that produce a delay before the reverberation is heard.

## pre-echo

1. A repeating of the sound before the reverberation is heard. Used to simulate reflections found in a stage environment. 2. In tape recording, a low-level leakage of sound coming later, caused by print-through (ie data leaking through onto the other side of the tape). 3. In disc recording, a similar sound caused by a groove deforming a later groove. 4. The positioning of an echo send control before the main channel fader.

## pre-emphasis

A boosting of high frequencies during the recording process in order to keep the signal above the level of noise at high frequencies.

## pre-fader

The positioning of a send or other control before the main channel fader.

## pre-fader listen

A solo circuit that allows a channel signal to be heard (and often metered) before the channel fader.

## pre-mix

1. The same as *pong* (ie to play several recorded tacks with sync playback through a console in order to mix them together and record them on an open track). 2. To mix together the audio of several devices before sending the composite mix to the main console. 3. The composite mix of definitions 1 or 2.

## pre-/post-switch

A switch on an input module which determines whether the echo send control comes before or after the main channel fader.

## presence

The quality in an instrument (or sound source) that makes it sound like it's right there next to you.

## presence frequencies

The range of audio frequencies between 4kHz and 6kHz that often, when boosted, increase the sense of presence, especially with voices.

## preset

1. A sound programmed into a device at the factory by the manufacturer. 2. A factory-set parameter that gives one effect on a signal-processing device. Some manufacturers distinguish between presets, programs and patches, each of which may contain a different set of parameters.

## pressure-gradient microphone

A microphone whose diaphragm that is exposed at the front and at the back and whose diaphragm movement is caused by the difference in pressure between its front and back.

## pressure microphone

A microphone whose diaphragm moves because the pressure of a sound wave causes one side of the diaphragm to work against the normal or controlled air pressure inside the mic case.

## pressure sensitivity

The feature in a synthesiser or keyboard controller of aftertouch (a control or operational function of a synthesiser where the exerting of pressure on a key after it has been pressed, and before it is released, will activate a control command that can be set by the player).

## pressure zone microphone (PZM)

Barrier microphone manufactured by Crown. The head of the mic is attached closely to a plate designed to be attached to a larger surface and which has a half-omni pick-up pattern.

## preview

1. To play an edit in a digital-audio editing system before committing to save it. 2. In a computer-assisted punch in, to have the computer play over the area while switching the monitoring so that the effect of the punch in can be heard before it is performed. 3. Short for *preview signal*.

## preview signal

A signal in disc recording that matches and occurs earlier than the signal being recorded.

## processor

The part of a computer that actually performs task and calculations.

## producer

The director of an audio-recording project and the person responsible for obtaining a final product of desired quality within a budget.

## program change

A MIDI message sent to a receiving device that will change its presets, causing a synthesiser or other device to switch to a new program (also called a preset or patch) contained in its memory.

## program equalisation

Changing the level of any signal in a certain range of frequencies to emphasise or de-emphasise certain elements in the frequency of an instrument or sound source and change its tone.

## program time

In DAT recording, the time indication from the top of one selection.

## prompt

A set of instructions that appear on a computer screen as a guide for the user to follow.

## proprietary

Describing a function, feature or characteristic owned by one company and available only in units manufactured by that company.

## protocol

A system of digital data where the positioning of the data, and the significance of each bit in the data stream, is determined according to a standardised format so that all devices can properly interpret the data.

## proximity effect

In directional microphones, this is the boost in the microphone's output for bass frequencies as the mic is moved closer to the sound source.

## psychoacoustics

The study of how things sound to individuals because of mental or emotional factors.

## pulse

A rise and then fall in amplitude, similar to a square wave, but one which stays up for less time than it stays down.

## pulse-code modulation

The use of amplitude pulses in magnetic tape to record the digital information bits of digital audio.

## pulse-wave modulation

Moving smoothly from a square wave to a pulse wave, in response to a control-voltage input (usually from a LFO).

## pulse width

The amount of time that a pulse is at maximum voltage.

## pumping breathing

The sound of noise changing volume as a limiter or compressor operates.

## punching in

Putting a recorder/sequencer in Record mode on a previously-recorded track while the track is playing in Sync Playback mode and the singer or musician is singing or playing along.

## pure tone

A tone without harmonic frequencies (except for the fundamental frequency) and with a sine-wave shape.

## PZM

A trademark belonging to Crown for its barrier microphone. (See *pressure zone microphone.*)

## Q

The sharpness of the peak response in an equalisation circuit.

## quality factor

The ratio of reactance to resistance in a coil which affects Q.

## quantisation distortion/error

A modulation noise (also perceived as a distortion) that occurs in digital processing and recording and is caused by the sample levels being altered to conform to standard quantisation levels.

## quantisation/quantising levels/increments

A standard level that can be recognised by a digital recording system.

## quantisation noise

A modulation noise (also perceived as distortion) that occurs in digital processing and recording and is caused by the sample levels being altered to conform to standard quantisation levels. This is one of the types of error introduced into an analogue audio signal by encoding it in digital form. The digital equivalent of tape hiss, quantisation noise is caused by the small differences between the actual amplitudes of the points being sampled and the bit resolution of the analogue-to-digital converter.

## quantise

The conversion of the values of an analogue wave or random occurrence into steps. Quantising is a function found on sequencers and drum machines and causes notes played at odd times to be "rounded off" to regular rhythmic values.

## rack

1. The physical setting of a head in the direction toward or away from the tape, therefore affecting how much pressure is applied on the head by the tape. 2. Short for *equipment rack*, a cabinet with rails, or free-standing rails, that have holes in them to accept screws at standard spaces. Used to house outboard gear.

## rack space

A standardised size of the front mounting plate in outboard gear, equal to approximately one and three quarter inches tall by 19 inches wide.

## radiation

The angle and pattern of a speaker's coverage.

## radiation pattern

A polar graph of the coverage of a speaker.

## RAM

Abbreviation of *random access memory*. Used for storing user-programmed patch parameter settings in synthesisers and sample waveforms in samplers. A constant source of power (usually a long-lasting battery) is required for RAM to maintain its contents when the main power is switched off.

## ramp wave

A waveform that is similar to a sawtooth waveform but differs in that it starts at zero level and gradually rises to its peak level and then instantly drops back to zero level to form one cycle.

## random-note generator

A device that generates unpredictable pitches at a set rate. Used in synthesisers.

## random phase

The presence of many signals or reflections where some of the signals are in phase and some out of phase. The overall effect is that of being between in phase and out of phase.

## rap

To perform a spoken rhythmic part to a music or percussion performance. Considered by some to be people talking bollocks.

## rarefaction

The spreading apart of air particles in the formation of a sound-pressure wave.

## rated load impedance

The input impedance (ie the opposition to current flow by a device's input) that a piece of equipment is designed to feed.

## R-DAT

Abbreviation of *rotating-head digital audio tape*, a standard format for the recording of digital audio. Comprises a very small tape cassette and the recording process employs a rotating head.

## real time

Occurring at the same time as other, usually human, activities. In real-time sequence recording, timing information is encoded, along with the note data, as the computer analyses the timing of the input. In real-time editing, changes in parameter settings can be heard immediately, without the need to play a new note or wait for computational processes to be completed.

## recording session

Any period where music is being recorded, especially the first such period, where the rhythm instruments are being recorded.

## recording solo

A switch or function which routes the signal of a channel to the monitor system by itself, and yet the signals out of the console to the recorder are uninterrupted.

## reference level

1. A standard value used to describe the amount of level present in decibels above or below this reference. 2. The same as *operating level* (ie the maximum average level, which should not be exceeded in normal operation).

## reflected sound

Sound that reaches a mic or listener after reflecting once or more from surrounding surfaces.

## regeneration

1. The same as *jam sync*, ie a generation of a new SMPTE time-code signal according to the input SMPTE signal, giving an identical SMPTE signal out as the one that came in. 2. Feedback, especially around a delay line.

## register

A user-modified program, with changed parameters, that is stored in the memory of an effects unit or sound module.

## regulated power supply

A device that supplies power to electronic equipment to ensure that the output voltage won't fluctuate when more equipment is turned on or if there is a change in voltage of the power line.

## release

1. The rate at which the volume of a synthesiser drops to silence once a key is released. 2. The portion of an envelope that begins after a key is lifted.

## release time

The time it takes for a dynamics-processing device to change gain when the input signal crosses the threshold level while decreasing.

## release velocity

The speed with which a key is raised and the type of MIDI data used to encode that speed.

Release-velocity sensing is found on some instruments, although it is rare. It's usually used to control the rate of the release segments of an envelope or envelopes.

## remote

1. Short for *remote control*, a device with which an operator can control a tape machine some distance away. 2. The recording taken at the site of a performance, rather than in a recording studio.

## repeat echo

An echo effect caused by discrete repetitions of a program source by using a long delay time and feedback on a delay line. Also called *space echo*.

## resonance

1. The prolonging of a sound at a certain frequency and the tendency of something to vibrate at a particular frequency after the source of energy is removed. 2. A function on a filter in which a narrow band of frequencies (the resonance peak) becomes relatively more prominent. If the resonance peak is high enough, the filter will begin to oscillate and produce an audio output, even in the absence of input. Filter resonance is also known as *emphasis and Q*, and on some older instruments is also known as *regeneration* or *feedback* (because feedback was used in the circuit to produce a resonance peak).

## resonant frequency

The frequency at which a physical item tends to vibrate after the source of energy (which causes the vibration) is removed.

## resonate

1. To vibrate at the resonant frequency. 2. To linger on, as in reverberation. In this respect, the term is used in terms of sound in a room or is used to describe a room or other area that produces reverberation with a long reverb time.

## return

Short for *echo return* or *auxiliary return*, ie the input of a console which brings the effect signal back from an echo chamber or other reverberation device.

## reverb

1. The persistence of a sound after the source stops emitting it. 2. A function on a filter in which a narrow band of frequencies (the resonance peak) becomes relatively more prominent. If the resonance peak is high enough, the filter will begin to oscillate and produce an audio output, even in the absence of input. Filter resonance is also known as *emphasis and Q*, and on some older instruments is also known as *regeneration* or *feedback* (because feedback was used in the circuit to produce a resonance peak).

## reverb(eration) time

The time it takes for the reverberation or echoes of a sound source to decrease by 60dB after the direct sound from the source stops.

## reverberant field

The area away from a sound source at which reverberation is louder than the direct sound from the sound source.

## reverberation envelope

Literally, the attack, decay, sustain and release of the reverberation volume. In other words, the time it takes for the reverberation to reach its peak level and its rate of decay. (See also *ADSR*.)

## reverb-time contour

A graph of reverberation time for signals of different audio frequencies.

## rhythm track

The section of recording that features rhythm instruments.

## ribbon microphone

A microphone with a thin, conductive ribbon as both the diaphragm and the generating element (the device that generates the electricity).

## riff

A short melody repeatedly played in a tune, sometimes with variation and often between vocal lines.

## ringing

An undesirable resonance at the cut-off frequency of a filter that has a high rate of cut-off.

## ringing out a room

A test often carried out at the setting-up stage before a performance, where pink noise is sent through the speakers and the microphones are turned up until feedback occurs.

## ring modulator

A special type of mixer that accepts two signals as audio inputs and produces their sum-and-difference tones at its output but doesn't pass on the frequencies found in the original signals themselves. (See *clangorous*.)

## roll-off

The reduction of signal level as a signal's frequency moves away from the cut-off frequency, especially when the cut-off rate is mild.

## ROM

Abbreviation of *read-only memory*, a type of data storage where the contents can't be altered by the user. An instrument's operating system and, in some cases, its waveforms and factory presets are stored in ROM. (See also *RAM*.)

## room equalisation

An equaliser inserted in a monitor system that attempts to compensate for changes in frequency response caused by the acoustics of a room.

## room sound

The ambience of a room, including reverberation and background noise.

## room tone

The background noise in a room where there are no people speaking and no music playing.

## RT

Abbreviation of *reverb time*, ie the time it takes for the reverberation or echoes of a sound source to decrease by 60dB after the direct sound from the source stops.

## rumble

A low-frequency noise, especially that caused by earth/floor vibration or by uneven surfaces in the drive mechanism of a recorder or playback unit.

## run-off

A quick reference mix recorded on cassette or some other format after a multitrack recording or overdubbing session so that the client can listen to what was recorded.

## run through

Musicians run through a tune before the recording process begins so that the engineer can calibrate levels and check the sound quality.

## sample

1. In digital recording, to measure the level of a waveform at a given instant. 2. To record a short segment of audio for the purpose of playback later. 3. The short recording made in definition 2.

## sample and hold

1. In digital recording, a term used to describe the measuring of the level of a waveform at a given instant and then converting it to a voltage at that level, which will then be held until another sample is taken. When triggered (usually by a clock pulse), a circuit on an analogue synthesiser looks at (samples) the voltage at its input and then passes it on to its output unchanged, regardless of what the input voltage does in the meantime (the hold period), until the next trigger is received. In one familiar application, the input was a noise source and the output was connected to oscillator pitch, which caused the pitch to change in a random staircase pattern. The sample-and-hold effect is often emulated by digital synthesisers through an LFO waveshape called "random".

## sample dump

The copying of a digitally recorded sample without converting it to analogue between different storage units or sound modules through a MIDI transmission.

## sample playback

The reproduction (in analogue signal form) of a recorded sample, the pitch and sustain of which is controlled by a MIDI signal.

## sampler

A device that records and plays samples, often including features for the editing and storage of the samples, usually by allowing them to be distributed across a keyboard and played back at various pitches.

## sample rate

In digital recording, this refers to the number of times that samples are taken each second.

## sample-rate conversion

The conversion of digital audio data at one sample rate to digital audio data at a different sample rate without first converting the signal to analogue.

## sampling

The process of encoding an analogue signal in digital form by reading (sampling) its level at precisely spaced time intervals.

## sampling frequency

The same as *sample rate*, ie the number samples taken each second. Typical sampling rates are usually between 11kHz and 48kHz.

## sampling synchronisation signal

A stream of synchronisation pulses that are generated by a digital audio tape recorder, recorded onto tape and then used as a clock signal to time the sampling of the sampling circuits.

## sawtooth waveform

A waveform that jumps from a zero value to a peak value and then gradually diminishes to a zero value to complete the cycle.

## scratch

1. A descriptive term meaning "temporary". 2. A scratch vocal is taken during a basic recording session to help the other musicians play their parts. At a later date, the final vocal track is overdubbed. 3. The action of a musician or disc jockey quickly moving a record back and forth with a phono cartridge reproducing the stylus motion in order to create a rhythmic pattern of sound.

## scrub

1. To shuttle (ie move the sound track) either forward or backward when a control is moved off a centre point either left or right. 2. To move backward and forward through an audio waveform under manual control in order to find a precise point in a wave (for editing purposes).

# SCSI

Abbreviation of *small-computer systems interface*, a high-speed communications protocol that allows computers, samplers and disk drives to communicate with one another. Pronounced "scuzzy".

# SDII

Abbreviation of *Sound Designer II*, an audio file format and the native format of Digidesign's Sound Designer II graphic audio waveform editing program for the Macintosh.

# SDS

The standard MIDI sample dump. SDS is used to transfer digital audio samples from one instrument to another over a MIDI cable.

# send

A control and bus designed to feed signals from console channels to an outboard device, such as a reverberation unit.

# send level

A control determining the signal level sent to a send bus.

# sensitivity

In microphones, the output level produced by a standard amount of sound-pressure level.

# separation

A term used to describe the pick-up of a desired signal compared to that of an undesired signal.

# sequence

1. An automatic playing of musical events (such as pitches, sounding of samples and rests) by a device in a step-by-step order. 2. The action of programming a computer to play musical events automatically, in a stepped order.

# sequencer

1. A computer which can be programmed to play and record a stepped order of musical events. 2. A device or program that records and plays back user-determined sets of music-performance commands, usually in the form of MIDI data. Most sequencers also allow this data to be edited in various ways and stored on disk.

# serial data

Digital data where all of the bits are transmitted one after another over a single wire/connection.

# serial interface

A plug and cable for a computer that sends and receives data one bit after the other.

## serial port

A jack that sends out or receives digital data one bit after another through a single pin.

## series connection

Equipment (especially circuit elements) connected so that the electrical signal flows from one device to the next and to the next and so forth.

## set up

To position microphones, instruments and the controls on recorders/consoles etc prior to recording.

## set-up

An arrangement where microphones, instruments and controls on recorders, consoles, etc, are positioned for recording.

## shelf

The frequency response of an equalisation circuit where the boost or cut-off frequencies form a shelf on a frequency response graph. A high-frequency shelf control will affect signal levels at the set frequency and all higher frequencies, while a low-frequency shelf control will affect signal levels at the set frequency and at all lower frequencies.

## shelf filter

The circuit in an equaliser used to obtain the shelf.

## shield

1. The outer, conductive wrapping around an inner wire or wires in a cable. 2. To protect the inner wire or wires in a cable from picking up energy given off by such things as fluorescent lights.

## shielded cable

Cable that has a shield around an inner conductor or conductors.

## shock mount

An elastic microphone mount that reduces the microphone's movement when the stand vibrates in response to floor vibrations from footsteps, etc.

## short delay

Delay times under 20ms.

## shortest digital path

The routing of a digital-audio signal so that there is a minimum amount of digital-to-analogue, analogue-to-digital or sample-rate conversion.

## shortest path

A technique in recording by which a signal is routed through the least amount of active (amplified) devices during recording.

## shotgun microphone

A microphone with a long line filter (a tube that acoustically cancels sound arriving from the side), thus allowing the microphone to pick up sound in one direction much better than in any other direction.

## sibilance

Energy from a voice centred at around 7kHz, caused by pronouncing "s", "sh" or "ch" sounds.

## side bands

Frequency components outside the natural harmonic series, generally introduced to a tone by using an audio-range wave for modulation. (See *clangorous*.)

## side chain

The control circuit of a dynamics-processing device.

## signal

1. In audio, an alternating current or voltage matching the waveform of, or being originally obtained from, a sound-pressure wave. 2. In audio, an alternating current or voltage between 20Hz and 20kHz. 3. A digital-audio bit stream.

## signal processing

Changing the sound of an instrument or some other sound source with equalisers, limiters, compressors and other devices, thereby "processing" the sound ready to be recorded onto a master.

## signal-to-error ratio

The difference in level between the signal and the noise and distortion caused by converting analogue audio signals into digital audio and then back into analogue.

## signal-to-noise ratio

The difference in decibels between the levels of signal and noise.

## sine wave

The waveform produced by a sound source vibrating at just one frequency (ie making a pure tone).

## single D

Abbreviation of *single port distance*, used to describe a microphone in which there is one distance between the port and the diaphragm.

## Single-Step mode

A method of loading events (such as notes) into memory one event at a time. Also called *step mode* and *step time*, compared with real time.

## slap echo

One distinct repeat added to one or more instrument sounds in a mix that creates a very live sound, similar to what you'd hear in an arena.

## smart FSK

An FSK (Frequency Shift Key) sync signal where the beginning of each measure has an identification message giving the measure number.

## SMDI

Abbreviation of *SCSI musical data interchange*, a specification for sending MIDI sample dumps over the SCSI bus.

## SMPTE

1. Society of Motion Picture and Television Engineers, a professional society. 2. A term loosely used to mean *SMPTE time code*, a standardised timing and sync signal specified by this society.

## SND

Sound resource, a Macintosh audio file format.

## soft key

Abbreviation of *software key*, another name for a function key (ie a key that has a different function depending on the programming of a computer and as shown on a menu screen), especially when it's on a device that has an internal computer.

## soft knee

Generic name for the DBX Corporation's registered trade name of Over-Easy, named for the gradual change of compression ratio around the threshold, which makes it difficult to detect when compression is taking place.

## soft knob

Abbreviation of *software knob*, a knob used in a computer-controlled device which has a different function depending on the programming of the computer.

## soft sound source

A low-volume instrument, such as an acoustic guitar.

## solid state

In electronics, solid-state devices use transistors and semiconductors rather than tubes.

## solo

1. A circuit in a console that allows just one channel (or several selected channels) to be heard or reach the output. 2. In music, an instrument or section where an instrument is the featured instrument for a short period, often playing a melody. 3. An original Copy Code (protective digital signal recorded with digital audio bits) that was developed by Philips to prevent the making of digital copies of a copy made from a CD, thereby helping to prevent bootlegging.

## solo switch

A switch that activates the solo function, which allows only selected channels to be heard or to reach the output.

## song position pointer

1. Short for *MIDI clock with song pointer*, ie the time data contained in the MIDI signal used to sync two sequencers together. The song position pointer advances one step each $1/24$ of a beat, and also has a number signal for each measure or bar which indicates the number of measures or bars you are into the tune. 2. A type of MIDI data that tells a device how many 16th-notes have passed since the beginning of a song. An SPP message is generally sent in conjunction with a MIDI Continue message in order to start playback from the middle of a song.

## sostenuto pedal

A pedal found on grand pianos and mimicked on some synthesisers, which only sustain notes if they are already being held down on the keyboard at the moment when the pedal is pressed.

## sound

1. Moving pressure variations in air caused by something vibrating between 20 times and 20,000 times a second, or similar variations in other substances, like water. 2. Loosely, any audio signal, regardless of its energy form.

## sound absorption

The same as *acoustical absorption*, ie the quality of a surface or substance which takes in a sound wave rather than reflecting it.

## sound blanket

A thick blanket that can be put on floors or hung to help prevent sound from reflecting from hard surfaces.

## soundcard

A circuit board that is installed inside a computer (typically an IBM-compatible machine) providing new sound capabilities. These capabilities can include an FM or wavetable synthesiser and audio inputs and outputs. MIDI inputs and outputs are also normally included.

## sound file (soundfile)

A digital-audio recording that can be stored in a computer or on a digital storage medium, such as a hard disk.

## sound-pressure level (SPL)

A measure of the sound pressure present, measured in decibels above the threshold of hearing (.0002 microbars).

## sound-pressure wave

Alternate compressions (compacting together) and rarefactions (spreading apart) of air particles moving away from something that is vibrating at between 20 and 20,000 times a second, or a similar occurrence in another substance, such as water.

## sound quality

A characteristic of how well the diaphragm movement in a microphone matches the pressure changes of a sound wave reaching it, particularly sudden changes.

## sound source

Something that vibrates between 20 and 20,000 times a second, producing a sound-pressure wave.

## SoundTools

Digidesign's digital-audio-editing system.

## sound wave

Abbreviation of *sound-pressure wave*, ie a wave of pressure changes moving away from something that is vibrating between 20 and 20,000 times a second.

## source

Input mode on a tape machine/computer sequencer where the meters and the output of the machine's electronics will be the signal arriving at the input connector.

## spaced cardioid pair

A far-distant miking technique of placing two cardioid microphones a distance apart (usually about six inches) and pointing away from each other by 90°.

## spaced omni pair

Placing two microphones with omni-directional patterns between four and eight feet apart, so that one microphone picks up the sound coming from the left and the other from the right.

## spaced pair

Any two microphones spaced apart to obtain a stereo pick-up, especially using the spaced omni or spaced cardioid techniques.

## space echo

An effect of repeating echoes of a sound.

## SPDIF

Shortened from the first letters of Sony/Philips Digital Interface, a standard for sending and receiving digital audio signals using the common RCA connector.

## speaker

A device that converts electrical signals into audible sound. Alternatively, a transducer that converts an electrical audio signal into a sound-pressure wave.

## speaker out direct

Term used to refer to the practice of feeding the signal from a speaker output of an instrument amplifier to the recording console without using a microphone.

## speed of sound

The wave velocity (ie the time it takes for one point of the waveform to travel a certain distance) of a sound-pressure wave (1,130 feet per second at 70° Fahrenheit).

## SPL

Abbreviation of *sound-pressure level*, referring to a pressure of .0002 microbars, considered to be the threshold of hearing (ie the lowest level at which people begin to hear sound).

## split keyboard

A single keyboard divided electronically so that it acts as if it were two or more separate keyboards. The output of each note range is routed into a separate signal path in the keyboard's internal sound-producing circuitr, or transmitted over one or more separate MIDI channels. Applications include playing a bass sound with the left hand while playing a piano sound with the right.

## spring reverb

A device that simulates reverberation by driving a spring (in the same way that a loudspeaker cone is driven) and picking up the spring's vibrations with a contact microphone (a device that converts physical vibrations into audio signals).

## square wave

A wave shape produced when voltage rises instantly to one level, stays at that level, instantly falls to another level and stays at that level, and finally rises back to its original level to complete the cycle.

## standing wave

An acoustic signal between two reflective surfaces with a distance that is an even multiple of half of the signal's frequency wavelength.

## status byte

A MIDI byte that defines the meaning of the data bytes that follow it. MIDI status bytes always begin with a one (hex eight through to F), while data bytes always begin with a zero (hex zero through to seven).

## step input

In sequencing, a technique that allows you to enter notes one step at a time, also called *step recording*. Common step values are 16th- and eighth-notes. After each entry, the sequencer's clock (ie its position in the sequence) will advance one step and then stop, awaiting new input. Recording while the clock is running is called *real-time input*.

## step program/mode/time

To program a sequencer one note (or event) at a time in accordance with the rhythm to which the time value of one step is set.

## stereo

A recording or reproduction of at least two channels where the positions of instrument sounds from left to right can be perceived.

## stereo image

The perception of different sound sources being far left, far right or any place in between.

## stereo miking

The positioning of two or more microphones in such a way that their outputs generate a stereo image.

## stretched-string instruments

Instruments that use stretched strings to generate tones, such as guitars, violins and pianos.

## submix

A combination of audio signals treated as one or two channels (for a stereo image) in a mix.

## subtractive synthesis

The generation of harmonically rich waveforms by various methods and then the filtering of these waveforms in order to remove unwanted harmonics and thus create sound. Alternatively, the technique of arriving at a desired tone colour by filtering waveforms rich in harmonics. Subtractive synthesis is the type generally used on analogue synthesisers.

## sum

A signal comprising a combination of two stereo channels that are both equal in level and in phase.

## sum and difference signals

When two stereo channels are mixed at equal levels and in phase, a sum signal is created. A difference signal is one where the mixture of the signals from the two channels has one channel phase-reversed so that any signal exactly the same in both channels will be cancelled.

## super-cardioid pattern

A microphone pattern that has maximum sensitivity on axis and least sensitivity around 150° off axis.

## surround sound

A technique of recording and playing back sound used in film, where the sound has a front-to-back quality as well as a side-to-side perspective.

## sustain

1. A holding-out of the sounding of a pitch by an instrument. 2. The level at which a sound will continue to play when a synthesiser key is held down.

## sustain pedal

The electronic equivalent of a piano's *sostenuto* (damper) pedal. In most synthesisers, the sustain pedal latches the envelopes of any currently playing or subsequently played notes at their sustain levels, even if the keys are lifted.

## sweetening

Musical parts that are overdubbed in order to complete the music of a recording, especially the melodic instruments, such as strings and horns.

## switch

A device that makes and/or breaks electrical connections.

## switchable-pattern microphone

A microphone that has more than one directional pattern, depending on the position of the Pattern switch.

## switch matrix

A series of switches – usually arranged in rows and columns of buttons – that allow any input module to be connected to any output bus.

## synthesiser

A musical instrument that artificially generates signals (using oscillators) to simulate the sounds of real instruments or to create other sounds impossible to manufacture with "real" instruments and is designed according to certain principles developed by Robert Moog and others in the 1960s. A synthesiser is distinguished from an electronic piano or electronic organ by the fact that its sounds can be programmed by the user, and from a sampler by the fact that the sampler allows the user to make digital recordings of external sound sources.

## system common

A type of MIDI data used to control certain aspects of the operation of an entire MIDI system. System-common messages include Song Position Pointer messages, as well as Song Select, Tune Request, and End Of System Exclusive messages.

## system exclusive (sysex)

A type of MIDI data that allows messages to be sent over a MIDI cable, which will then be responded to only by devices of a specific type. Sysex data is used most commonly for sending patch parameter data to and from an editor/librarian program.

## system-exclusive bulk dump

A system-exclusive bulk dump is the transmission of internal synthesiser settings as a manufacturer-specified system-exclusive file from a synth to a sequencer or from a sequencer to a synth.

## system real time

A type of MIDI data used for timing references. Because of its timing-critical nature, a system real-time byte can be inserted into the middle of any multibyte MIDI message. System real-time messages include MIDI Clock, Start, Stop, Continue, Active Sensing, and System Reset messages.

## take

A recording taken between one start and the following stop of a track.

## take sheet

A sheet used to note the number of takes made on each tune, along with comments.

## talkback

The system that allows an engineer to talk into a microphone in the control room and have his voice sound over the studio monitors and/or headphones so that he can talk to the musicians.

## talk box

A guitar effects unit that allows a voice to modulate (control) a guitar signal. Operated by a vocalist talking with a tube in his mouth.

## tempo

The rate at which the music progresses, measured in beats per minute (ie the number of steady, even pulses that occur in each minute of the music).

## tempo mapping

Programming a sequencer to follow the tempo variations of a recorded performance.

## THD

Abbreviation for *Total Harmonic Distortion*, an audio measurement specification used to determine the accuracy with which a device can reproduce an input signal at its output. THD describes the cumulative level of harmonic overtones that the device being tested adds to an input sine wave. THD + $n$ is a specification that includes both harmonic distortion of the sine wave and non-harmonic noise.

## thin sound

A sound that doesn't have all frequencies present. Especially refers to a sound that is deficient in low frequencies.

## three-to-one rule

The rule which states that the distance between microphones must be at least three times the distance between either microphone and the sound source.

## three-way speaker

A speaker system that has separate speakers to reproduce the bass, mid-range and treble frequencies.

## threshold

The level at which a dynamics-processing unit begins to change gain.

## threshold control

The control on a dynamics-processing device that adjusts the threshold level (ie the level at which it begins to change gain).

## threshold of feeling

The sound-pressure level at which people experience discomfort for 50% of the time.

## threshold of hearing

The sound-pressure level at which people can hear for only 50% of the time.

## threshold of pain

The sound-pressure level at which people feel actual pain for 50% of the time.

## throat

A small opening in a horn or driver through which a sound wave passes from the driver to the horn.

## throw

In speakers and microphones, the amount of movement that the diaphragm can make (without restriction) in order to produce or pick up a sound wave.

## thru box

A unit with one MIDI In port and several MIDI Out ports. Each MIDI Out port has the same signal as the MIDI In port, but with a delay of the signal (usually around 4ms).

## thru port

A connector that puts out a MIDI signal identical to the input MIDI signal.

## tight/hyped sound

The sound obtained by close-miking well-isolated instruments.

## timbre

1. The timbre of the instrument is what makes it sound like that particular instrument and not like any other, even though the other instrument may be playing the same pitch. 2. One of the building blocks of a patch in a Roland synthesiser. Pronounced "tam-br".

## time base

The number of pulses/advances per beat in a simple clock signal.

## time code

Short for *SMPTE time code*, a standardised timing and sync signal specified by the Society of Motion Picture and Television Engineers. Alternatively, a type of signal that contains information about location in time and used for a synchronisation reference point when synchronising two or more machines together, such as sequencers, drum machines and tape decks.

## time-code generator

A unit that generates SMPTE time-code signals.

## time compression/expansion

The speeding up or slowing down of an audio recording without causing a change in the pitch.

## time constant

In a circuit that has reactance, the time it takes for the current or voltage to substantially stabilise in the circuit when the voltage or current is changing.

## timing clock

1. An even pulse signal used for syncing purposes. 2. The same as MIDI Clock, ie time data in a MIDI signal that advances one step each $1/24$ of a beat and can be used to sync two sequencers together.

## tone

1. One of several single-frequency signals found at the beginning of a tape reel at the magnetic reference level that will be used to record a program. 2. Any single-frequency signal or sound.

3. The sound quality of an instrument's sound relative to the amount of energy present at different frequencies. 4. In some synthesisers, a term meaning the audio signal that will be put out by the unit which would be similar to the sound of an instrument.

## touch sensitive

Used to describe a synthesiser keyboard's ability to generate a MIDI Velocity signal. Not all synthesiser keyboards are touch sensitive.

## track

1. One audio recording made on a portion of the width of a multitrack tape. 2. One set of control commands in a sequencer recorded in a similar manner to an audio track and often controlling one synthesiser over one MIDI channel. 3. A term with the same meaning as the term *band track* (ie the part of a song without the lead vocal or without the lead and background vocals). 4. To be controlled by or to follow in some proportional relationship, such as when a filter's cut-off frequency tracks the keyboard, moving up or down depending on the note being played.

## tracking

Recording the individual tracks of a multitrack recording.

## transformer matrix

A device that uses transformers to take two audio channel inputs and change them to a sum signal (ie a mix of the signals on the two channels) and a difference signal (ie the mixture of the two signals with the phase of one channel reversed so that any signal exactly the same in both channels will be cancelled).

## transient

The initial high-energy peak that occurs at the beginning of a waveform, such as one caused by the percussive action of a pick or hammer hitting a string.

## transient response

Response to signals with amplitudes which rise very quickly, such as drum beats and waveforms produced by percussive instruments.

## transmit

In MIDI, to send a MIDI command to another device.

## transposing

The act of changing the musical register of an entire piece of music by the space of an interval.

## trap

A filter designed to reject audio signals at certain frequencies.

## treble frequencies

Higher audio frequencies.

## tremolo

An even, repeated change in volume of a musical tone. A periodic change in amplitude, usually controlled by an LFO, with a periodicity of less than 20Hz.

## triangular wave

A waveform that looks triangular.

## trigger

1. The signal or action of sending a signal to control the start of an event. 2. A device that emits a signal to control the start of an event, including a device that puts out such a signal when struck.

## trim control

A device that reduces the strength of a signal produced by an amplifier, often over a restricted range.

## trim status

Solid State Logic's Console Automation mode, which operates as follows: when a slide is at its trim point, the gain variations (fader movements) last programmed in the computer will be in effect; when the slide is moved from the trim point, gain or loss is added to or subtracted from the program.

## truncation

The editing of a sample playback so that only the desired portion of the sample is played. Effected by moving the start and end points of the sample playback.

## tube

An abbreviation of *vacuum tube*, ie an amplifying device that has elements to send and control current through a vacuum in a glass or metal tube.

## tuned

A term used with reference to a circuit or device which is most sensitive to a certain frequency.

## tuned cavity

A cavity which, because of its physical dimensions, will resonate at a particular frequency (ie it will tend to reinforce the energy at certain frequencies of vibration).

## tuned pipe instrument

An instrument that uses a pipe of certain dimensions as a sound generator.

## turnover frequency

The same as *cut-off frequency*, ie the highest or lowest frequency in the pass band of a filter.

## turntable

1. A device that supports and rotates a phonograph record during playback. 2. One of the round disc platters that holds a reel and reel lock and is driven by a reel motor (also known as a *deck*).

## tweak

A slang term meaning to calibrate (ie to set all operating controls and adjustments in order to obtain a device's optimum performance), particularly in terms of very precise calibration.

## tweeter

A speaker designed to reproduce only higher frequencies.

## two-way speaker

A speaker system fitted with separate speakers – a woofer and a tweeter – in order to reproduce lower and higher frequencies respectively.

## μ

1. The Greek letter *mu*, which is actually a forerunner of the English M, although lower-case *u* is often used in place of it, because of its similar appearance. 2. A symbol used to represent the prefix micro (ie one millionth).

## unbalanced

Used to describe a method of interconnecting recorders, amplifiers and other electronic gear using twin-conductor cable.

## uni

A prefix meaning "one".

## unidirectional

A pick-up pattern that's more sensitive to sound arriving from one direction than from any other.

## unison

Several performers, instruments or sound sources sounding at the same time and with the same pitch.

## unity gain

No increase or decrease in signal strength at the output of an amplifier or device when compared to the signal strength at the input.

## update by absolute

Solid State Logic name for the action of rewriting the settings of an automated console control.

## Update mode

A mode of console automation that allows the programming of a console channel to be modified so that, when the slide of the fader is at a predetermined point (usually the point marked "0"), the gain variations (fader movements) last programmed into the computer will be in effect, but when the engineer moves the slide up or down from this point, gain or loss is added to or subtracted from the programmed level.

## vamp

The repeated part of a tune at its end, usually the chorus or part of the chorus.

## vamp and fade

A method of ending a recording of a tune where part of the music is repeated and the engineer reduces volume until the music fades out.

## Variable-D

A patented invention of Electrovoice where several ports are inserted in the casing of a microphone. These ports are increasingly less sensitive to high frequencies, as they are further away from the diaphragm, reducing the proximity effect.

## VCA

Abbreviation for *voltage-controlled amplifier*, ie an amplifier that will change gain according to the level of control voltage sent to it.

## VCA automation

A system of channel gain (or other functions) controlled by a computer via the use of voltage-controlled amplifiers, which change gain according to the level of control voltages sent to them by the computer.

## VCA fader

A fader with a VCA in its casing arranged so that, in manual operation, the slide of the fader controls how much control voltage is sent to the VCA and therefore controls the channel gain.

## VCA group

Several VCA faders that are fed control voltages from a group master slide.

## VCA master

A slider that feeds control voltages to several VCAs in order to control the gain in several audio channels.

## VCA trim

A control in an audio system (such as a console) that can adjust the control voltage feeding all VCAs, usually with a limited range.

## VCF

1. Abbreviation of *voltage-controlled filter*, the cut-off frequency of which can be changed by altering the amount of voltage being sent to its control input. 2. The digital equivalent of a VCF.

## VCO

1. Abbreviation of *foltage-control oscillator*, which generates an AC control voltage, usually in the form of a low-frequency oscillator putting out a signal between .1Hz and 10Hz. 2. Abbreviation of *voltage-controlled oscillator*, which changes its frequency according to a control voltage fed to its control input.

## velocity

In synthesisers and keyboard controllers, a MIDI message giving data on how hard a key is struck. Alternatively, a type of MIDI data (ranging between 1 and 127) usually used to indicate how quickly a key is pushed down (attack velocity) or allowed to rise (release velocity). (A Note-On message with a velocity value of zero is equivalent to a Note-Off message.)

## velocity curve

A map that translates incoming velocity values into other velocities in order to alter the feel or response of a keyboard or tone module.

## velocity microphone

Another name for *pressure-gradient microphone*, ie one whose diaphragm is exposed at the front and back and the movement of which is caused by small differences in pressure between the front and back of the diaphragm.

## velocity sensitive

The same as *touch sensitive*, used to describe a synthesiser keyboard's ability to generate a MIDI Velocity signal. Not all synthesiser keyboards are velocity sensitive.

## vibrato

1. A smooth and repeated changing of pitch up and down from the regular musical pitch, often practised by singers. 2. A periodic change in frequency, often controlled by an LFO, with a periodicity of less than 20Hz.

## virtual

Existing only in software.

## virtual tracking

Having a MIDI sequencer operating in sync with a multitrack tape and controlling the playing of synthesisers along with recorded parts.

## vocal booth

A isolation room used to record a vocal track so that other instruments in the studio don't leak into the vocal microphone. Also used to reduce ambience and reverberation in a vocal recording.

## vocoder

An effects device that will modulate (control) one signal with another.

## voice

1. In synthesisers, a pitch that can be played at the same time as other pitches. 2. In Yamaha synths, a term meaning the same thing as *sound patch*, ie a sound that can be created by the synth.

## voice channel

A signal path containing (as a minimum) an oscillator and VCA, or their digital equivalent, and capable of producing a note. On a typical synthesiser, two or more voice channels – each with their own waveform and parameter settings – can be combined to form a single note.

## voice stealing

A process by which a synthesiser that is being required to play more notes than it has available voices switches off some of the voices that are currently sounding (typically those that have been sounding the longest or are the lowest amplitude) in order to assign them to play new notes.

## voltage-controlled amplifier

The same as *VCA*, ie an amp that changes gain according to the level of control voltage sent to it.

## voltage-controlled attenuator

Similar to a voltage-controlled amplifier, except that, with no control voltage sent to it, the amplifier will have no gain and no loss. As an increasing control voltage is sent to it, the amplifier reduces gain, causing a loss of signal strength.

## voltage-controlled fader

The same as *VCA fader*, ie a fader with a VCA in its casing arranged so that, in manual operation, the slide of the fader controls how much control voltage is sent to the VCA and therefore controls the channel gain.

## voltage-controlled filter

A filter (especially a low-pass filter) that will change its cut-off frequency according to the level of the control voltage being fed to its control input.

## voltage-controlled oscillator

The same as definition 2 of *VCO*, ie an oscillator that changes its frequency according to a control voltage fed to its control input.

## voltage-control oscillator

The same as *VCO* (definition 1), ie an oscillator that generates an AC control voltage, usually a low-frequency signal between .1Hz and 10Hz.

## volume

1. A common, non-technical term equivalent to level of sound pressure and loosely applied to also mean audio voltage level. 2. Abbreviation of the term *volume control*.

## volume control

An amplifier's gain control.

## volume envelope

The way in which a note sounded by a musical instrument changes in volume over time.

## volume pedal

A guitar pedal used to change the volume of an instrument or a similar device used with other instruments, such as an organ.

## volume unit

A unit designed to measure perceived changes in loudness in audio material. The unit is basically the decibel change of the average level, as read by a volume unit (VU) meter. The movement of the VU meter is designed to approximately match the ear's response to changes in level.

## vox

Latin for "voice", used on track logs to denote a vocal track.

## VSO

Another term for a *vacuum-tube voltmeter*, ie a device that measures the electrical voltage and uses a vacuum tube to drive the indicator so that testing the circuit does not load the circuit.

## VU

1. Abbreviation of the term *volume unit*, ie a unit designed to measure perceived changes in loudness in audio material. 2. A meter that reads levels of audio voltage fed into or out of a piece of equipment and is designed to match the ear's response to sudden changes in level.

## wah/wah-wah

A changing filter that filters either more or less of an instrument's harmonics.

## WAV

The Windows audio file format. Typically encountered as "filename.wav".

## wave

A continuous fluctuation in the amplitude of a quantity with respect to time.

## waveform/waveshape

The shape made by fluctuations in a wave over a period over time.

## wavelength

The length of one cycle (in feet, inches, etc) of a wave.

## wavetable synthesis

A common method for generating sound electronically on a synthesiser or PC. Output is produced using a table of sound samples (actual recorded sounds) which are digitised and played back as needed. By continuously re-reading samples and looping them together at different pitches, highly complex tones can be generated from a minimum of stored data without overtaxing the processor.

## wave velocity

The time it takes for one point of a waveform to travel a certain distance.

## weber

A unit that describes a number of magnetic lines of force. Used in the measurement or statement of magnetic flux density (the strength of magnetism).

## weighting

An equalisation curve used in audio tests that compensates for the Fletcher Munson effect at various levels.

## wet

Having reverberation or ambience. Alternatively, consisting entirely of processed sound. The output of an effects device is 100% wet when only the output of the processor itself is being heard, with none of the dry (unprocessed) signal.

## wheel

A controller used for pitch bending or modulation, normally mounted on the left-hand side of the keyboard and played with the left hand.

## white noise

Random energy distributed so that the amount of energy is the same for each cycle, causing the noise level to increase with frequency.

## wide-band noise

Noise that has energy over a wide range of frequencies.

## width

Another term for *depth*, ie the amount of change in a controlled signal exerted by the control signal.

## wild sound

Sound recordings that are taken completely separately from the master recording (or *picture recording*), and therefore can't be synced to the master recording.

## windscreen

A device that reduces or eliminates wind noise from the microphone being moved or from blowing into the microphone on remote-location recordings.

## wireless microphone

A microphone with an FM radio transmitter inside its casing that transmits a signal to an offstage FM receiver.

## woodwind controller

A device that plays like a woodwind instrument, controlling a sound module by putting out a control voltage or MIDI command.

## woofer

A speaker designed to reproduce only bass frequencies.

## word

A shortening of the term *digital word*, ie a number of information bits that communicate one value.

## workstation

A device that controls a variety of functions and is designed to be operated by one person, comprising a synthesiser or sampler in which several of the tasks usually associated with electronic music production – such as sequencing, effects processing, rhythm programming and storing data on disk – can all be performed by components found within a single physical device.

## wow

A low pitch change that occurs because the speed of a recorder or playback machine fluctuates slowly.

## wrap

The angle formed by the tape as it bends around the head.

## XLR connector

1. A common three-pin connector used in balanced audio connections. 2. A microphone cable.

## XY miking

A method of arranged two cardioid microphones for stereo pick-up, with the two mic heads positioned as close together as possible without touching, pointing 90° away from each other and 45° to the centre of the sound source.

## Y-cord/lead

A cable fitted with three connectors, so that one output may be sent to two inputs.

## zero-crossing point

The point at which a digitally encoded waveform crosses the centre of its amplitude range.